BUILDING COACHES

A Complete Guide for Railway Modellers

ROKET

RAPID

etting, medium
uty cyano glue.
5-10 sec.   20

uxematerials.com   AD-

STAINLESS
NONMAGNETIC

Va
Earlier
coaches,

BUILDING COACHES

A Complete Guide for Railway Modellers

GEORGE DENT

THE CROWOOD PRESS

First published in 2016 by
The Crowood Press Ltd
Ramsbury, Marlborough
Wiltshire SN8 2HR

www.crowood.com

British Library Cataloguing-in-Publication Data
A catalogue record for this book is available from the British Library.

ISBN 978 1 78500 205 2

Acknowledgements
For their help in the production of this book, I'm indebted to a variety of folks within the model and craft trade. My sincere thanks go, in no particular order, to Julie Lightburn (York Modelmaking), Jacqueline Hunt (Axminster Tools), John Peck (Precision Labels), David Palmer (Train-Tech), John Bristow (Deluxe Materials), Matthew John (Albion Alloys), Steve Bell (Railtec Models), Ralph Robertson (Palatine Models), Dave Mylett and Dave Martin (Hatton's), David and Ron (SMTF model shop, Poynton), Lisa Munro and Alex Medwell (The Airbrush Company) and Tim Murrell (Everything Airbrush). Thanks are also due to Peter Harvey (PH Designs), along with Brian Hanson and the chaps at Shawplan/Extreme Etchings.

My colleagues at *Model Rail* magazine – Richard Foster, Chris Leigh, Dave Lowery, Chris Nevard, Mike Harris and Peter Marriott – have provided support and inspiration over the years, for which I'm grateful. So too has Ben Jones of *British Railway Modelling*.

I must also register my appreciation for the patience of the staff at Crowood and, in particular, all the various members of the Dent Collective.

Disclaimer
The author and the publisher do not accept any responsibility in any manner whatsoever for any error or omission, or any loss, damage, injury, adverse outcome, or liability of any kind incurred as a result of the use of any of the information contained in this book, or reliance upon it. If in doubt about any aspect of railway modelling readers are advised to seek professional advice.

Typeset by Jean Cussons Typesetting, Diss, Norfolk
Printed and bound in Malaysia by Times Offset (M) Sdn Bhd

CONTENTS

INTRODUCTION 6

CHAPTER 1 RESEARCH, TOOLS & EQUIPMENT 12

CHAPTER 2 EASY UPGRADES FOR READY-TO-RUN STOCK 24

CHAPTER 3 MORE READY-TO-RUN UPGRADES 35

CHAPTER 4 SUPERDETAILING 47

CHAPTER 5 MAKING A START WITH KITS 58

CHAPTER 6 RESIN & LASER-CUT KITS 74

CHAPTER 7 WOOD-BASED MATERIALS & 3D PRINTING 85

CHAPTER 8 CONVERSIONS 94

CHAPTER 9 COUPLINGS, GANGWAYS, LIGHTS & POWER 104

CHAPTER 10 FOUNDATIONS IN METAL 118

CHAPTER 11 METALWORK IN PRACTICE 136

CHAPTER 12 ROOFS, BOGIES & FIXED AXLES 149

CHAPTER 13 DOING IT YOURSELF 162

CHAPTER 14 PAINTING 178

CHAPTER 15 FURTHER FINISHING 198

CHAPTER 16 WEATHERING 217

CHAPTER 17 FINISHING TOUCHES 232

BIBLIOGRAPHY & SUGGESTED READING 246

USEFUL ADDRESSES 248

INDEX 253

INTRODUCTION

Although railways have their origin in man's desire to move freight, carriages for fare-paying passengers were in use as early as 1807, pre-dating the introduction of locomotives. Developments in carriage design were fairly slow, even following the opening of the Liverpool & Manchester Railway in 1830, widely regarded as the first true passenger railway. Indeed, carriages remained similar in style to the stagecoaches they were soon to render obsolete.

Not until forty years later did the first bogie coaches appear, on the narrow gauge Ffestiniog Railway, of all places. The increased passenger capacity of longer, articulated vehicles soon saw mainline railway companies developing the bogie principle, although four- and six-wheel rigid underframes continued in use well into the twentieth century.

With the introduction of British Railways' iconic Mark I stock in 1951, the use of all-steel construction finally became standard, albeit continuing the tradition of a separate underframe and bodyshell. The 1960s saw the development of the Mark 2, with its integral construction and improved crash-worthiness, enhanced further by the adoption of electric heating and air conditioning in later batches.

Mark 3 and Mark 4 stock, built in the late 1970s and 1980s, was designed for higher speed, increased passenger density and improved safety. Moreover, the introduction of push-pull locomotive working, in conjunction with Mk3 and Mk4 DVTs (Driving Van Trailers) and Mk2 DBSOs (Driving Brake Second Open) eventually paved the way for the mass 'unitization' of Britain's railways, with the use of locomotive-hauled passenger stock dwindling in favour of multiple units.

Given the importance of coaching stock to the real railway, it's not surprising that it also forms a vital part of the model railway hobby. Coaching stock, in a variety of forms, has been a key fixture in the ranges of virtually all ready-to-run (RTR) manufacturers, across the popular modelling scales. Only since the turn of the millennium, however, has the quality, accuracy and breadth of choice matched that of contemporary locomotives, especially for modellers of the UK scene. Up to the 1990s, Hornby and Bachmann Branchline offered a limited range of British Railways and Big Four (LMS, GWR, Southern and LNER) carriages in 'OO' gauge, many of which were models from former brands such as Airfix, Tri-ang and Mainline. Such products were variable in terms of detail and authenticity, some dating back to the early 1970s. Lima also offered a range of BR MkI stock, of dubious realism, while Jouef's Mk3 stock was impressive for its time and remains sought after today.

In contrast, modellers in 'N' gauge enjoyed much less in the way of choice, with the predominant Graham Farish range developing little from the 1970s until the 2000s. Mass-market RTR 'O' gauge coaching stock has only recently emerged as a realistic proposition, thanks mostly to the efforts of the Danish brand Heljan.

Ready-to-run carriages have come a long way in terms of fidelity and production quality. Although the outline of this late 1930s Hornby 'O' gauge carriage is basic, the quality of the painted finish is actually very high. Have railway modellers always been a demanding customer group?

The move towards all-plastic RTR models in the 1970s saw a rise in refinement and accuracy, with Lima, Tri-ang, Hornby, Airfix, Replica and Mainline producing some impressive models for the time. Some are still in production today, albeit under different guises.

A blast from my past: as a young enthusiast in the 1980s, much of my pocket money went on BR coaching stock of the day. While Lima's Mk1 and Mk2 stock was just about passable, it was for the more authentic Replica and Airfix models that I yearned. The Jouef 'OO' Mk3 also gained a reputation for a high standard of finish and detail at the time of its release.

Airfix's air-conditioned Mk2D stock, released in 1977, was especially good for the time. Continued under the Hornby brand, they have recently been superseded by a newly tooled version of the similar Mk2E.

Models with a long pedigree have been improved greatly with twenty-first-century standards of painting and lining, as evinced by this Hornby Collett carriage. There is a pleasant amount of relief in some of the mouldings, especially the bogies, but the chunky couplings and rudimentary end detail hark back to a different era.

These days there is a comparative wealth of choice, with Bachmann's popular BR Mk1s (released 1999) and Hornby's LNER 'Gresleys' (2004) each marking important watersheds in 'OO' gauge coaching stock production. With the market's expectations thus raised, we've since been treated to even higher-grade models, such as Hornby's Hawksworth, Maunsell and LMS 'Period III' stock, and Bachmann's LMS 'porthole' carriages and BR Mk2s. In 'N', Farish and Dapol have taken standards to new heights with much-improved steam- and diesel-age carriages, and we've even seen the first RTR 'OO9' narrow gauge stock, courtesy of Peco.

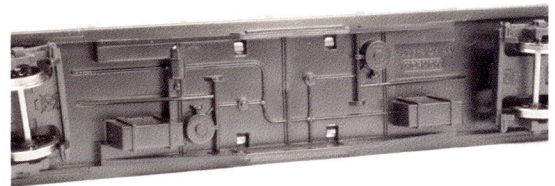

The spartan nature of the Collett's underframe is also a throwback to an earlier era. The shunting of stock like this into Hornby's budget Railroad range, however, makes them great value, especially as a basis for detailing and repainting projects.

Although far from perfect, Hornby's Gresley stock proved to be a game-changing release. Hitherto, only Bachmann's BR Mk1 range had reached such heights of detail and finish.

Hornby's rendition of the varnished teak finish surpasses anything achievable by even an expert modeller in a small scale, showcasing the best of modern printing techniques.

Bachmann has produced a wide variety of vehicle types within the iconic BR Mk1 family. We probably take them for granted now, but they're a great example of successful RTR product design.

Modellers in 'N' gauge have seen great leaps in quality in recent years. Compare the difference between these Graham Farish Mk1s: the older product on the right, with its flat, printed side overlays and basic underframe, looks a poor relation to the more recent version.

Choice amongst ready-to-run 'O' gauge is still limited, but Heljan has been offering various Mk1 vehicles with a decent array of fine detail, especially in terms of underframe equipment. In terms of kits, there is plenty more to choose from, including the excellent Just Like the Real Thing range.

All of this product development naturally comes at a price, with the cost of some of the more ornate carriages approaching eye-watering levels. Modern fitments such as automatic close-couplings, interior lighting and DCC compatibility are impressive additions that add value to each car, but may not actually be desired by some modellers. Happily, there are still bargains to be found, such as Hornby's recent BR Mk1 and Mk2E stock, plus the ex-Airfix LMS carriages now offered by Dapol. Such models may appear a little rough-and-ready in some respects, but they do offer great potential for the budding detailer.

Cost is a significant factor, with even a recreation of a sleepy branch line requiring at least a few carriages for each service. Furthermore, any attempt to replicate a main-line location will demand a significant investment in rolling stock. Talk of expensive UK-outline models should be tempered, however, by the prices that Continental and North American modellers have been expected to pay for decades. Brands such as Lilliput, Fleischmann and Rapido have long offered high levels of detail and specification at the kind of prices that some of us would be thinking of paying for a locomotive only.

The question of time is also pertinent, with a modest rake of improved RTR carriages potentially absorbing many hours of detailing work. When kit assembly is introduced, the time requirement increases exponentially.

KITS OR RTR?

While RTR choice has increased, surely the need for kit building has passed, especially in the ever-popular 'OO' gauge/4mm scale? This is far from the truth, as the sheer weight of numbers in terms of carriage types and sub-classes (even amongst the BR 'standard' marks) means that there remain a vast number of prototypes untouched by the RTR brands. Many slight variations can be modelled by using RTR models as a basis for conversion projects, or employing underframes to recreate different designs altogether, perhaps by fitting an etched brass or resin body kit.

Modellers with an interest in pre-Grouping railways, narrow-gauge or Irish railways, on the other hand, are still faced with kits as the primary source of their coaching stock. And that's just taking 'OO' as an example. For those working in other scales, kits or scratch-building may be the only routes available. Carriage kits remain available in a wide range of scales and media, ranging from plastic, metal and resin to laser-cut wood. Many offer a complete package, leaving only paints to be sourced separately, while others provide the bare bones, such as a basic bodyshell, and leave the modeller to fill in the gaps. Recently the growth in 3D printing has allowed an even greater range of obscure prototypes to be replicated, offering pre-formed bodies as a head start for the scratch-building process.

Some kits may demand significant extra work to match the best RTR models (it used to be that RTR models were substandard to kit-built models!) or simply to meet your own set of specifications and preferred coupling and operating practices. Whatever format that a model takes, there is nearly always room for further enhancement, whether it be in adding a more detailed interior or improving the finish by buffing up the paintwork and adding some weathering for a more lived-in appearance.

Adding new glazing to RTR models, such as the sublime laser-cut glazing packs from Extreme Etchings/Shawplan, produces a significant visual improvement for relatively little effort. Introducing some extra variety to your rolling stock may also be desired, perhaps by recreating a particular type of catering vehicle employed on the route that your layout depicts, or maybe even reproducing

Even Irish railways are now catered for by the RTR 'OO' market: Murphy Models produces a range of high quality 'OO' gauge carriages, taking away the hitherto necessity of RTR conversions or kit building.

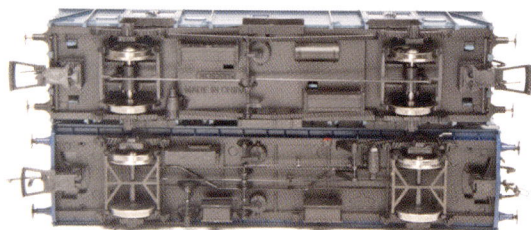

Although far from universal, this is the kind of underframe detail that we've now become accustomed to with 'OO' gauge RTR stock. Anything less is an inevitable disappointment. Have we become spoilt?

an unusual rake of non-passenger stock such as an overhead line maintenance train, both of which may only be possible by employing kits.

At the other end of the scale, maybe it's only a change of running number, regional prefix or livery that's required on a rake of RTR models. Either way, this book is intended as a broad guide to getting the best from ready-made and kit-built coaching stock.

WHAT'S IN THE BOOK

As with my previous books in the Crowood series, the onus is on techniques, hints and tips rather than simply a series of specific projects. There are, however, a few undertakings that can be followed if you so desire, but the main purpose of the work is to furnish the reader with a full range of skills that are transferrable to any coach modelling project, whatever the era, scale or region.

This book seeks to demonstrate how RTR models can be improved, modified and converted, as well as looking at a range of kits in various materials. Where kits and RTR still don't offer a solution, we'll look into the subject of scratch-building entire vehicles or the most vital components, such as underframes, bodysides and interior fittings.

Starting with a range of rudimentary techniques, including renumbering RTR stock (without the need for repainting) and adding passengers, we'll gradually move on to the more challenging pursuits of

soldering, shaping metal parts and casting your own components. All techniques are described and illustrated in full, with a complementary study of the most essential tools, equipment and adhesives. As with any practical pursuit, it helps to know something about the materials we'll be working with, so there is plenty of information on this scattered throughout the chapters.

Furthermore, the chapters are arranged roughly in order of difficulty, although the subject of painting and finishing is saved until Chapter 14. Readers who aren't yet ready for scratch-building or working with metal kits may prefer to skip straight to the later chapters for a look at applying the final touches. On the other hand, much of the content of the metalworking chapters will prove essential for anyone contemplating the use of etched brass detailing or conversion parts, as the subjects of soldering and shaping are covered in depth in Chapters 10 and 11.

Other interesting – yet often overlooked – subjects, such as interior lighting and couplings, are also discussed, helped by the proliferation of a wide range of innovative new products. The intricacies of finescale modelling are touched on, too, in an effort to whet modellers' appetites. The fundamental aspects of compensation, for example, is a topic attractive to most modellers who are aiming a little higher, so that is included in Chapter 12, along with other hints and tips to improve the appearance and performance of fixed-axle and bogie vehicles.

Changing running numbers, adding passengers and making a few detail enhancements to the exterior can drastically improve the look of even the best RTR products. A suitably weathered finish adds the finishing touch.

Kits offer the route to recreating a wider range of prototypes as well as a more rewarding experience than simply titivating a ready-made product.

Older kits remain a viable option, providing joy of a different kind, as well as many unique challenges. More up-to-date kits employ a multimedia approach, taking advantage of developments in photo-etching, 3D printing, laser cutting and resin casting.

ONE MORE THING …

It only remains for me to stress the importance of enjoyment in our hobby. Any undertaking that causes frustration and stress in our spare time hardly seems worth the hassle. On the other hand, learning new and unfamiliar skills always involves a degree of trepidation. What this book aims to do is to arm the reader with all of the necessary information and to illustrate a range of tried-and-trusted techniques. In other words, I'll show you how to avoid the many potential pitfalls, offering the benefits of my experience.

It is to be hoped you won't make the same mistakes that I did when I was starting out. But, even if you do, it's often the best way of learning. Just don't let it put you off!

The subject of scratch-building is also touched upon in this book. How else would a modeller set about recreating Queen Victoria's Royal Train? The late Cliff Newell – a master coachbuilder if ever there was one – crafted this 'EM' gauge depiction, which now resides in the National Railway Museum. See Chapter 13 for more details. IMAGE COURTESY OF MODEL RAIL

CHAPTER ONE

RESEARCH, TOOLS & EQUIPMENT

Getting started with any modelling endeavour involves differing degrees of enthusiasm and trepidation. By equipping yourself with a clear working plan, copious amounts of prototype information and a decent understanding of the tools and materials involved will lessen the amount of apprehension considerably. Furthermore, maintaining enthusiasm is essential, especially when embarking on more complex projects, where a greater number of challenges are likely to occur.

Thorough preparation has many benefits. Ensuring that all of the necessary resources are at hand, before work starts, should help the project to continue unhindered. Continual interruptions inevitably cause a waning of interest and will often lead to postponement or eventual abandonment. Ask any modeller how many unfinished projects are laying around their workshop and they'll have to admit to at least a handful – I've lost count!

Careful study of the prototype in terms of build details, differences between batches, equipment upgrades and refurbishment, liveries, interior details and eventual withdrawal dates provides invaluable titbits of information that will reveal what extra parts will be needed, especially for kit building, superdetailing or conversion projects.

Sourcing extra detailing or conversion kits and components may involve a number of different suppliers and, according to how intrepid the project, your shopping list may be a long one: bogies, wheels, bearings, underframe details, couplings, lighting units, transfers, paints, interior fittings, passengers, glazing, buffers and gangways are the most common items required. There are also a number of useful 'stock' materials to have at hand, such as fine metal wire for handrails and pipes, plus plastic and metal sheet, strip and section.

Adhesives, to suit different materials and applications, are crucial, along with a variety of tools.

If metal kits are involved, the need for soldering equipment and consumables must be added to the total cost, although, as will be explained in due course, this need not break the bank. Basic, intermediate and advanced modelling tasks demand a range of specific implements and in this opening chapter we'll consider the most fundamental of tools, with more specialized equipment discussed in later chapters.

RESEARCH

What do we need to look for and where can we find it? There's no doubt that researching railway history today is much easier than in the past, especially as much of it can be done from the comfort of one's armchair. The Internet places at our disposal a wealth of information, with plenty of historical sites, discussion forums and digitized archives. Apart from the latter, such sources may not be 100

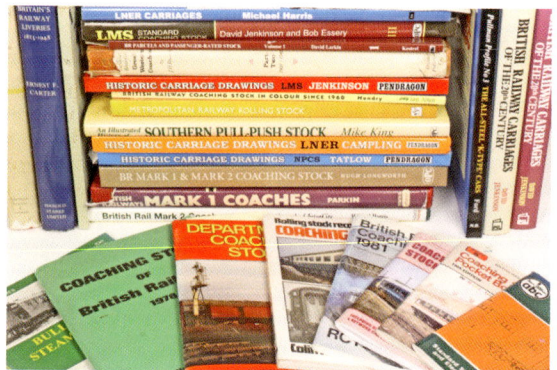

Knowledge is power: equipping yourself with plenty of prototype reference material will help enormously when assembling kits, improving RTR models or building carriages from scratch. There's an endless range of books, magazine and journal articles to be found, many available cheaply secondhand via the Internet.

per cent reliable, so a degree of crosschecking is recommended.

Photo-based websites, such as Flickr and Fotopic, contain countless collections of railway images, although sifting the wheat from the chaff can absorb many an hour. Books, magazines and the journals of specialist study societies (such as the Midland Railway Society) will provide plenty of visual, textual and statistical material and the Internet can help again with tracking down those hard to find, out of print titles from second-hand book dealers.

Municipal libraries (the few that retain a wide range of books), museums and archives are also worth investigating. The National Railway Museum's Search Engine facility offers the chance to browse an extensive online catalogue and archive, before arranging a visit in person or ordering reproductions.

For those of us who enjoy a more tangible link with the prototype, getting out and viewing the real thing, whether preserved or still in everyday service, is a sure-fire way to inject extra passion into a project. Gaining access to preserved vehicles can be a straightforward business, with a polite request usually sufficing (a donation to the cause in return is good manners). Just remember that a preserved vehicle may not be in authentic period condition, so some extra research into archive or published material is recommended.

What the carriage modeller needs most are plans, photographs and written information regarding specifications, liveries, numbers and dates. Much depends on your own quest for authenticity, with the more detailed knowledge being more difficult to locate, especially for pre-1930s prototypes. Details of upholstery and interior fittings can be difficult to discern from photographs alone, especially black and white images, so some descriptive information will be necessary unless fabric samples can be tracked down in a museum archive.

On occasion, a kit's instructions may possibly take care of much of the key elements of research, with some makers offering a wealth of illustrated material as part of the package. This is, sadly, not universal, and surrounding the workbench with plenty of illustrations will help to define exactly what goes where and why.

Collating large amounts of research material can sometimes prove a little overwhelming, so it pays

If you are lucky, you may be able to gain access to copies of official drawings, whether they're in an archive or via a current operator. Luckily, I managed to get access to the drawings and technical information for GNER's 'Mallard' update to its Mk4 stock in 2004, although these were supplemented by my own observations and sketches on the platform at Peterborough station.

Nothing beats getting out into the fresh air and looking over the real thing – but what to look out for? Prior study of books and articles will give a few pointers. In this case, the NRM's Mk1 support carriage carries equipment for both air and vacuum brakes, plus steam and electric heating systems. The air cylinder beneath the guard's door and the variety of hoses and cables at each end confirm this. The nearest compartment has also been converted to catering facilities, with extra vents on the roof and a tiny water filler cock at solebar level.

A closer look at the brake gear reveals the vertical vacuum cylinder on the left and the air tank at far right behind the access step. Note how the 'V' hanger is not set at an equal angle, with one side straighter than the other. Maintenance schedules and testing point legends have been stencilled on the solebar.

The battery box (left) looks a little worn in contrast to the immaculate bodywork, while the addition of the cooking gas storage boxes (right) are a later modification for this kitchen-equipped support coach.

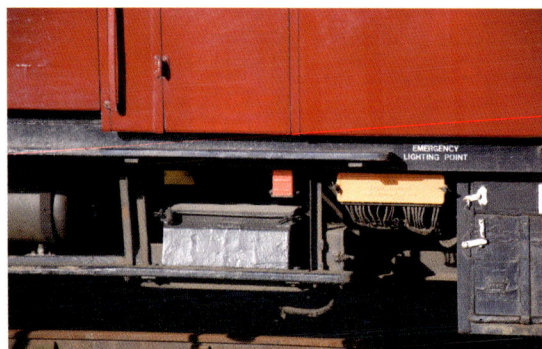

Fuseboxes and lighting distribution box are other interesting details, with more areas of detail painting and stencilling.

Pay attention to the bogies too, as Mk1s in particular could be found riding atop a range of different types, such as this Commonwealth bogie. Note how dusty the wheels and brake shoes appear compared to the shiny bogie frame.

Prototype images will also reveal how particular vehicles tended to weather and how they were cleaned. For instance, this air-conditioned Mk2 is typical of how I remember them in the early 1980s, with clean sides and ends, but with dusty brown underframes and grubby roofs. The yellow and black overhead warning stickers give the game away that this is actually a 'heritage' rake in the privatized era. The orange central locking door lights are also a much later addition.

to pick out the most relevant details, perhaps drawing up your own sketch plans and bullet points to complement the kit's instructions or to guide you through a RTR detailing or conversion exercise. Annotating photocopied images is one of my favoured modelling aids, while compiling an 'Order of Works', in conjunction with any instructions, helps one to gain a more focused impression of how an undertaking will take shape before any practical work begins.

TOOLS

Aside from a core set of measuring, cutting, shaping and joining tools, there are a few extra devices that will make carriage assembly projects more enjoyable. The tool sector of the hobby has witnessed plenty of innovation in the past few decades and, while I've never been one to collect tools willy-nilly, anything that can speed up a process, offer more consistent results or help me to gain more efficiencies in my work is worth serious consideration.

Most of the tools and working aids featured in this book may be seen as essentials. A few 'luxury' items are included by way of illustrating how they can make a particular task or skill more attainable, while a number of improvised or homemade devices are also demonstrated.

The tools that no modeller can live without include a good quality knife, some fine tweezers and pliers, plus mini hand and power drills with a range of bits down to 0.3mm diameter. A bench drill press is a luxury that will be greatly appreciated when working with metal kits or scratch-building, as will a precision milling table attachment, such as offered by Proxxon.

Images of the interior, if you can get them, are a real boon. This ex-LMS observation saloon has obviously seen better days, but the colour of the blinds, interior panelling and carpet is important.

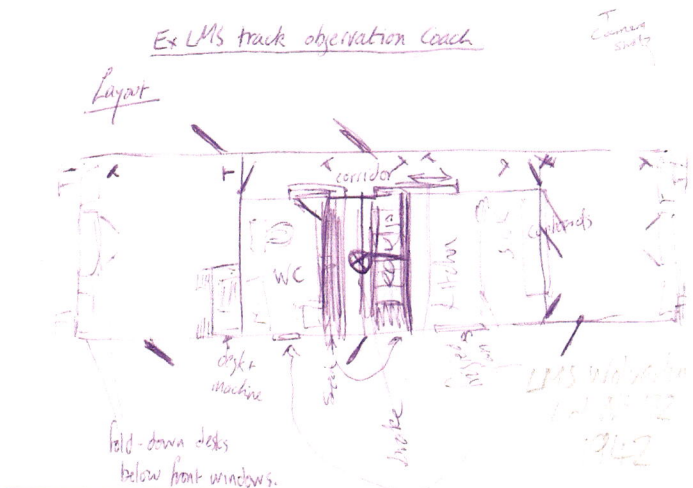

Whenever you're on site, taking endless photographs, it's worth keeping notes and sketches at the same time, to help jog your memory when you get home. This very rough sketch was taken while inside the observation saloon and shows the layout of the compartments and furniture. Crucially, it also records from where each photograph was taken.

These are likely to be the implements that you'll use for virtually every undertaking, so it's worth investing in good quality tools. A knife handle that is comfortable to hold, with the facility for interchangeable blades, will prove more economical in the long term. Indeed, it's important to only ever employ sharp blades, changing them on a regular basis, to ensure the best results and avoid accidents.

At the very least, you'll need a selection of marking, measuring, holding, cutting, abrading and drilling tools. Some will see plenty of use, others only occasional. But the quality of your modelling output can be improved by using the right tool for the right job.

Cutting tools will see plenty of use, especially on detailing and kit-building tasks. A fine scalpel with a selection of blades will prove to be your faithful servant, while a Stanley knife will be needed for heavier, less precise work. Cutting shears are required for work with sheet and etched metal components, while a razor saw and profile cutter will help when making more severe modifications to carriages and components. Razor blades make excellent scraping tools for flattening surface relief. Just watch those fingers!

It may seem contradictory, but a sharper tool is often a safer tool: forcing a blunt edge to cut material surrenders control, leaving the user more at risk of accidents. A light duty scalpel will be fine for most small-scale work in plastic, but for other materials and larger components a sturdier blade will be required. If a blade struggles to get through, why persist in the struggle when a small saw or serrated blade will do the job in a fraction of the time. Similarly, for the most intricate of cutting tasks, a set of precision shears is recommended, as they're likely to exert far less stress on the surface than a knife. As will be demonstrated throughout the book, cutting on the waste side and fettling to final size with abrasives affords much more control, despite the need to spend slightly longer on the job.

I prefer hand drills to powered tools for the most part, especially when creating holes of less than 1mm in diameter. Even in metal, where a pin vice will demand much wear on the fingers, greater precision is possible when working at a slower speed. Electric mini-drills do have an important role in my workshop, however, as will be seen in the ensuing pages. Drills alone aren't the answer to creating

A set of miniature drill bits and pin vices is essential. Working by hand can be time-consuming and tiring, especially where lots of repetition is involved, but a pin vice offers supreme control and accuracy, which more than makes up for the effort.

A mini power drill and accessories will make shorter work of drilling and shaping tasks. When used freehand, however, accuracy can sometimes suffer, so I tend to use these devices for fairly rough work that can be tidied up by hand. As well as a range of drill bits, sanding drums, milling bits and slitting blades will also come in useful.

Greater precision and safety is assured with a bench-mounted drill, especially when working on smaller components. This Proxxon device quickly converts into a milling table, allowing the quick and effective removal of unwanted material, even in the trickiest of locations.

precise apertures, with tapered reamers also being of massive value. These allow far greater facility for fine-tuning the size of a hole to fit a specific component, whereas trying to open out an existing hole with a regular drill bit runs the risk of losing the alignment and circularity.

Measuring and marking-out will also prove to be fundamental in creating accurate and reliable models. Good quality steel rulers, preferably with scale measurements, scribers and centre punches will be of more use than a sharp pencil, regardless of the materials at hand.

Soldering tools and equipment will be vital if any work in metal is envisaged, even if dealing only with etched brass detailing components, many of which will require shaping and assembly before fitting to the carriage. While most such tasks can be achieved with adhesives, the bond is seldom strong enough to withstand years of handling or operation, particularly when dealing with footsteps, gangways and similar projecting parts. Soldering still holds a foreboding aura amongst some modellers, but I've never understood why. My Dad showed me how to solder when I was about twelve years old, so I suppose the myths of it being a 'Dark Art' passed me by. But, if a pre-teen can manage it, I don't see why grown-ups can't. Most of the trepidation comes down to misinformation and, trust me, as long as you follow a couple of important rules, there's really nothing to it.

Nothing too fancy in the way of expensive tools and gear is needed for most soldering work, with a good quality iron costing less than £30. Only when working with white-metal – where there's a need to control the iron's temperature – will a greater cost be involved. A full rundown on tools, solders, fluxes and techniques is provided in Chapters 10 and 11.

Interested in adding etched metal detailing parts, installing working lights or building metal kits? If so, you'll need a basic soldering kit of iron, stand, flux and solder. Temperature-controlled irons and specialist solders will be necessary for more involved work, especially if materials like white-metal are involved.

ible sheets, pads, sticks and needles are available in graduated grit levels, with the finest grades able to create a highly polished surface on plastics, resin and metal. Each can be used wet or dry and the various shapes make them perfect for the most intricate work.

It's important to work patiently through each grade of abrasive, with clean water employed as a lubricant wherever possible. This prevents the abrasive 'teeth' from becoming clogged and causing scratching on the surface – just the thing that we're trying to remove. Each grade is designed to remove the marks left by the preceding grit and, by the time you're down to a 12,000-grit abrasive, the surface should be left almost flawless.

ABRASIVES

A selection of flat and shaped files, of varying sizes, are required to help prepare kit components or to modify existing models. Packs of needle files are cheap and readily available, but a few wider tools will also be necessary, such as half- or three-quarter-inch flat files to help render surfaces straight and true. Half-round and fully round files are also very handy.

In most cases, 'second' cut tools will suffice. However, files with coarser teeth, known as 'bastard' cut, will make shorter work of most materials and are helpful when more waste has to be removed, the rough finish then being refined with smoother tools. The teeth of files are likely to become blocked when working with soft materials such as plastics, resin and white-metal. Clearing them with a stiff wire brush or special cleaning tool, at regular intervals, is a must.

Abrasives, in a variety of grades, are also vital implements. Sheets of emery cloth, wet-or-dry and sanding paper will be of great help when working with metals, plastics and wood-based components. However, we also need some ultra-fine abrasives, such as Micro Mesh, Flex-i-File or those in the Squadron and Albion Alloys ranges. These flex-

Abrasives perform a vital role in coach building, with plenty of work involving fettling, smoothing and shaping of all materials. We're spoilt for choice amongst high-quality sanding pads, sticks, needles and sheets from the likes of Albion Alloys, Flex-i-File, Squadron and Micro Mesh, with a vast array of individual grades for heavy and super-fine polishing tasks alike.

HELPING HANDS

As well as tools, the workshop should also possess a means of safely holding models or components, allowing both hands to work freely. Clamps, vices and homemade jigs will be appearing throughout this book, employed for various assembly and modification tasks. As is the purpose of any holding device, their job is to keep the parts steady while gluing, soldering, drilling or cutting, without inflicting any damage to the surfaces.

Magnifying stands or headsets may also be helpful, especially when working in smaller scales or with more intricate components. Combined magnifiers and clamp sets kill two birds with one stone, while those with an inbuilt spotlight are also of great assistance. Indeed, lighting is an important issue, as there's nothing worse than trying to model in poor light. Plenty of the natural variety is always the preferred option, with daylight-simulating bulbs employed in lamps wherever possible. The location of your workstation is also important, so that you won't be working in shadows. Ventilation is vital, allowing nasty fumes to disperse harmlessly when working with paints, glues, fillers and solder.

Other necessary modelling aids include a set of gauges to suit your scale, permitting reliable and consistent setting of back-to-back measurements across your carriage wheelsets. Jigs for bending wire handrails, aligning axles, shaping roof and body profiles and myriad other assembly tasks can either be bought or fabricated as desired. It's easy to be sniffy about some of these things, but they can greatly speed up production as well as ensuring consistency, which is essential if a number of similar kits are being built.

One 'luxury' that I'd recommend, when working with any etched metal components, is a Hold 'n' Fold device. These versatile tools hold delicate parts securely and help in the formation of perfect folds and other intricate shaping tasks. They also double as effective clamps and are available in a wide range of sizes. A 'Nutter' tool is another great addition to the toolbox, designed for creating individual rivet and bolt heads – just the thing for detailing, conversion and scratch-building projects.

Vices will be required for holding parts during fettling, cutting and shaping tasks, while a variety of hand, sprung and screw clamps will help keep bits secure during assembly, especially when gluing or soldering.

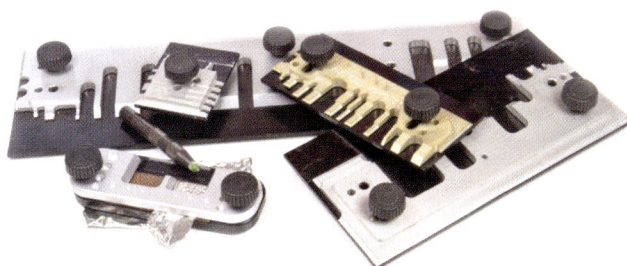

If your budget can accommodate one, I'd heartily recommend at least one Hold 'n' Fold in your tool collection. A Nutter punching kit, however, is more of a niche tool. Aimed at scratch-builders and super-detailers, a range of punches are included to produce individual nut, bolt and rivet heads in a soft metal foil.

Always protect yourself against dust, fumes, solvents and flying debris by wearing gloves, mask and eye protection.

ADHESIVES

It is not unreasonable to class adhesives as tools, as they have an equally important role to play in carriage modelling. Selecting the best glue to suit a particular task is vital for the longevity of the bond as well as the convenience of the builder. There are certainly plenty of brands and formulas to choose from. These can be separated roughly into two types: mechanical and non-mechanical. The former provide an intermediate layer between two materials in order to hold them together, while non-mechanical glues actually fuse the parts together before evaporating.

It will be appreciated that non-mechanical adhesives will require the mating surfaces to be as close as possible in order to be effective. Whatever type of adhesive is employed, ensuring that all joint surfaces are clean of debris, oil or other residues is of paramount importance, otherwise the glue will not be able to work effectively. Another point to remember is that cheap, general-purpose glues are seldom reliable for modelmaking purposes. With only a few exceptions, choosing a formula aimed specifically at craft and modelling use is to be recommended.

Store all adhesives in a stable environment, free from frost and high temperatures and away from direct sunlight. Many will have limited shelf lives, especially once opened. So only buy what you need, when you need it, as opposed to hoarding glues, along with kits, to be used 'on a rainy day'.

CYANOACRYLATE

Commonly referred to as superglue (after a leading brand name from years gone by), cyano will stick virtually anything to anything. A variety of formulas are tailored to particular jobs, with viscosity and curing times differing accordingly. Instant grab versions are great if the parts are already in contact or there's no need for gentle adjustments to ensure accurate alignment. Alternatively, slower curing versions allow parts to be manipulated for up to thirty seconds before the bond becomes permanent. Gel-type cyano also exists, combining slower drying times with a filling action, lending it to parts

that don't meet perfectly and the fully cured adhesive can be filed and abraded afterwards.

Cyano glue formulas are also available for use with particular materials, with some being optimized for use with plastics. In general though, cyano is great for bonding any material that we're likely to encounter. It can be applied straight from the tube or bottle or, for greater precision, there are precision applicators available. Decanting a small blob on a scrap of plastic or card and using a cocktail stick to apply the desired amount onto the part is my usual approach.

All cyano glues are hazardous and should be used with care, working in a well-ventilated area and avoiding skin contact. Never use cyano on parts likely to get hot, or where any soldering is to be undertaken. Heating will release noxious gases laced with cyanide, which can be unpleasant and decidedly unhealthy. Only a tiny amount is ever needed to effect a strong bond. In fact, applying too much can sometimes weaken a joint. Accelerating and de-bonding liquids are available, making cyano a more versatile adhesive than you might think.

CONTACT ADHESIVE

Intended for a range of materials, these adhesives are great for bonding larger metal, plastic or resin components, especially heavier parts like white-metal castings or ballast weights. They can be difficult to apply in small amounts, often being stringy and gloopy, so intricate work may be beyond them. Always read the label, as some contact glues may not be suitable for use with softer plastics, such as styrene.

For best results, apply a minimal amount of adhesive to both parts and leave aside to turn tacky for a few minutes before bringing them together. This results in a faster 'grab' and tidier joints. Any excess can be removed with white spirit.

EPOXY

Despite smelling like blocked drains, epoxy is a great adhesive, with many positive qualities. It can bond almost any material and provides a heat- and chemically resistant joint that also offers great durability.

Supplied as a pair of viscous liquids, equal amounts of each must be mixed thoroughly to create the adhesive. In common with cyano glues, different epoxy formulas offer a variety of working times, from five minutes up to an hour or so, while full bond strength is usually achieved within twenty-four hours.

The rapid cure versions are great for quick bonds or where there's little need for adjustment or clamping-up. However, it's only worth mixing up small amounts at a time as you'll get just a couple of minutes of working time before the glue hardens. A twenty-minute variety is often the most useful, especially if a number of parts are to be bonded at a time, leading to less time spent mixing small batches of glue and plenty of time to get the components aligned correctly. Although a slower 'grab' time results, clamping the parts with masking tape, clothes pegs or other devices will keep them from moving.

PVA

Polyvinyl acetate (PVA) is best known as an adhesive for woodwork, but it's also suitable for bonding card, paper, fabric and plastics. Countless variations are available, including many aimed specifically at the modelling market. Some PVAs cure to a milky film, while others will dry crystal clear, lending them to work with clear plastics. Furthermore, certain PVA-based formulas can also be used to create glazing films.

ALIPHATIC RESIN

Sharing some similar qualities as PVA, aliphatic glues cure faster, harder and offer greater resistance to moisture. Titebond wood adhesive is the choice of many a professional cabinetmaker, while aliphatic hobby glues such as Super Phatic and Roket Card Glue are thinner, penetrating adhesives for use with paper, card or wood components. They can also be employed to join wood-based materials to most plastics.

PLASTIC CEMENT

Liquid plastic cements are very different to the 'mechanical' adhesives already discussed, as they're basically a powerful solvent designed to chemically 'weld' plastic surfaces together. Having broken

Keeping a selection of adhesives at hand will allow for a variety of materials to be bonded in a neat and effective manner.

Johnson's Klear acrylic floor polish is an unlikely addition to a modeller's workbench, but it's an excellent adhesive medium for small detail components or glazing. It's also ideal for repairing scratched clear plastic.

seconds but there is a window of opportunity to make fine adjustments before the parts harden completely, usually after an hour or so. Once fully cured, the plastic will be fused together, so any attempt at breaking the joint apart will have to be undertaken with a saw.

Gentle clamping of the assembly with masking tape or rubber bands will keep everything together while the glue is applied, preventing any movement or distortion during curing. Where parts do not meet snugly, or where it's necessary to apply glue before they're brought together, a thicker formula of cement is required, such as Humbrol's Precision Poly, Revell's Contacta or Deluxe Materials' Roket Plastic.

FILL THE GAPS

It's always nice to achieve perfect joints between components, but it can be a rare occurrence with many older kits. Where gaps exist or the parts have been sullied in any way, recourse to filler is inevitable. There are plenty of putty formulas available that make application and manipulation easier.

Acrylic-based fillers, such as offered by Vallejo and Deluxe Materials, can be applied via a pinpoint syringe or needle tip, allowing the material to be deposited exactly where it's needed. A damp swab can then be employed to smooth the putty and remove any excess, leaving far less in the way of clearing up later, once the filler is dry.

Alternatively, solvent-based putties cure more quickly and are more durable, being particularly suited to larger cavities. These can also be manipulated with a swab soaked in an appropriate solvent, such as cellulose thinners. Delicate, brushable fillers, such as Mr Surfacer from Gunze Sangyo, are great for hairline cracks or surface imperfections and they tend to dry in minutes, allowing the job to continue without undue delay. Care is demanded, however, as the strong solvents in some formulas may damage the soft plastic surface if applied in heavy quantities. Therefore, apply a little at a time and build up deeper recesses gradually.

down the plastics enough for them to fuse together, the solvent eventually disperses leaving behind no traces. Different formulas are offered to cope with a variety of plastics, such as styrene, ABS and butyrate. Brand names such as Plastic Magic, Plastic Weld and Mek Pak are amongst the best known. Humbrol and Tamiya also offer thin liquid cements that offer great results. Application can be via a small brush or pinpoint applicator and the parts must be fettled carefully to meet as closely as possible.

As the solvent evaporates quickly, application must be made when the parts are already in contact with each other. The parts will 'grab' within a few

Epoxy putty, such as Milliput, is inert enough to be safe with all plastics and can be applied into deep cavities without any problems. Curing overnight into a rock-hard finish, it can then be sanded, carved and drilled.

As already mentioned, thicker formulas of cyano adhesives are also viable mediums for repairing small gaps and holes. Gel-type cyano offers the convenience of a bonding and filling agent in one shot and is ideal for use when plastic parts don't fit quite so well. Thinner cyano glues can be mixed with talcum powder to form a rapid-drying paste, while Deluxe's Roket Powder is designed to perform the same task. When fully cured, cyano can be filed and sanded smooth, with the ability to withstand drilling and shaping.

All fillers and putties tend to shrink to some degree as they dry out, so it's important to anticipate this by applying the material to sit just proud of the surface. Once fully cured, file and sand the filler flush with the surrounding area.

TAKING THE PLUNGE

Armed with our prototype research and a working knowledge of tools and adhesives, we can now make a start on the practical side of the hobby. There's no point running before we can walk, though, so the next couple of chapters will look at RTR models and how they can be improved to create more authentic and refined replicas of the real thing.

Fillers and putties help to ensure that all surfaces are perfectly prepared, especially if assembling kits or modifying RTR models.

CHAPTER TWO

EASY UPGRADES FOR READY-TO-RUN STOCK

While there's no doubting that ready-to-run (RTR) carriages have improved dramatically over the past decade, there's still plenty of scope for adding detail enhancements and customization. Expanding your fleet, by means of changing factory-applied numbers, is a worthwhile task and the glaring omission of what the vehicles were built to carry – passengers – can also be addressed.

The purpose of this chapter is to illustrate what can be done to improve RTR models with the minimum of fuss. Avoiding anything too invasive or destructive, or that may demand expensive tools, we can still achieve some impressive results.

FITTING SUPPLIED DETAILS

A logical starting point is to fit any separate detailing components that may be supplied. Although not so common with UK-outline carriages, many Continental and North American models frequently feature packs of extra handrails, brake pipes and other delicate parts that may not survive transit if fitted in the factory. Alternatively, fitment may be left to the modeller's discretion as they may impede the function of the couplings or bogies once installed.

A good example of a recent British carriage model with a host of exquisite plastic detailing parts is the Invicta/Bachmann 'OO' gauge Mk1 CCT van. Dummy screw couplings, brake and steam heat pipes, plus brake rodding and end door enhancements are bundled together in a plastic bag within the box. Fitting is a straightforward exercise, with the pre-formed holes being just wide enough for a snug – but not tight – fit.

A tiny dab of adhesive applied to the mounting lugs with a cocktail stick will be effective and a fine set of tweezers will help get the parts in the right place. Epoxy glue is probably the safest formula to employ, but the hassle of mixing the two components and the general gloopy nature are definite marks against it. Contact adhesive has similar drawbacks.

Instead, I prefer to use cyano glue for such tasks. Used in very small amounts it should not cause any adverse reactions to paintwork or any glazing components in the vicinity. An important precaution is required, however, in that the model must not be placed within a confined area (its box for instance) for twenty-four hours, so that any solvent fumes can disperse safely. To reduce the risks even further, try an odourless formula of cyano, although curing time may be about twice as long.

Ready-to-run carriages can be greatly improved with only a modicum of effort. Simply enhancing the interior and adding passengers can have a subtle but telling effect.

When fitting any separate detailing parts, or if anything has broken off during dismantling, my preference is to employ a tiny amount of cyano glue, applied to the component with a cocktail stick or pinpoint applicator. A tail lamp sets off the end of the rear carriage in a rake nicely.

Fitting brake pipes and a dummy scale coupling at the tail end of a permanently fixed rake of carriages or vans, perhaps with a tail lamp, adds a welcome touch to any passenger or parcels train if your layout's operations permit it. There's plenty of choice in terms of miniature lamps, with Springside in particular offering a wide variety of patterns and colours across the scales. There's even the option of working lamps, as will be discussed in Chapter 17.

Choosing the right time to fit any delicate parts is important: there's little point fixing them in place before dismantling and adding passengers to the interior, for instance.

LOOKING INSIDE

Although there's a limit to what may be visible through a carriage window, it's still important to give the impression that everything that should be there is present. The presence of figures alone seldom conveys the bustle of a real carriage, with luggage and the flotsam and jetsam associated with commuters, holidaymakers and catering facilities.

Plain moulded interiors also lack the variety to be found on the prototypes, with different coloured fittings for First Class and Standard Class, or the

myriad interior design upgrades and re-upholstering of the privatized age.

Starting with the innards of a modern carriage is easier said than done. How I miss the days when you could take a coach apart with only a fingernail! With delicate fittings adorning roof, ends and underframe, simply handling the model can be tricky. Dismantling methods differ according to specific models and brands, although Hornby tend to stick to the idea of having the bodyshell clipped to the chassis via several mounting points along each side. In contrast, other models may have to be accessed via the roof.

Holding the model safely is vital, reducing the risk of accidents. A sheet of packaging foam will allow a model to be laid on its side without damage to paintwork, glazing or fine details. Purpose-made foam cradles are available that hold the model securely, leaving both hands free.

Getting into many RTR carriages can be tricky. Hornby tends to favour sets of retaining tabs at each corner, partially hidden by the bogies. Depressing these tabs will allow the underframe to be partially released.

Safely cradling the model while it is being taken apart is a good idea, with soft packaging foam or similar materials being ideal to prevent scratches or broken components. If parts need to be prised apart, try to avoid hard metal tools, such as screwdrivers or blades. Stiff plastic shims, filed to a wedge profile, will prove far less injurious to soft plastics and paintwork. Once one corner has been released, insert more shims along the length of the side or roof, repeating the trick on the other side until the parts are released.

One of the worst dismantling procedures is the need to depress the glazing in order to push the roof upwards, as employed on Hornby's Mk3 and Mk4 stock. As the roof is rendered in the same clear, brittle plastic as the windows, there's a greater risk of damage unless handled carefully.

TOP: **With the corner tabs freed, insert a couple of card or plastic shims to maintain the gap between body and chassis while working a fine flat blade along one side to free the remaining clips. Repeat the process along the other side.**

MIDDLE: **Bachmann employed a different method of assembly for its 'OO' gauge MkI range. First task is to pull out the wire tank-filling pipes that link the body to the roof.**

BOTTOM: **By inserting a fingernail or blade between the roof and side at one corner, the roof can be unclipped. Work along one side at a time to release each clip in turn. The latest Farish 'N' gauge MkIs are also accessed via the roof in similar fashion.**

With the roof lifted off, the sides can be unclipped, pushing the ends outwards slightly to free the tabs at each corner. This method is suitable for virtually all Bachmann Mk1 stock and being able to work on the sides separately offers greater convenience.

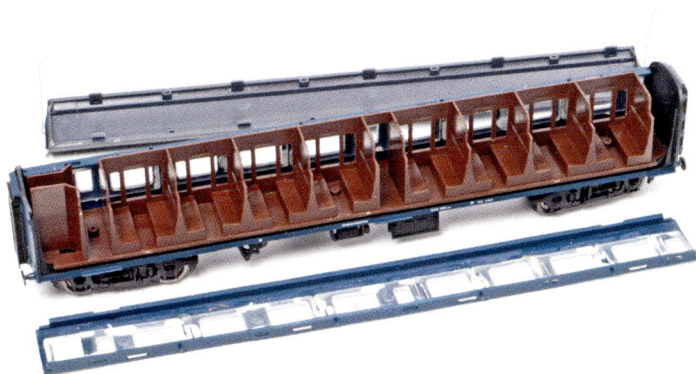

If small parts have come adrift, intentionally or otherwise, pop them into a sealed container and label them as to their purpose and location. There's little point fixing them back on too soon, as they're likely to get damaged again during reassembly, so they may as well wait until later.

INTERIORS

Once inside, we can decide to what extent we want to improve matters. The standard fitting across all scales is a simple self-coloured plastic moulding, depicting bulkheads, partitions, seats and tables. Picking out the various fixtures and fittings in the appropriate paint shades is a simple enough task that will have a dramatic effect on the finished model, especially once passengers have also been installed.

Older models are likely to feature one-piece bodyshells, fixed to the underframe via screws or hidden locating tabs. A typical example is the Hornby/Dapol/Airfix Mk2D stock, where the gangways have to be prized off before the underframe tabs can be levered out of the ends.

Painted interiors are pretty rare. At best, the seating may have been picked out in approximations of the fabric shades. They're simple enough to paint yourself, though. Spray a primer coat over the plastic moulding and apply suitable wood-type effects where appropriate. This Bachmann interior has been painted largely by airbrush (for speed), with the blue Second Class seating added by hand. A stippling action and subtle variations in shade produce a more textured finish, redolent of heavy fabric.

An alternative to painting interiors is offered by printed overlays, along with downloadable 'textures' from Scalescenes that mimic wood grain and tiled floor effects (ideal for some buffet and dining cars). Framed carriage prints are also handy, where the prototype warrants their inclusion.

Other fittings, such as mirrors and posters, add to the general ambience of a working carriage and there are countless other small details that we can add, according to the internal appointments of the prototype. Curtains and blinds are just the tip of the iceberg.

This self-adhesive printed interior is from LHP Products, available via eBay (see Useful Addresses). Simply cut out each element and stick in place. The BR standard mirrors are cut from kitchen foil backed with double-sided tape.

RTR carriages seldom include curtains in the appropriate compartments or saloons. If they are present, they're in the form of flat printed detail whereas the real things feature plenty of texture and depth. Cast metal curtains are available from Comet and MJT and look great when painted and 'washed' in a similar way to the passengers. Making your own curtains is also possible, using coloured paper folded concertina-like and with thin strips acting as tiebacks.

The cast curtains required trimming to fit within this Bachmann Mk1, being fixed with Glue 'n' Glaze adhesive. The edge of the seats also needed trimming slightly to give adequate clearance before reassembly could commence.

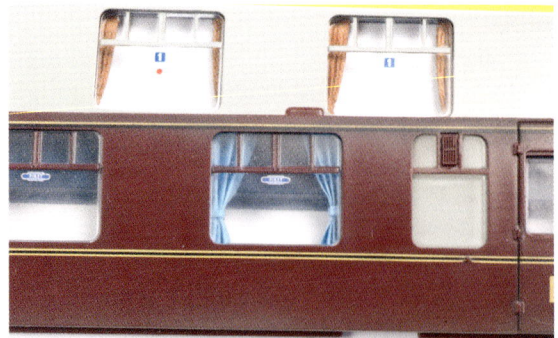

Once in place, the new curtains look incredibly realistic, especially the homemade versions. I didn't have the right shade of blue card to hand, but you get the idea.

PASSENGER FOCUS

The quality of passenger figures varies, especially in 'OO' and 'N' gauges where their smaller size and limited visibility within a carriage can be forgiven. Moreover, as cost will be an important factor when populating a rolling stock fleet, we can be forgiven for basing our choices on economic grounds rather than fidelity. It can be surprising how much money, time and effort can be expended purely on providing passengers for even the most humble of branch line trains, with the need to paint and install them individually. As the vast majority of figures will need a little surgery to enable them to fit within a RTR interior, that adds even more to the workload.

Pre-painted options exist across a number of figure manufacturers, but the cost may be prohibitive to most of us. Unpainted plastic figures are often the cheapest option and bulk packs, such as those offered in 'HO' scale from Preiser, can be tempting. Furthermore, the use of 'HO' passengers within 'OO' stock is to be recommended as their smaller stature suits the restricted space and many come without lower limbs to facilitate fitting into a moulded interior with a shallow floor.

Cast metal figures are more difficult to trim, but they do offer extra ballast. This may be a blessing or a curse, as a relatively full carriage may end up weighing significantly more than an empty version. Compensating by removing some or all of the factory-fitted weights may be necessary to avoid traction problems or derailments. We'll talk more about weight in later chapters, especially in regard to kit building, but it's worth mentioning here the importance of ensuring a consistent mass across a rake of carriages. Any anomalies, be they lighter or heavier than the rest, are likely to cause problems.

Whatever figures are chosen, the mouldings or castings will need any unsightly deposits of excess material or mould seams tidying with a needle file. After a rinse in warm water to remove any debris and production residues, they can be treated to a coat of primer, preferably from an aerosol, before painting can begin in earnest.

Batch painting, with the figures fixed temporarily to a scrap of timber, can prove an enjoyable evening pursuit. Or it might feel like the most boring endeavour in history, depending on your outlook. I have to be in the mood for this job, but if there's a football match on the radio or an audio book to listen to, then I'm happy to while away a winter evening or two painting a few dozen miniatures.

My preference is to employ acrylic paints, as they can be blended readily on the model's surface, to create rudimentary highlights and shadows, to bring out the best in the moulded detail. As they dry quickly, progress can be made more readily than with enamels. *(continued overleaf)*

Seated passenger figures are widely available in all scales, mostly in unpainted form and rendered in plastic or cast metal. Metal figures can add considerable extra weight to a carriage.

Although the exact contents of every carriage are unlikely to be scrutinized too closely, it's important nonetheless to get the passengers looking as authentic as possible. Creating plenty of variety in terms of clothing colours, within the limits of the period's fashions, will be effective, as will subtle changes in skin tone and hair colour across the board. It's tempting to simply 'knock out' batches of painted figures, but they can look very samey all too easily, although hordes of men in dark suits and hats may not be too unrealistic for a city commuter train.

Think also about how busy a particular train is likely to be. A peak-hour suburban service nearing a city terminus is likely to be packed to the rafters, while a sleepy branch line service ought to be more lightly loaded. Those sitting in First Class or, especially, Pullman saloons are certain to be dressed in their finery while a humble Third Class or workman's train would be awash with men in flat caps.

Once the people have been 'coloured in' and the paint has dried overnight, a final flourish is to treat them to an overall wash with a dilute mix of grey paint. This will sit within the seams of the clothes and the moulded relief, exaggerating shadows and taking the edge off any brightly coloured areas. Any excess is immediately wiped away and the figures left to dry overnight.

After checking the fit of each character and snipping away any unwanted material, the figures can be fixed in place. A strong, resilient adhesive is required to withstand minor bumps over the years, but not too potent as to cause damage to any surrounding fixtures and fittings, especially if clear plastic glazing is in attendance. Contact

Lightly affix the passengers to a block of wood using a drop of cyanoacrylate glue. A coat of aerosol-based primer will then render the figures ready for painting.

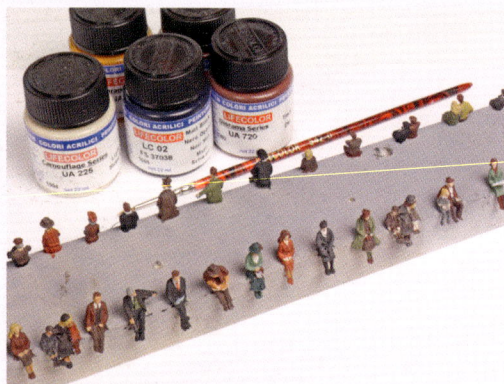

Take the time to paint your figures as carefully as possible, paying attention to period fashions and colours.

Allow the paint to dry overnight before enhancing the passengers with an overall weathering wash. MIG Productions Neutral Wash will settle into the moulded detail, bringing the figures to life. Wipe away excess with a cotton bud and allow to dry overnight.

adhesive, epoxy and cyano can be employed, the latter only with great care and in the minimum quantity possible. Ensure that the parts are well ventilated and that they're not placed into an enclosed space until a few days later.

PVA adhesive is also suitable, especially for plastic figures. My glue of choice in these instances is Glue 'n' Glaze from Deluxe Materials, as it dries completely clear, is odourless and the bond remains flexible enough to withstand the rigours of layout operations and handling. A small blob is applied to both the seat and the backside of the passenger and allowed to turn tacky for a few minutes before the bond is made. After an hour or two, the glue will have cured enough for the interior to be handled, but an overnight wait should be observed before the carriage is reassembled.

Depending on the carriage interior, it may be necessary to trim the figures to fit into the seats. Test-fit before committing yourself to any adhesive just yet.

My preference is to secure the passengers with Glue 'n' Glaze, a PVA-type adhesive that dries to a flexible yet resilient bond. Alternatively, thick cyano adhesive is suitable, if used with care. An accelerant, such as Roket Blaster, speeds up the bond and reduces the risk of 'blooming' to the surrounding surfaces.

Other internal elements such as newspapers and magazines strewn across tables add extra life. These are from a lorry cab detailing set from Ten Commandments, while the white mugs are cut from Evergreen plastic rod.

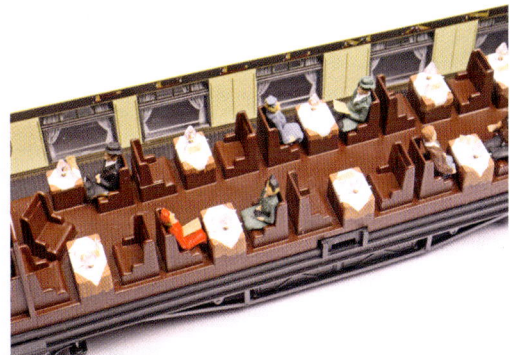

Cups, crockery and cutlery are also deceptively simple to recreate from plastic rod, tube and fine metal wire. These Pullman tables have also been painted to replicate the tablecloths, with menus and napkins cut from paper.

REBRANDING

Being able to change a carriage's running number, without any drastic recourse to paints, is a useful skill to have in reserve. Seldom do RTR manufacturers offer the exact identities that we're after, nor do they provide enough examples with the correct regional prefixes to properly equip a modest mainline layout. Multi-pack bundles of the same carriage type, as offered by many retailers, usually include multiples of the same number, so wiping away and replacing the factory-printed digits will be a commonplace undertaking.

Adding extra markings, such as Inter-City or regional logos to later BR stock, or simply instating missing markings from the carriage ends or underframes may also be desired. Again, reference to prototypes is essential as variations in markings

Factory-printed legends can be removed by gently rubbing over with T-Cut paint restorer. Working patiently, with only a small amount of T-Cut on a cotton bud, the numbers will soon disappear. Protect other markings with masking tape where necessary.

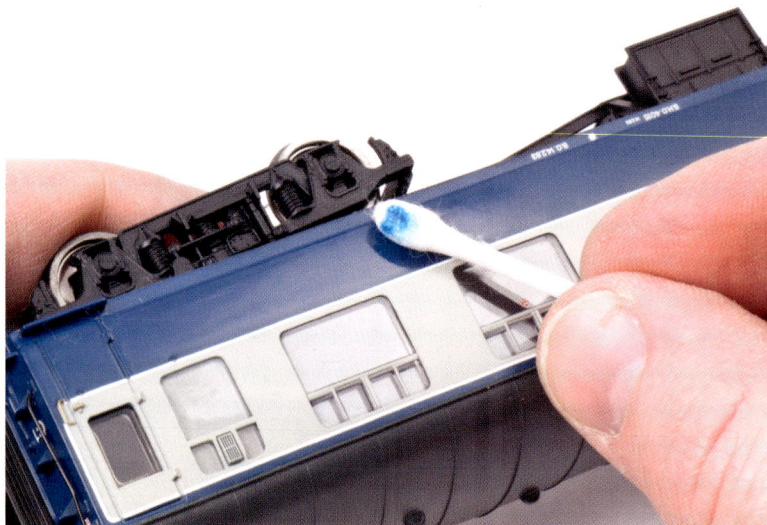

Once the numbers and letters have gone, the surface can be buffed with a dry cotton swab. This will remove any traces of the T-Cut, while also leaving the surface smooth.

Employ a strip of low-tack masking tape as a guide for the new numbers. Dry rubdown decals are the easiest to apply. After rubbing over with a pencil, gently peel the film away. Seal the new legends in place by rubbing the pencil over the supplied tracing paper.

Carefully remove the masking tape guide. I always repeat the pencil-and-tracing paper rubbing, just to make doubly sure that the transfers are secure.

Waterslide decals are a little more labour intensive, but worth the effort. The surface must be as clean and glossy as possible (varnished if necessary) and a prior coat of Micro Set solution greatly helps adhesion.

Soak the transfer in water and, once it becomes loose, slide it onto the model's surface. A blunt cocktail stick aids positioning without risk of damaging the delicate film.

Once the decal is in place, dab away the excess moisture with a cotton swab, gently remove the tape and apply a further coat of Micro Sol to help the transfer settle. Allow it to dry naturally overnight before sealing with a light coat of varnish. For a uniform finish, apply the varnish over the whole side, whether by hand, aerosol or airbrush.

and their positions abounded, especially as vehicles passed through works for intermediate overhauls or *ad hoc* repairs.

Dry rubdown transfers make the job of adding new markings simple, with little in the way of surface preparation, bar the need to remove the originals and ensure that the area is smooth and clean. A softer lead is recommended for rubbing over the transfer film, something along the lines of a 2B for example, which will be less likely to pierce the film or leave any traces on the plastic bodyshell. I have found that Replica Railways produce some of the best rubdown numbers for BR coaching stock in 4mm scale.

Waterslide decals, on the other hand, demand a high gloss surface on which to adhere, so either the paintwork needs polishing or a gloss varnish must be applied. One of the benefits of my preferred renumbering method is that the T-Cut automotive paint restorer used to remove the original characters also acts as a polishing agent. Some gentle burnishing with cotton swabs will result in a beautifully shiny finish that lends itself perfectly to the application of waterslide transfers.

Once in place and thoroughly dry, the decals will also need a sealing coat of varnish. By treating the whole vehicle, any traces of interference with the original finish can be removed. Some masking of glazing and moving parts will be necessary if the varnish is sprayed, but the results will be worth the extra effort involved.

REASSEMBLY

Putting coaches back together should, in theory, be a straightforward reverse of the dismantling process. Be sure that any adhesives and paints employed on the interior are completely dry and that all solvent fumes have dispersed, and check that everything will fit back inside the bodyshell. Errant elbows, knees and heads of passengers can sometimes catch you out once the glazing and other impedimenta of the inner bodyshell and roof are encountered. It also helps to check that the interior and body are the right way around in relation to the underframe, although some RTR models are designed so that they can only be reassembled in the correct way.

When you're sure that everything will do, clip the parts back together and refit any screws where necessary. At this point, if any further handling is to be minimal, any parts that were broken during dismantling can be reaffixed.

WHAT NEXT?

The modifications suggested here are fairly simple, yet they combine to produce a dramatic improvement in the appearance of a RTR coach. We can go further, of course. Something as small as swapping a set of wheels or replacing 'sunken' glazing in favour of superior flush-fitting windows has a massive, transformative effect. These subjects, and more, will be covered in the following chapter.

CHAPTER THREE

MORE READY-TO-RUN UPGRADES

There's always the possibility of going one step further with detailing work. Peering closely at prototype images will reveal all manner of tiny details that will be lacking from even the best RTR offerings. Most commonly brought about by compromises in the production process, certain fittings may either be missing or rendered in a rudimentary fashion, requiring some degree of surgery to put right.

Older models can look somewhat out of place beside the more recent products and, therefore, making them more at home on a twenty-first century layout may be your priority. This can be achieved with a modicum of detailing work and maybe a new set of wheels. Handrails and buffers are the type of fixture that's commonly ripe for improvement. Or perhaps your chosen prototype has a few features different to those on the RTR model, such as an alternative pattern of roof vents. The glazing is another point where older models suffer but, again, there are ways and means of curing these minor ills.

Upgrades or modifications throughout a coach's working life will see a few changes here and there. Carriage types built in huge numbers, across a variety of different workshops, are likely to see detail variations, many of which a RTR model can't hope to capture. Adding variety to our passenger fleets is a worthwhile endeavour, as a typical train seldom has every carriage looking exactly the same, especially in the pre-privatization era. Furthermore, it's the knack of being able to identify such tiny variations that is a key attribute of the avid detailer.

Removing the original and inferior moulded detail, making good the surrounding surface and adding new components is the fundamental process behind upgrading RTR products. Mounting holes may need to be marked out and drilled, with replacement parts carefully shaped before installation, while the appropriate adhesive must be selected.

This chapter sets out to explore each of these topics, demonstrating the various processes and offering plenty of hints and tips along the way.

GLAZING

Models with a longer pedigree, some of which are still being produced in the mainstream RTR market, rarely feature flush-fitting glazing, this being something of a post-1990s phenomenon. Vacuum-formed flush glazing packs were once the staple of enthusiastic coach detailers, with South Eastern Finecast offering packs tailored to specific 'OO' gauge models.

In the twenty-first century, however, we now have laser-cut plastic replacement glazing, from Extreme

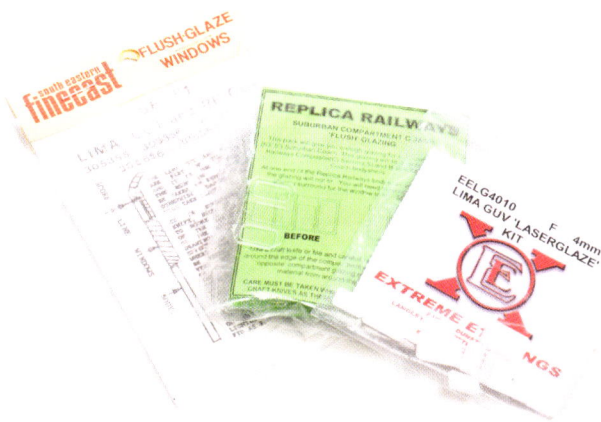

Replacement flush glazing has been around for many years, most notably via South Eastern Finecast's (SEF) vacuum-formed plastic packs for specific 'OO' RTR models. More recently, Extreme Etchings/Shawplan has raised the bar with a range of laser-cut acrylic glazing.

Removing the original glazing varies in difficulty according to the model. In most cases it can be snapped away with a stout blade used for leverage. Just be very careful not to damage the bodyshell or your fingers.

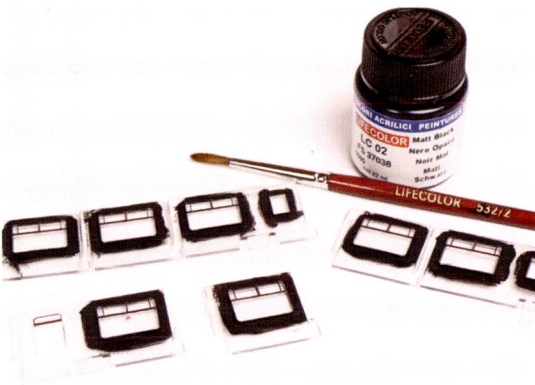

A great tip for improving the supplied glazing is to remove it and paint around each pane with matt black acrylic paint. Two coats are often required for full opacity.

Etchings/Shawplan and York Modelmaking. This is designed to fit from the front of the carriage, being cut with a tapered edge for an interference fit within each aperture. With minimal fettling, it produces an astoundingly realistic effect and an overall coat of gloss acrylic varnish will provide a durable bond.

Talking of acrylic varnish, Johnson Klear floor polish (also branded under the 'Future' or 'Pledge Klear' labels) is an ideal medium for fixing laser-cut glazing in place. Thin and crystal clear, it can be run into the joint around the glazing components for a reliable and seamless bond. Furthermore, it can also be brushed over the clear parts to improve their appearance and provide a tough, scratch-resistant coating.

Older Graham Farish coaches, along with a handful of 'OO' kits, made use of clear plastic body-shells, with the livery painted over the top, thus rendering the glazing flush with the outer faces. This sounds like a good idea in theory but the effect is a little one-dimensional as there should be a raised beading around most windows, while pre-1950s stock did actually sport slightly recessed windows within steel or wooden frames.

It is possible to fashion your own flush glazing from clear acctate, plastic card or by modifying the model's existing glazing so that individual panes can be fitted flush into each aperture. After polishing the faces and edges of the clear plastic, dipping in Klear will restore the translucence and remove any last vestiges of tool marks or blemishes.

Allow the paint to cure fully before re-fixing the glazing, using a PVA-type adhesive such as Glue 'n' Glaze. The black paint effectively minimizes the prismatic effect caused around the edges of the moulded glazing.

There's no doubt that cutting and fettling individual windows can be a tiresome exercise. It may not be so bad if only a couple of vehicles are being treated, or if we're dealing with parcels vans featuring only a few apertures per side. It all depends on your own personal whims, budget and desire for authenticity.

Even the fancy flush glazing fitted as standard to contemporary RTR stock can be improved, simply by removing it from the body and running a black marker pen or paint around the edges. This reduces the prismatic reflection of light that fools the eye into thinking the glazing is thicker than it actually is. Indeed, when adding off-the-shelf laser-cut or vacuum-formed flush glazing packs, the same trick will improve matters considerably.

Getting the factory-fitted glazing out of the bodyshell is not always easy, as the clear plastic is inherently brittle and prone to cracking. Often it depends on how much glue the operative on the production line has applied to individual carriages; some may simply pop out, while others will be stuck fast. In the latter case, it's often best to leave well alone rather than risk irreversible damage, although there are times when I've persevered with a miniature, flexible razor saw blade, but don't blame me if it all goes wrong!

Finally, adding 'frosting' to obscured windows in toilets or catering vehicles can be achieved in a number of ways. Either the inside face of the glazing can be painted with an off-white shade of acrylic or enamel paint, or a piece of tracing paper fixed behind the clear plastic with Spray Mount adhesive. Each technique produces a notably different result that may be suited to different circumstances. For example, the painted-out version

The SEF flush glazing is simple to install. Cut out the individual 'panes' with scissors, leaving a small amount of material around the outside for the glue to work on. A thin bead of glazing adhesive, left to turn slightly tacky before fixing in place from the inside of the body, will provide a strong and crystal clear bond.

Test-fit each window to gauge whether the aperture requires a little fettling with a needle file to effect a snug fit. The appearance is certainly an improvement, but the vacuum forming process inevitably leaves a rounded edge to the glazing.

In contrast, Extreme Etchings's Laserglaze is fitted from the outside of the vehicle, with a slight taper being cut into the edges for a precise 'plug-type' fit. Fitting the parts with the chamfer correctly oriented is critical, so keeping a magnifier at hand may be helpful. Run an indelible marker pen around the edges of each pane, either in black or a close approximation of the carriage's livery shade.

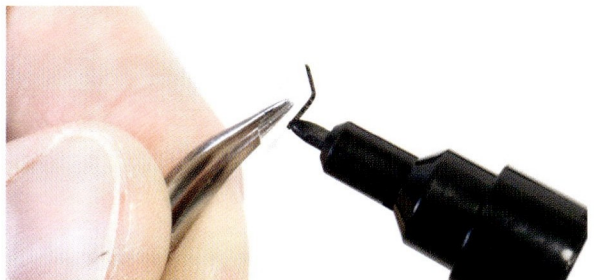

Place the glazing into position, with the narrower edge of the taper facing downwards. Invariably a snug, accurate fit will result. Wrap tape around the tips of your tweezers to prevent damaging the clear acrylic.

Seal the glazing in place by running a thin clear acrylic varnish around the edges, allowing it to flow into the window surround. Johnson Klear floor polish is perfect for this job. Applied over the entire pane, it also improves the transparency of the plastic.

Creating your own flush-fitting glazing is a viable option, if time-consuming. Mark out and cut the glazing from a thin sheet of clear styrene, using a fresh blade and gentle pressure to avoid shattering the brittle plastic.

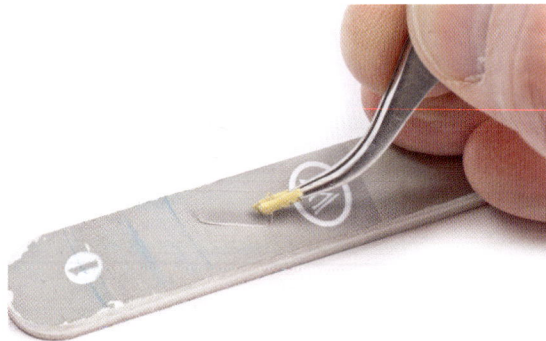

Start out with each pane slightly oversized and fettle the edges until a close fit is achieved, rounding over the corners carefully where necessary. After test fitting, the plastic can be polished on fine abrasive pads. Dip the glazing into Johnson Klear for an ultra-clear appearance.

Secure the glazing with a thin bead of adhesive around the inside of the aperture. Mop up any excess glue with a damp swab, although it will dry crystal clear anyway.

is more appropriate for post-1950 stock, while the more subtle effect of the tracing paper is redolent of earlier practices.

REWHEELING

Another facet of pre-millennium RTR rolling stock is the prevalence of coarse scale wheels and flanges. These may be fine for your layout, especially if running on Code 100 ('OO') or 80 ('N') track. For users of finer specification rail systems or those simply wanting something more pleasing on the eye, these wheelsets will have to be replaced.

Besides, installing high-quality wheels and axles, from the likes of Gibson, Markits, Romford or Ultrascale, will result in smoother, quieter and more reliable running, without the risk of oversized flanges catching on rail chairs, check rails or point frogs. A better-running carriage also means less drag on the locomotive, which can be important when running scale-length trains.

Choose turned metal wheels wherever possible, as these offer the best running characteristics and appearance. Gibson wheels are of note, as they feature plastic centres fitted into turned metal rims. Although there's usually a little excess plastic to trim away from the moulding process, the material is much easier to paint than all-metal wheels. Additionally, the plastic inserts also serve to reduce running noise.

The main RTR manufacturers offer bulk value packs of carriage wheels and these are by far the most economical option. Be discerning, however, as many are produced as metal pressings and their roundness may not be as precise as those turned on a lathe.

Once again, prototype reference is pertinent, as wheel sizes and patterns differed across a range of vehicles, particularly in the pre-1950s era. Spoke, plain disc, disc with holes, plain with brake discs or the distinctive wood-centred Mansell pattern are the most common, with each type being available in most scales from a number of sources.

Although it's a bonus if we can install wheels of true scale dimensions to our models, we may have

Enhance the glazing further by adding any necessary information stickers for non-smoking compartments, Class designations or coach lettering, as per your prototype and operating period. These wonderful waterslide decals from Precision Labels are double-sided, showing the same legend on both sides of the glazing. Once in position, apply a coat of Johnson Klear for a flawless finish.

Obscure toilet compartment windows by either painting or fixing tracing paper to the inside face of the glazing. Use a 'dry' adhesive such as Spray Mount.

to compromise in some areas. Those of us with second radius curves and less-than-finescale track specifications will see true-scale wheels struggle to cope with the cramped confines of bogies and underframes. In this case, choosing slightly smaller wheels will be necessary.

In order to achieve a modicum of standardization, the NMRA (National Model Railroad Association) and NEM (Normen Europäischer Modellbahnen) have set out guideline specifications for each mod-

Upgrading a model's wheels can offer superior performance as well as appearance. Deep flanges and inconsistent back-to-back measurements lead to unreliable running, while good quality metal wheels reduce the amount of dirt building up on the rails.

elling scale, governing such factors as wheel profiles and other key dimensions. One of the most relevant specifications is Recommended Practice document 25 (RP-25), which sets out the optimum wheel dimensions to suit each rail 'code', as described in thousandths of an inch (Code 75 rails are 0.075in high and so on). Not all wheel manufacturers actively follow these guidelines, however, but it's worth consulting the specifications and checking the wheels with a set of calipers (*see* Useful Addresses for NMRS website address).

GAUGING OPINION

Back-to-back measurements and wheel profiles can be a thorny issue amongst purists and finescale adherents. Those with more of a model engineering bent will be aware of the tolerances involved with the wheel–rail interface but, for the more aesthetically inclined, as long as the carriages stay on the tracks and don't wobble around, we're happy enough.

I suppose I straddle both camps to a degree, although I'm probably more inclined towards a relaxed approach to scale. Indeed, I seldom model to finescale standards, insofar as the 'mechanics' are concerned. Like many of us, I want the wheels and

rails to look as realistic as possible but, as a confirmed 'OO' modeller, I'm happy to live with a few necessary compromises.

In order to ensure reliable running, setting the wheel back-to-backs to a consistent measurement is recommended, as the variances between RTR wheels and those supplied from the aftermarket trade can be significant. Even between manufacturers, or even between axles on the same RTR coach, there is likely to be some variance and this is usually the cause of mysterious derailments, especially on finer grade track and points.

Checking the wheels of every item of stock before it enters service with a set of calipers will reveal some anomalies, while a purpose-made back-to-back gauge will also discern whether a wheel is slightly out of true on the axle. But what should the back-to-back measurement be? Here is a list of the most widely accepted specifications for each of the most popular standard gauge scales. However, these should be treated as guidelines only, as a number of modelling societies state slightly different specifications. For more detailed information, *see* the NMRA and NEM websites, or contact some of the specialist societies for your chosen scale (*see* Useful Addresses).

Back-to-back Measurements for the Popular Gauges

'N'	7.4mm
'HO'	14.5mm
'OO'	14.4mm (Standard 'OO') or
	14.8mm (Double O Gauge Association finescale standard)
'EM'	16.5mm
'P4'	17.75mm
'O'	29mm

Seldom do new wheels drop straight into RTR model bogies, as the axles are invariably slightly longer. Handy axle reaming tools, available for 'OO' and 'EM/P4' from DCC Concepts, allow for a quick modification. Drop it into the axle holes and twist until it turns freely.

Slot the new wheels into the bogie and check that they rotate freely. A tiny amount (1mm) of side-play in 'OO' stock is advantageous. Take the time to check the back-to-back measurement of each set of wheels.

A final test is to place the bogie onto a sheet of glass. This will reveal whether all four wheels are aligned concentrically: if the bogie rocks, then something has gone awry and performance will suffer. Check whether the bogie itself has become twisted and re-ream the axle holes if necessary.

Replacement wheels are available in various sizes and patterns (spoke, disc and so on). Etched and cast metal inserts cater for modern air-brake disc-fitted stock (left) and Mansell wood-centred wheels (right) for a variety of pre-war carriage types.

What a difference a new set of wheels makes. These old Lima bogies are actually quite good in terms of moulded detail, but the original wheels (right) and massive tension lock couplings date back to another age. DCCconcepts metal wheels offer a more refined appearance as well as superior – and quieter – running.

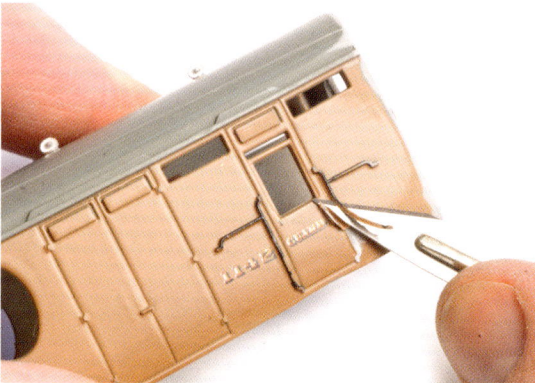

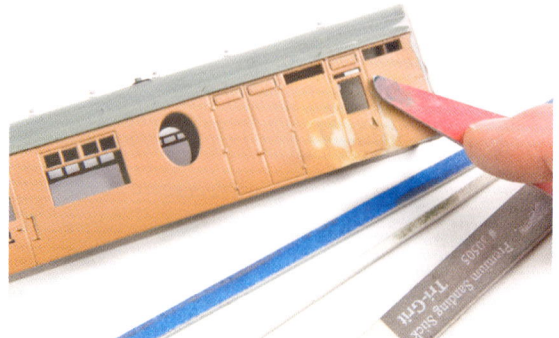

Moulded handrails are seen as something of a throwback these days. Their removal, and any other unwanted surface detail, is not too onerous a task. The key to success is to remove the plastic relief gradually with a fresh, razor-sharp blade. Don't try and render the surface flush with the blade.

Use sanding sticks and fine abrasives to work away the last of the moulded detail, employing increasingly fine grades until the surface is free from blemishes and tool marks. It is rare that the factory-applied livery will survive these attentions.

SURGICAL MATTERS

Having taken the time to identify the features to be removed or modified, we can set to work. Draw up a list of jobs, with accompanying sketches, to ensure that you don't miss anything. Trying to intervene with a knife or drill after installing delicate detailing parts can prove an awkward task, so try to get all the 'heavy' work done at the same time, tidying up the surfaces with abrasives where necessary, leaving the model as a blank canvas.

A fresh scalpel blade will take care of most of the unwanted plastic detail, with the surface rendered flush either with a scraping action or with the use of needle files and abrasive strips. If the livery is to be preserved, employ masking tape to protect the surrounding area from tool marks and accidental damage.

Once all of the unwanted detail has been removed, check the surface for any imperfections that might show up once the paint has been touched in. As plastic is a soft material, it's easy to remove too much with the knife or abrasives, creating a hollowed-out area. If this is the case, apply a little model filler and allow it to cure before rubbing down gently. Again, if the paintwork is to be disturbed as little as pos-

Another unsightly feature of some older models is a prominent seam where the sides and ends meet. Bachmann's LNER Thompson stock is a prime example and a little work with hobby filler will make a dramatic difference. Spread on the filler and, once fully cured, sand the surface flush and smooth.

sible, then choose an acrylic-based filler or Milliput epoxy putty. These won't react against the factory finish, whereas solvent-based fillers will cause blistering. Being more tenacious and curing rock-hard, Milliput is recommended when blanking-out small holes, especially if the area is to be re-drilled or reshaped in any way.

ADDING DETAILS

Don't be tempted to rush the marking-out stage. I often do just that – and end up regretting it. A sharp scriber tool is preferred to a pencil, being far more reliable when fractions of a millimetre are at stake. Get things slightly out of kilter at this stage and the model can take on a wonky air, with pairs of handrails not lining up, or door hinges askew. The scriber also acts as a centre punch, marking the exact location for a hole to be drilled and this indentation then guides the drill bit.

A variety of steel set squares and a steel rule with clearly printed gradations are essential tools for this job. A scale rule to match that of your model avoids any head scratching and mental arithmetic, provided that you have the prototype dimensions at hand. Knowing, for example, that a handrail was 4ft 6in long on the real thing can readily be marked out using the scaled gradations.

On the subject of handrails, fashioning replacements from fine brass wire is a simple task, with the most difficult aspect being the attainment of the correct length. With the corners shaped in the mouth of a set of round-nose pliers, it can be deceptively tricky to get the two mounting tails set at exactly the right length apart. Creating a modest jig, using a pair of nails driven into a scrap of hardwood and set at the correct distance apart, around which the wire can be bent, will do the trick. Alternatively, simple bending jigs are available from Bill Bedford with a wide range of handrail lengths instantly available.

Another simple aid can be employed to ensure that the handrails are secured at a consistent height above the surface. Nothing more than a scrap of plastic card or sheet brass, of the appropriate thickness, placed beneath the wire as it's pushed home, will produce perfect results.

An important factor regarding handrails is the choice of wire. Coiled brass, copper, nickel and lead wire have many uses in detailing models, being easy to form into intricate shapes (especially lead and copper wire), but rendering straight sections will be difficult. Once wire has taken on a curved shape, it's nigh on impossible to straighten it. Instead, invest in packs of stiff brass wire from Alan Gibson or Albion Alloys for such tasks.

The sourcing of replacement detail components, such as roof ventilators, door hinges and handles, buffers and underframe fittings, is best done before any of the original details are removed. If you're lucky,

Once all of the filling and abrading tasks have been completed, the locations for new details can be marked out and any mounting holes drilled. Always use a fine-tipped scriber to mark the position of a hole before drilling, giving the bit a head-start and ensuring complete accuracy.

Handrails are best formed from straight sections of brass wire. Gibson and Albion Alloys offer a selection of wire in various sizes, with 0.35 and 0.4mm being especially suited to 4mm scale vehicles. A set of round-nose pliers is the perfect tool for forming the handrails. It's best to make the 'tails' too long as the waste can be snipped away later.

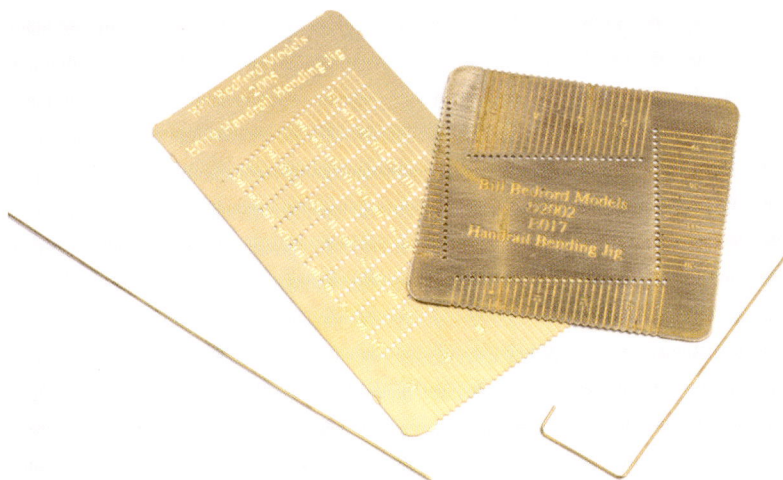

For consistently accurate handrails, try a bending jig, such as one of these from Bill Bedford.

Insert a plastic or metal shim (40thou' plastic card for this 'OO' van) to attain a uniform height above the body for the handrails. Fix the wire with a drop of cyano glue and snip away the waste.

New handrails can be complemented with a set of superior door fittings (these are from MJT). Again, drill a small mounting hole and fix with a tiny amount of cyano.

you'll be able to buy a single detailing pack aimed at a specific type of vehicle. In reality, however, it's more likely that a number of separate packs will have to be obtained, perhaps from multiple suppliers. There's certainly plenty to choose from, with Comet, MJT, Gibson, Markits and Bill Bedford being just a handful of names in the detailing supplies field.

Fixing the superior details in place needs to be done with the minimum of adhesive. A strong, durable bond is essential, but so too is a neat joint. Blobs of excess glue are difficult to remove without damaging surrounding paintwork, so use a pinpoint applicator or cocktail stick to place just enough adhesive exactly where it's needed. With most detail components, whatever the material, cyano glue is my usual preference. Epoxy is second choice, despite being safer around clear glazing and existing paintwork, but the hassle of mixing the two elements and the general gloopy nature are marks against it. Besides, when used carefully (in tiny quantities) cyano should not cause any problems.

A common choice of material for detailing components is white-metal. It can be cast into ornate patterns and, being fairly soft, is easy to work with. Typical applications are buffers, roof vents and underframe equipment.

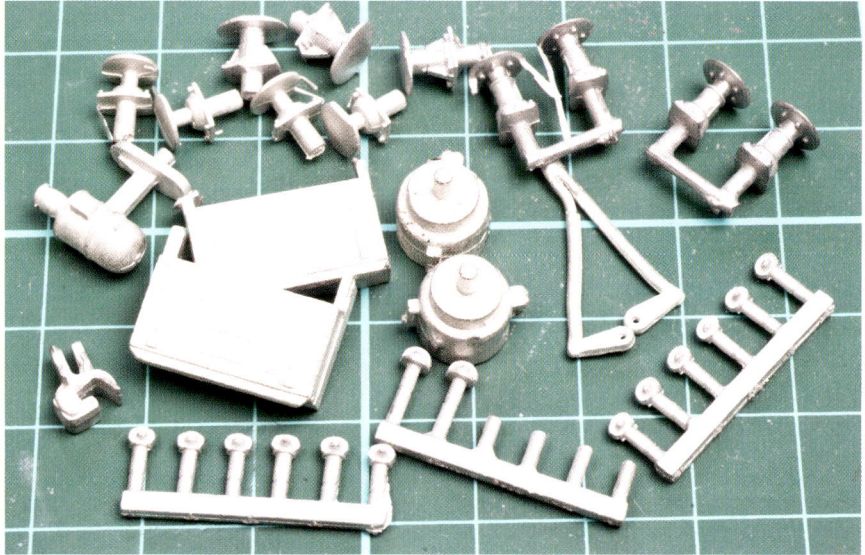

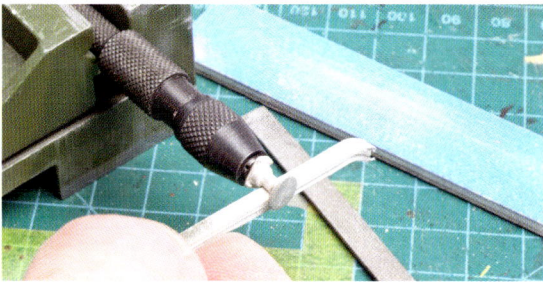

An inevitable facet of employing white-metal is the need to clean up the castings before use. Mounting the part in a pin vice makes the job easier and needle files or abrasive sticks will make short work of removing casting seams or blemishes.

Improving poorly moulded roof vents, or adding a different pattern, follows the same procedure as the handrails. Cut away the offending material gradually with a blade and follow with files and abrasives until the surface is perfectly smooth.

Take your time marking out the position of the new vents after establishing a longitudinal centre line. Use a fine punch to help locate the drill bit and form the mounting holes to suit the lugs of the detailing parts for a snug fit.

Place a drop of cyano glue into the hole with a cocktail stick and pop the new vents into place, ensuring that they're correctly aligned.

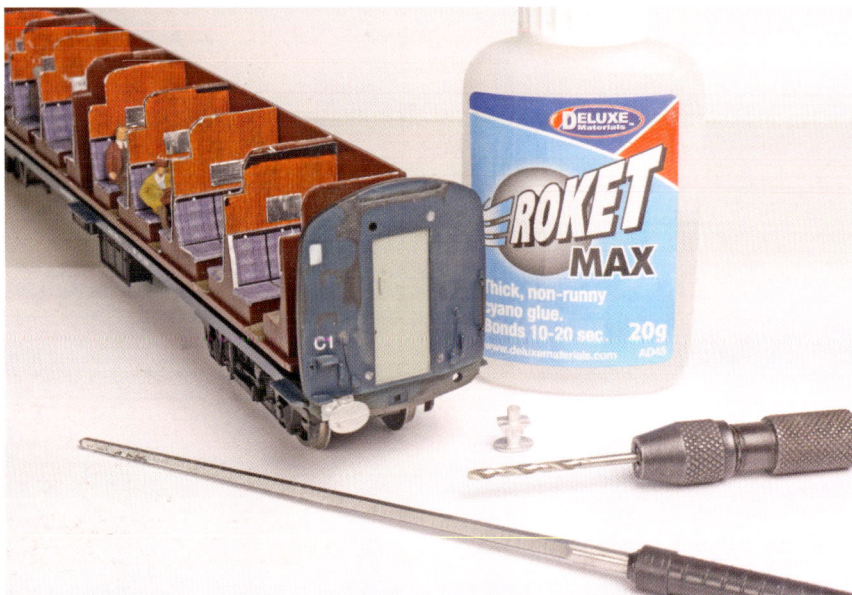

Buffers are a common item to be replaced, either through damage or because the original parts aren't too convincing. Adding an extended set of buffers at the outer end of a fixed rake, with retracted units on the 'inside' ends, also makes for greater realism. After cutting and filing away the waste, a tapered reamer is most effective for opening the holes to the exact size required.

KEY SKILLS

The art of removing unwanted features and replacing them with superior parts fashioned from a range of materials, all installed accurately and neatly, while making good the modified surface areas and paint finish, are the main key skills required to upgrade RTR carriages. Also essential is a modicum of proto-typical knowledge, putting the fruits of your research to good use, and developing an appreciation of how a particular model can be improved.

From now on, it's a matter of developing these core techniques in order to push our modelling forward into the realms of superdetailing, where finely etched metal parts will be encountered, along with more in the way of underframe detailing.

CHAPTER FOUR

SUPERDETAILING

When a model is referred to as being 'superde-tailed', it suggests something very special. Cutting through the grandiose terminology, though, what does superdetailing actually entail? The answer is rather simple, in principle at least: we're trying to achieve the very best, most authentic recreation of a prototype as possible, using an existing model as a basis.

Building on what we have already covered in the previous two chapters, here we'll be taking things a little further in our quest for realism. The amount of work necessary depends as much on the base model as it does on the modeller's attitude and aspiration. Individual handrails, doorknobs, hinges, dynamo belts and improved brake gear greatly improve the exterior, along with more authentic textured roof surfaces for pre-war stock. Perhaps most of the original underframe and body detail will need to be removed before new parts are added, or it may only be a case of tweaking what's already there.

Some of the work requires precision, but mostly it demands patience and a willingness to invest

When trimming unwanted detail, cure any resulting blemishes with filler. Mr Surfacer liquid putty offers a quick and convenient solution. It can be sanded and polished and is less cumbersome than most tube-based fillers.

Mk1 carriage-ends were modified from the mid-1960s, with most of the treads removed and the handrails shortened. I find it easier to flatten the whole end, reinstating the remaining steps with 'U' channel styrene. Trim the channel to replicate the angled brackets and fix with liquid poly cement.

New jumper cables have been installed, along with the revised handrails. As this will be the tail end of a fixed rake of carriages, extended buffers, dummy buckeye and brake hoses give a more refined air. Check if your prototype had dual brakes and/or dual heating, as the number of pipes and jumper cables will have to reflect this.

hours in an individual vehicle. This may seem untenable if you have a large layout and numerous nine- or ten-car rakes. But smaller branch trains are well worth the effort and, who knows, you may get hooked on the experience and roll out the improvements across your whole fleet.

Superdetailing also offers a route to correcting serious flaws in a RTR model, or to create period-specific detail not otherwise available. One such example is the later condition of BR MkI coaching stock, with most RTR models failing to note the modifications carried out from the mid-1960s onwards. Additionally, models with a longer pedigree can be brought closer to contemporary standards, allowing them to blend more seamlessly with newer stock and traction.

There are drawbacks to such obsessive detailing work. The finished models are likely to be even more fragile and some modifications to underframes, coupling systems and gangways will reduce the vehicle's ability to cope with tight curves and short radius points, so you'll have to decide what will be compatible with the needs of your layout.

There's also the issue of cost: the extra detailing parts and materials will add significantly to your investment. However, savings can be made if treating several vehicles at once or if a comprehensive detailing kit is chosen. Parts can also be improvised or crafted from stock materials rather than relying on etched or cast components from a third party.

WORKING WITH ETCHED PARTS

Whereas the previous chapter briefly introduced cast metal detailing components, here we'll delve into some of the issues relevant to etched metal parts. This medium is ideally suited to the rendering of thinner, more delicate items such as doorknobs, hinges, ventilation grilles, lamp brackets, footsteps and gangway covers. Brake linkages and 'V' hangers are also far more lifelike in etched brass or nickel silver than plastic or metal castings.

Having obtained the necessary etched parts from the likes of MJT, Comet and Bill Bedford, they need to be handled, shaped and fitted with great care.

Cutting components away from the surrounding fret can be tricky and a good-quality set of fine-nosed metal shears is an essential tool to have at hand. Keep such cutters for fine work on etched frets only, as we need a razor sharp set of jaws that won't distort the fragile parts as they cut.

Once the component is free, the edges need dressing with files or sanding sticks to remove the inevitable ridge caused by the two-stage etching

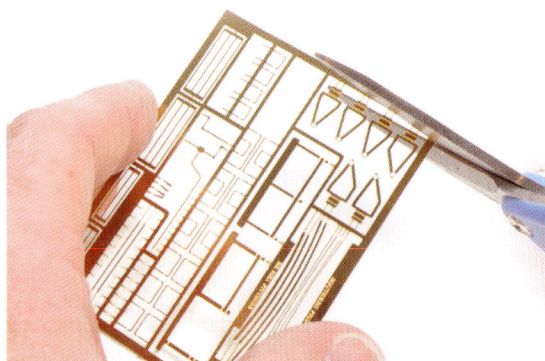

Cutting etched parts away from the fret without damaging them is one of the most important techniques to master. A set of good-quality, super-sharp shears is essential. This set is from DCCconcepts and the long blades are great for reaching into awkward areas of the fret. Gently dress the edges of the components with a needle file to remove any burrs.

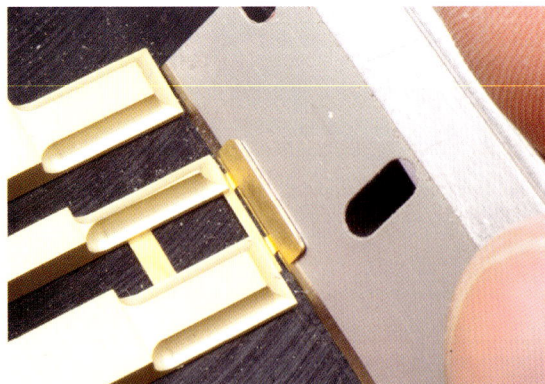

Shape the parts carefully in a vice or Hold 'n' Fold. While the metal is firmly clamped, a flat blade creates the fold.

Once shaped, the parts can be installed. Items at risk of occasional knocks, such as steps, benefit from fixing into drilled holes.

While etched footboards are available, you can improvise your own with plastic strip. These bogie footboards are formed from 10 × 100 thou' Evergreen strip, with lengths of 10 × 20 thou' fixed along one edge. Make up long lengths of this L-shaped combination and, when cured, simply cut to the sizes required.

process. In order to render half relief detail (such as rivet or bolt heads) and folding guidelines, the metal is etched in multiple stages and this results in rough edges. Clamping the parts securely while filing the edges smooth and square is essential to avoid damage, with a mini bench vice proving a great help.

As for folding the metal parts to shape, a Hold 'n' Fold device is another welcome luxury, especially for complex or 'box'-type forms where shaping with pliers would prove too clumsy. I'm not a fan of employing pliers for smaller parts anyway, as they seldom create sharp folds and are more likely to distort the soft metal.

Handling small fittings is never easy and a set of fine self-closing tweezers will help to avoid footsteps or lamp brackets being swallowed up by the carpet monster. Indeed, sitting well under the table or work-bench, rather than perching near the edge, is to be recommended to lessen the risk of dropping components into the abyss. Working over a shallow, lipped container also helps.

Fixing the new parts into position must be achieved cleanly and with the minimum of fuss. There's little

point fitting tiny detail parts with a thick gloopy adhesive, so a medium-grade cyano glue will do the trick. Remember that only a tiny amount is required, applied via pinpoint applicator or a cocktail stick. Once the layers of primer and paint have been applied, the smaller parts will be given even more security.

Fixing styrene to the tougher plastic commonly employed for bogies and underframes can sometimes be a problem. Simply brush Roket Tricky Stick onto the plastic and, a few moments later, fix the parts with a tiny drop of cyano glue. The bond will be extremely strong.

Older RTR models (and some still in production today) feature raised door seams instead of recesses. An Olfa profile cutting tool is a perfect device for correcting this. Dress the surface smooth with files and abrasives and draw the Olfa tool gently along the door seam, using a set square as a guide. A few passes with a sharp blade will be enough. For very fine seams, try grinding the point of the blade on an oilstone to a narrower point.

Add the necessary hinges from either tiny lengths of 10thou' Microstrip styrene or, preferably, etched brass hinges. Avoid adhesives for this task, as application is likely to be fiddly. Instead, acrylic varnish or Johnson Klear floor polish will provide a secure bond. Apply a drop of Klear, pick up and position the parts with a wet brush and add a further drop of the fluid after a few minutes to seal the part in place.

Door bump stops are also available in etched form, but I prefer punching my own with a Nutter rivet-forming tool. Strips of fine metal foil are fed into the device and formed with the appropriate sized punch. Again, Johnson Klear is the perfect adhesive.

Etched brass door handles and grab rails add the finishing touch, looking far superior to any moulded equivalent. Often it's best to leave fitting such parts until after the carriage has been painted to preserve their natural brass appearance.

Toilet water tank filling pipes can be tricky to form, as they have to follow the profile of the roof and ends, starting and terminating in the right place. Shaping them to follow the moulded originals before they're cut away will remove much of the guesswork.

Filler pipes set much further inboard are more challenging. Make the job easier by taping them into position while they're being shaped. These pipes have been retained with mounting brackets formed from thinner wire, shaped into loops and fixed into drilled holes. The loop tails are pulled tight from the inside and secured with a drop of cyano.

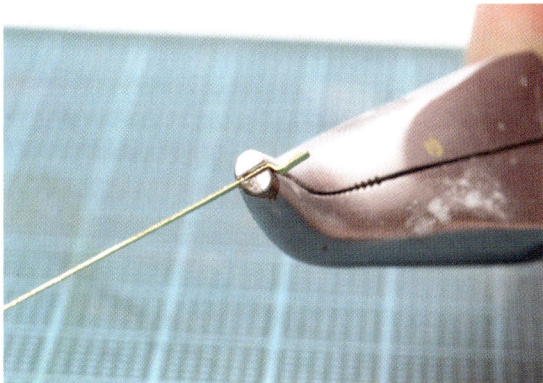

Forming your own lamp brackets from brass strip (1mm wide, 10 thou' thick in 'OO') is cheap and simple. A set of fine pliers or a Hold 'n' Fold will help to form the profile. Before trimming to length, mount in a mini-vice and shape the head into a gentle taper. Finish by polishing with a fine sanding pad to remove any burrs.

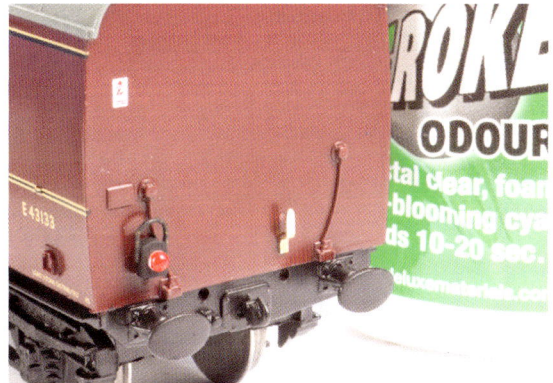

Trim the bracket with shears and fix with a drop of cyano glue. Alternatively, extend the mounting bracket and fold to a right angle before inserting into a small slot drilled into the body. This will give a more secure fixing.

Larger parts, or those subject to greater risk of damage, especially underframe components, can be fixed with epoxy or thicker cyano formulas. The longer working time of these adhesives also allow more scope for adjustment.

For the smallest parts that lay flat on the surface, such as etched window frames, door hinges and bump stops, a super-clean bond can be achieved with a thin acrylic varnish or Johnson Klear polish.

HOMEMADE PARTS

In an effort to save my pennies, I've been making more of my own detailing parts recently. I've always found improvisation one of the most rewarding and fun aspects of modelling, although I can't profess to be churning out high-grade etchings or castings. Rather, it's been a case of fabricating bits from plastic or brass sheet, strip, rod or section, with various metal wires also proving invaluable.

Although it requires an initial outlay to stock up on the raw materials, my humble supply will probably last for years. Surprisingly, it can take much less in the way of time and effort than you may think,

especially after a little practice. As well as the financial savings, this approach also avoids the frustration of a project coming to a halt because you've run out of certain off-the-shelf parts.

Common parts that I'll happily knock up myself include train heating jumper cables and connectors, brake gear, various bits of pipework, door furniture, lamp brackets, footsteps, interior fittings and underframe trussing.

There's more on building your own stuff in Chapter 13.

Lamp brackets can be formed in a variety of patterns to suit different vehicles. Here, the same brass strip has been folded over onto itself to create a flat right-angled bracket. Remove any burrs and tool marks with abrasives while it's clamped securely.

The brackets can then be installed into the side of the gangways, having drilled the necessary mounting holes.

Electric Train Heating (ETH) cables and sockets are available from 'the trade', but I like to fashion my own from various sizes of styrene rod and strip, drilled and fixed to lengths of flexible brass jewellers' wire. I can churn these out in a few minutes and they probably cost less than a penny each in terms of materials.

As well as jumper cables and sockets, air brake cylinders are also simple to fabricate from plastic rod or tube. The ends are filled with Milliput and sanded to shape, while straps are cut from insulation tape. Wound steel guitar strings are perfect for fashioning vacuum brake and steam heating hoses.

The completed Bachmann Mk1 end, after touching in the missing blue paintwork and picking out the various new details. The repositioned lamp brackets, new jumper cables and orange ETH sockets bring the model to life.

Dual-braked and air-braked Mk1 stock featured specific underfloor equipment and Bachmann offer the vertical actuator valve on some models, but not the adjacent reservoir tank. Fine jewellers' nickel wire forms the 'plumbing'.

A simple task, such as adding clear glazing to the partitions, also adds a touch of class. Either cut strips of clear styrene or employ a liquid glazing medium, such as Glue 'n' Glaze, that will dry crystal clear. Run the glue around the edge of the aperture and draw the film across with a cocktail stick.

Other parts that can be rustled up from plastic rod and brass wire include lamps for wall or table mounting. They may not be illuminated, but they still add some extra realism to the interior.

UNDERFRAMES

Making the most of the underframe can be a challenge, with older models likely to sport heavily moulded components that bear only a passing resemblance to the real thing. In contrast, there might be very little there at all, which actually makes our job easier, as removing lumps of plastic without damaging the sur-rounding area is no fun. Perhaps it would be simpler to replace the underframe altogether? If so, we'll look at etched metal chassis in Chapter 11, as well as scratch-built versions in Chapter 13.

In some instances, other RTR products may provide donor underframes, with a handy example presented here in the form of a BR 57ft Mk1 chassis. While the bodyshells of Bachmann's Mk1 'suburbans' can be readily improved with a modicum of detail enhancement, the underframes are a bit primitive by today's standards. However, the superior chassis from a Bachmann or Hornby Mk1 BG van is the same length and can be substituted pretty easily. Furthermore, with Hornby now having a creditable Mk1 BG in its budget Railroad range, it offers an economical solution.

Potential underframe improvements include refinement of the trussing, adding cross-sections if they're absent. New brake cylinders, 'V' hangers and linkages can make a tremendous difference to the carriage's outward appearance. Coupled with new battery boxes and other equipment (if they're all rendered in metal) can add some welcome extra ballast to a vehicle too. The issue of weight is an important one and will be covered properly in Chapter 5.

Even the best RTR underframes don't include everything that should be there. Dynamo belts are a typical example. We can't attach them to the axles if the bogies are to rotate, but we can make a representative version. Sketching a template to follow when treating several identical vehicles makes life easier.

The belt fits around the dynamo and is secured to the underside of the floor for strength. Choose the length to get the belt as close as possible while allowing free movement of the bogie. Adding part of the brake linkage from brass wire also greatly improves realism.

Sometimes it's easier to replace an underframe rather than modify the existing unit. If you're lucky, there's a ready-made RTR alternative. In this case, a Bachmann suburban Mk1 (lower) is to receive a far superior chassis from a new Hornby Railroad Mk1 BG. Apart from repositioning a battery box and removing the bufferbeams, there is little else to do.

With a set square and Olfa cutter, the Hornby bufferbeams were gradually cut away while leaving the ends at a perfect right angle. The original Bachmann body mounting clips are now redundant and the chassis will have to be retained by other means.

After the body had been detailed and re-glazed, the chassis could be fitted permanently. A small amount of Glue 'n' Glaze adhesive was used for simplicity. This will be resilient enough to cope with everyday layout operation and gentle handling. If access is required, the glue bond can be easily broken with a scalpel blade. Note the new footboard along the solebar, formed from plastic strip. Once a dynamo belt and brake linkages are added, the model will look even more superior.

Without recourse to a whole new chassis, there's still plenty of hope, even for the most basic of underframes. This Dapol LMS carriage chassis is showing its age, but a start has been made on the removal of what moulded detail there was. The underside of the floor will need flattening and the trussing refined with needle files and abrasive sticks.

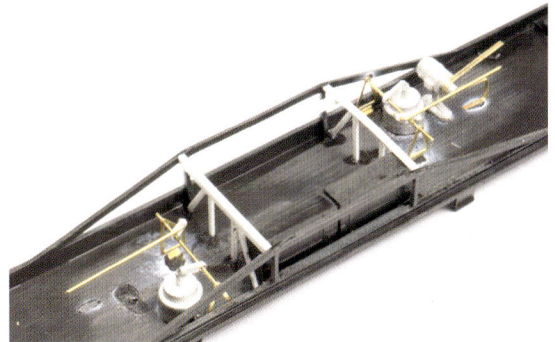

The trussing has been enhanced with the missing transverse girders (plastic angle), which also add extra strength to the frames. New battery boxes, brake cylinders and linkages, dynamo and drive belt are all in place.

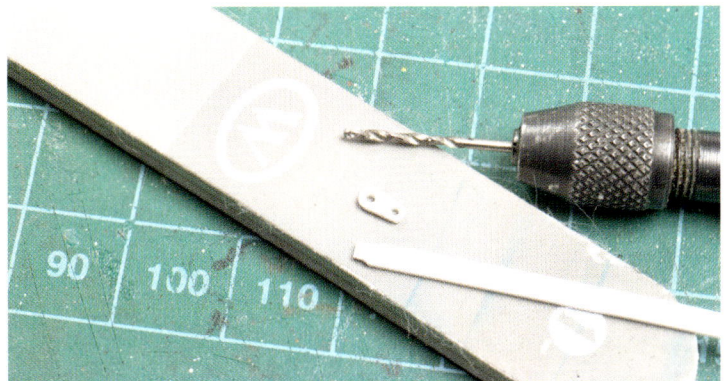

Having run out of etched brass brake linkages, I decided to form my own from thin plastic strip. The holes were drilled initially, before the shaping took place.

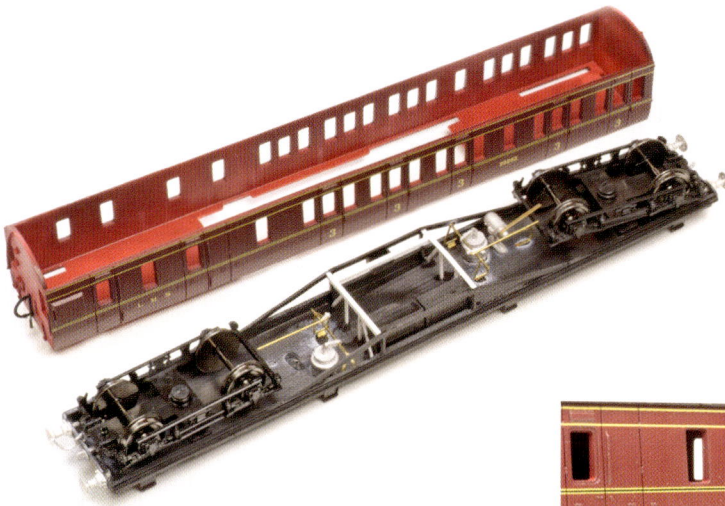

LEFT: **With the bogies installed (with superior wheels fitted), along with new buffers, dummy coupling hooks and brake pipes, the aged Dapol underframe is starting to look more purposeful.**

RIGHT: **I had thought about replacing the entire trussing but was glad that I persisted in tidying up the original moulding, despite the effort involved. Just the body, roof and interior to do now!**

UP TOP

In the days before all-steel carriage construction, wood planking was employed for the roof, laid over curved bulkheads and covered with stretched and waterproofed canvas. Possessing a distinct texture that is seldom captured by model carriages, it's not too difficult to replicate, especially in 'OO' and larger scales.

One option is to wait until the painting stage and apply an undercoat using textured paint. Mixing dry pigments, such as weathering powders, with acrylic paint is an ideal solution, adding a little thinners if necessary until the paint can be brushed evenly over the surface, preferably before the vents, pipes and other smaller details are installed.

A quicker and tidier method is to overlay the roof with paper. A heavily textured paper may be suitable for large scale models, but regular 80gsm printer paper seems to do the trick for my 'OO' models, offering a subtle but effective result. Surprisingly, liquid poly cement has proven ideal for fixing the paper to bare plastic roofs. Strip away any paint with abrasives beforehand, removing also any raised

details such as ribs, gutter strips, vents, handrails and pipes.

With the paper cut roughly oversize, it can be wrapped around the roof before the liquid poly is liberally brushed on. Use a good-quality, strong solvent, such as Plastic Magic, Mek Pak or Tamiya's Extra Thin Cement, as we're relying on it to penetrate the paper, yet still be strong enough to 'melt' the surface of the plastic beneath. Several coats of solvent will be required and the workspace will soon become very smelly, so make sure that there's an open window and plenty of fresh air.

Pay extra attention to the edges and corners, applying more liquid cement until the paper bonds firmly to the plastic and then set it aside to dry overnight. Check that the covering is secure before trimming the paper flush with the edges with a sharp scalpel blade. The extra details can then be added, with rain-gutter strips formed from Microstrip styrene (10 × 20thou' for 'OO'), having marked out the locations and profile carefully with a fine pencil. Making up a card template to ensure consistent results is a good idea, especially if working on a few carriages of a similar type. Again, the liquid poly cement will be effective for bonding the plastic strip, applied with a fine brush for neat results. The locations of vents, handrails and other fittings can also be marked out, drilled and the new detailing parts installed.

If lateral ribs are required (being more common on steel-skinned roofs), they can be added using Microstrip in a similar fashion to the gutters, or formed from thin strips of electrical insulation tape. This is a good way of replacing moulded ribs, which are regularly far too pronounced on RTR stock, though it can be laborious.

Once primed and painted, the texture of the paper roof can look highly effective, especially once weathering has been applied. The lack of a smooth, uniform surface offers a telling – and authentic – contrast with the smooth and shiny body sides. There's also the possibility of picking at the paper or distressing the surface slightly to create areas of peeling or damaged canvas, which can be just the thing for a neglected carriage nearing the end of its service life.

As always, careful study of the prototype will reveal what is missing or deemed inferior on your chosen model. Endless opportunities exist for improving RTR coaching stock and there's every reason to take a similar approach to kit-built vehicles too, as few kits, as we shall soon discover, offer a truly comprehensive package, leaving plenty of room for improvement.

Create a realistic texture to the roof by overlaying with paper. Apply a generous amount of liquid poly cement to bond the paper to the plastic roof, trimming the edges once the solvent has cured.

Having marked out the position of the various roof details, the rain gutter strips can be formed from thin Microstrip, again secured with liquid poly cement.

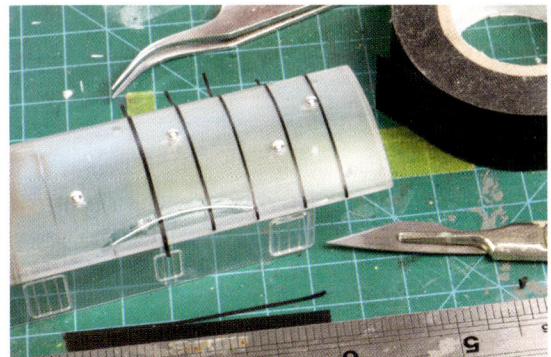

Drill mounting holes for the roof vents and any other necessary details, such as tank filler pipes and access handrails, checking prototype images and diagrams wherever possible.

For later, steel-plated roofs, raised lateral ribs are often moulded too tall or too fat – or both. File and abrade the roof back to bare plastic and start again, using thin strips of tape to form superior ribs and Microstrip again for the gutters.

CHAPTER FIVE

MAKING A START WITH KITS

Taking the plunge into kit building offers many potential challenges and rewards. The chance to learn new techniques should always be embraced, while working with different tools and materials will keep us on our toes. Rare is the kit that simply falls together as soon as the box is opened, so problem solving will be another skill we can add to our collection.

Beginning with plastic kits offers the cheapest option, both in terms of the kits themselves and the small number of tools and materials required. Without the stress of working with expensive parts and equipment, we can take our time and enjoy the learning process. Plastic is also a relatively easy medium to work with, being simple to cut, drill and bond with adhesives.

WHY?

We've already seen how well the modern modeller is served by the RTR market, for the post-1930s enthusiast in 'N' and 'OO' at least. But for those with a need for something more appropriate to their location and period, kit building still offers the best opportunity to add some variety to our rolling stock fleets.

Necessity is not the only reason, however. Kit building is a rewarding hobby in itself, as I argued in the two volumes of *Kit Building for Railway Modellers* (The Crowood Press, 2013). The satisfaction to be had from taking a variety of disparate, flat components and creating a three-dimensional, functioning miniature vehicle can't be overstated.

WHAT?

For this introduction to the subject, we'll stick with the humble plastic kit for now. Rendered by means of the tried-and-trusted pressure injection

moulding process, superbly detailed parts can be created in a variety of plastic compounds, although the quality of components depends mainly on the skill of the toolmaker.

Moulds (or 'tools') are usually manufactured from high-quality steel and the two halves must be carefully aligned before the molten plastic is injected through a series of small apertures. The siting of these injection holes is important as they invariably lead to imperfections in the resultant plastic parts, either in the form of raised 'pips' or depressed 'sink' marks. If these marks are in areas where they won't be seen on the finished model, such as the underside of a chassis or roof, then they can be largely ignored. It's even better if they're limited to the waste material, or 'sprue', but this is rare. If the main structural parts, joint faces or intricate detailing components feature such blemishes, then the modeller is left with the onerous task of remedying the situation.

As well as the quality of the toolmaking, the condition and age of the moulds is also relevant. If the faces of the tools no longer meet precisely, plenty of excess material will seep into the tiny gap, resulting in heavy mould seams and areas of 'flash'. Again, remedial work is necessary. Perhaps the worst scenario is when the alignment of the moulds is compromised, with parts emerging in an asymmetrical form. They may be salvageable, but hours of laborious filling and shaping will be demanded, leading to a frustrating and not entirely pleasurable experience.

The choice of plastic is tailored to the demands of the moulding process and the job that the moulded parts will ultimately need to perform. Underframe parts require a certain amount of rigidity, as the integrity of the chassis is dependent upon their strength. On the other hand, they must have a degree of flexibility and resistance to oils, solvents and mechanical wear.

For these reasons, ABS (Acrylonitrile Butadiene Styrene) is commonly employed for bogie frames and underframe components. It is capable of being formed into highly complex shapes and boasts a superior surface finish to most other plastics. Its high resistance to chemical attack also means that it demands a powerful solvent with which to bond it. Additionally, it can sometimes be tricky to paint, hence why most ABS parts are produced in self-coloured form.

Aside from the underframe fittings, plastic kit components are most likely to be rendered in poly-styrene (often referred to as styrene). This is the pliable, easy-to-work material that most of us grew up with, being a staple of Airfix and most other hobby-kit brands.

As well as being easy to cut, drill and shape, styrene is also readily bonded with itself and other plastics. Liquid solvents act to chemically 'weld' the parts together, forming incredibly strong bonds. Styrene is not perfect, though. It has a low resistance to oils and high temperatures and long, thin parts have a tendency to warp if not stored correctly. However, its sensitivity to heat allows parts to be manipulated after soaking in hot water.

Butyrate is another plastic that kit-builders are likely to come across. With high impact strength, it offers some of the flexibility of styrene and the durability of ABS, but takes paint better than the latter. Plastruct plastic strip, rod and section are formed from butyrate and it's also suitable for injection moulding, often being found in high quality, limited production kits.

HOW?

One of the first jobs is to give all the parts a good clean in warm water with a dash of general household detergent (not washing-up liquid). The plastic parts will doubtless carry residues of mould-releasing agents and, unless these are removed, paints and adhesives will struggle to adhere to the surface. It makes sense to clean these away at the beginning, while the parts are still attached to the sprues, although we'll still have to clean the model again at

Dedicated plastic sprue cutter tools are great, but may struggle to reach between narrow sprue gates. In such instances, try a Stanley knife with a fresh blade, cutting well away from the edge of the component. Make several light passes with the blade, if necessary, and don't force it.

a later stage. Having gently scrubbed the parts with an old toothbrush, rinse them thoroughly in clean water and set aside to dry out completely.

While they dry, take the opportunity to read the kit's instructions, identifying the locations and purpose of each part and gaining an idea of how assembly will proceed. Once you're confident that you know what you're doing, start removing parts from the sprue, preferably with a set of plastic cutting shears. A stout knife will do the job, but shears offer more control, especially around small, delicate components, provided the jaws of the shears can reach between the sprue gates.

Only remove the parts needed for each stage of construction, lest any be lost or confused. Don't worry about cutting away all of the waste material at the same time as removing the component from the sprue. It's safer to tidy up any flash or moulding imperfections gradually with a sharp knife, file or abrasives.

When dealing with long, thin or intricate components, it may be wise to do most of the fettling while they're still attached to the sprue. This will give the parts added protection from distortion as well as giving you, or your vice, more to hold on to.

Don't be too disheartened if some of the parts are damaged, as they can be readily repaired either before or during assembly. For underframe parts (solebars in particular) rebuilding shattered components *in situ* is a surer way to getting them correctly aligned. Moreover, aiming for an accurate, square and true outline and optimum running qualities are our primary goal and damaged parts may end up not going back together seamlessly. But no matter, we can deal with imperfections with filler, plastic shims and abrasives.

If parts are twisted or bowed, they can be reshaped gently after soaking in hot (not boiling) water, clamping them to a sheet of wood to ensure their straightness as they cool. Any unsightly injection pin or sink marks from the moulding process can also be addressed before assembly commences. If detail upgrades are envisioned, such as replace-

If possible, mount the component in a vice, adding protective covers to the jaws. Gently dress the edges flush, square and true with a flat file, being careful not to remove too much material.

Keep checking the edges with a set square to ensure the correct angles. Be aware that corner joints may be designed to meet at a 45° angle and must be dressed accordingly.

Before going any further, the choice of couplings ought to be considered as it is often easier to modify underframe parts before assembly. This long-wheelbase van is receiving a set of Symoba pivoting NEM-type coupling pockets and the underfloor ribbing must be flattened in order to accommodate them. However, the coupling units will not be installed until the van has been fully assembled. Couplings are discussed fully in Chapter 9.

Test fit the body sections around the floor, ensuring that the corners are square. It is not unusual for the floor to be slightly undersize, so be prepared to add thin plastic shims. Erect one side and one end around the floor, running liquid poly cement into the joint. Check the angles of the corner and floor.

Add the other side and end, again checking the exterior and interior angles. In many cases, especially for baggage cars with few windows, I like to reinforce the corners with plastic angle and the sides with plastic card strips. Clamp the whole thing up with masking tape, rechecking the angles as you go, and leave overnight to cure.

Solebars can take time to fettle before fitting. Mounting the file in a vice and rubbing the parts gently across the tool makes life easier. Keep the components at a right angle to the file, checking with a set square at regular intervals.

ment underframe equipment, handrails and door furniture, then removing the original fittings at this early stage is also recommended.

A stock of sharp blades, an improvised miniature chisel (a sharpened screwdriver blade) and abrasive pads, in various grades and shapes, will make short work of these tasks, with model filler employed wherever necessary. Take care not to damage any of the surface relief that is to be retained, although many features can be reinstated if necessary, either by re-scribing recesses or fabricating new parts.

Remember, though, that installing raised features like handrails and door knobs is best left until much later, perhaps after the painting stage, to simplify any masking, painting and lining tasks.

GLUES

Plastic adhesives were discussed in Chapter 1, but it's worth reiterating a couple of factors here. The use of thin, penetrating poly cements, such as offered by Tamiya, Deluxe Materials and Mek-Pak, is recommended for most tasks where the parts can be brought together closely. Apply with a fine brush or, for greater accuracy and neatness, a special pin-point applicator. These latter devices are excellent, but they are prone to clogging with softened plastic unless kept scrupulously clean during use. A little practice and the adoption of good habits vis-à-vis wiping the tip after every application should prevent any problems.

If the parts do not meet perfectly, or if a slower-setting formula is preferred to allow for more precise placement, a thicker grade of cement is required. However, these can be a little messier to deal with.

Another issue to consider is the compatibility of different cements with certain plastics. Tougher materials, such as ABS and butyrate, require a more powerful solvent, so be sure to read the kit's instructions and the adhesive's label before use.

All poly cements will damage painted surfaces, so if you're planning on creating and finishing a host of sub-assemblies, an alternative adhesive will be required when the parts are brought together. In these instances, plastic-friendly cyano glues are recommended.

GET YOUR FOUNDATIONS RIGHT

It's imperative that kits are assembled with all parts sitting square and true to each other. Once the bonds have cured, it's nigh on impossible to rectify

It is not uncommon for long, thin parts such as solebars to break in the packaging or while cutting from the sprue. No matter, they can be reconstructed in situ. Press the brass bearings into the apertures, securing with a tiny blob of cyano glue if they feel at all loose.

Cement one solebar to the underframe and ensure that it stands at a right angle. Leave for ten minutes and then position the other solebar. Pop the wheels into place, check that they rotate freely and that the axles are concentric to the sides of the vehicle. Apply liquid poly to the other solebar and make any adjustments where necessary.

Before the glue hardens, place the model on a sheet of glass or other flat surface and see that it moves freely, with all four wheel flanges in contact with the ground at all times. When happy, invert the model again and allow the cement to harden.

any alignment problems and a warped chassis or bogie will cause no end of problems on the track. From the beginning, therefore, we need to ensure that the parts are dressed correctly and that they all meet cleanly without pulling other sections of the assembly out of true. Ideally, there should be no need for heavy-duty clamps to bring everything back into line while the glue sets. Plastic has a strong 'memory' and will undoubtedly try to force its way back to the shape in which it began. If the parts are distorted when removed from the sprue, they must be rectified before any assembly takes place.

Checking how the parts fit together without adhesive will reveal where intervention is needed and working on a completely flat surface is essential. A sheet of glass, large tile or a stone slab will act as a reference surface. A simple wooden jig, with cheeks set at right angles, will also help to achieve perfect corner joints while allowing for easy clamping-up when the glue is applied.

My usual methodology consists of erecting the bodyshell in two halves, matching up one side and one end in my simple jig. After much in the way of fettling and dry runs to make sure they meet as cleanly as possible, the parts are clamped securely to maintain the correct angles while the adhesive is applied to the inside of the joint. The parts are then checked again for alignment and allowed to cure fully for several hours. Ideally, using a pair of identical jigs, the other side and end can be assembled in the same way before the two sections are brought together.

The kit may suggest building the body around the floor or roof, but relying on these parts to be of exactly the correct size and shape, especially after tools have been used to remove flash, is not recommended. Indeed, once the main walls of the body are assembled, it will become apparent if the floor is of the correct dimensions. Even if the underframe is to be made detachable, a snug fit for the body is still desired to aid alignment and to avoid any distortion of the long sides during handling.

If the floor is oversize, we have the bodyshell as a reference from which to work, fettling away the excess material. If it's too small, a fillet may be required. Discern the gap and divide the measurement in two, adding the appropriate size of thin plastic strip to either side of the floor to maintain any moulded locating points in their correct position. Fix the fillets either to the floor or to the inner faces of the carriage sides and ends; this latter approach offers extra rigidity when the body is intended to be demountable from the underframe.

If the corner joints offer only a minimal amount of material on which to make the bonds, they can be strengthened discreetly. Plastic angle is perfect for this job, fixed to the interior, with plenty of sizes available in the Plastruct and Evergreen ranges to ensure that the extra material does not interfere with other parts or window apertures. The body will become fairly rigid once the roof or floor is attached but, as the corners of any carriage are always the most prone to damage, some extra reinforcement will not be wasted. Don't forget to keep checking that the shell remains square at each stage of assembly.

FILL THE GAPS

It's always nice to achieve perfect joints between components, but it can also be a rare occurrence, especially with older kits. Where gaps exist or the parts have been sullied in any way, recourse to filler is inevitable.

We have mentioned fillers a few times already, although there are application methods that haven't been touched upon yet. For example, acrylic-based fillers, such as offered by Vallejo and Deluxe Materials, can be applied via a pinpoint syringe or needle tip, allowing the material to be deposited exactly where it's needed. A damp swab can then be employed to smooth the putty and remove any excess, leaving far less clearing up work to do once the filler is dry.

Alternatively, quicker drying and more durable solvent-based putties may be preferred and these can also be manipulated with a swab soaked in an appropriate solvent, such as cellulose thinners. Thin, brushable fillers, such as Mr Surfacer or Mr Dissolved Putty from Gunze Sangyo, are great for

hairline cracks, minor surface imperfections or for filling around new etched or fabricated detail components. Drying in minutes, they allow assembly to continue without undue delay.

Care is demanded, however, as the strong solvents in some formulas may damage the soft plastic surface if applied in heavy quantities. Therefore, apply a little at a time and build up deeper recesses gradually. Epoxy putties, such as Milliput, are inert enough to be safe with all plastics and can be applied into deep cavities without any problems. Curing rock-hard over twenty-four hours, it can then be sanded, carved and drilled.

When abrading, reaching into awkward crevices or around delicate detail demands care, but with a variety of shaped abrasive tools, the job is eased considerably. Resisting the urge to install smaller parts until the basic fabric of the vehicle has been assembled, filled and abraded will help even further.

BUILDING UNDERFRAMES

Having assembled the main bodyshell, the chassis can now be tackled. Whether the carriage features fixed axles or bogies, the need for a perfectly straight underframe is paramount. Any errors in the vehicle's foundations will lead to the carriage listing, wobbling or repeatedly derailing.

For bogie stock, I prefer to start with the underframe rather than the body. The solebars may be intricate affairs, with underframe trussing and footsteps integrally moulded. The trussing on this venerable Ratio kit is being cut and filed away before replacement with brass wire.

In order to achieve a square chassis, I like to mount the floor unit on a slab of MDF, drilling two mounting holes slightly inboard at each end. These holes will later be employed for attaching the bodyshell. Add one solebar, checking that it sits at the correct angle and flush with each end of the floor.

The other solebar can then be affixed and, once the liquid poly has cured, the new brass-wire trussing is formed and installed with cyano glue. The wire was shaped earlier to match the moulded detail before it was removed, ensuring a uniform appearance and adequate clearance for the bogies in due course. Note how the assembly jig has been marked with the centre line of the carriage for quick reference.

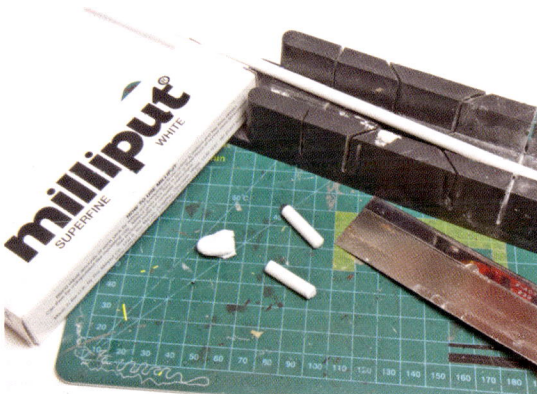

Another improvement over the Ratio kit's original parts is the replacement of the gas tanks. Plastic tube has been cut to size and filled with Milliput. Once cured, the ends will be filed flat and square.

Electrical insulation tape has been cut into 1mm-wide strips and added to the tanks, along with small lengths of brass wire to mimic the pipework. Etched brass brake hangers replace the moulded kit parts, although the Ratio vacuum cylinders have been retained.

Once again, working on a flat reference surface will help to avoid problems. Fitting brass bearings into the plastic axleguards or bogies promotes smoother running with less risk of wear and tear from the metal axles. The type of bearings employed depends on the kit, with many packages providing, or at least recommending, suitable parts. This isn't universal, however, with many longstanding kits

offering only moulded recesses. These may need drilling or reaming out to accept brass bearings, which is a job that demands care.

Flanged, or 'top hat', bearings are the easiest to fit, designed for use with metal pinpoint axles. By measuring the outside diameter and length of the main body of the bearing, the moulded depressions can be opened up with a drill bit, employing a simple depth gauge of masking tape to prevent the tool from passing right through the bogie frame or axle-guard.

Choose a drill bit of the same diameter to promote a snug fit and fix with a tiny drop of cyano glue, ensuring that the flange rests squarely on the surface. Bearings ought to be fitted before the frames are assembled, so that the holes can be drilled with the parts laid flat on the workbench for greater accuracy.

The overall length of axles tends to vary between manufacturers and it may be necessary to adjust the distance between the frames to accommodate your choice of wheels. Often the frames can simply be shimmed by a couple of thou', using plastic strip as a spacer in each side to ensure equidistance from the vehicle's longitudinal centreline.

Of greatest importance is the ability of the wheels to turn freely. Unless you're a dedicated finescale modeller, a degree of side-play ought to be allowed,

Plastic bogies are commonly made up of two side members and a main stretcher, with other detail fittings depending on the vagaries of your particular kit. Open out the bearing holes if necessary, but the fit ought to be snug. A strip of masking tape around the drill bit will act as a handy depth gauge. If glue is necessary, add a tiny dab of cyano into the hole.

Fix one side frame to the stretcher and check that it sits at a right angle before allowing the adhesive to cure for an hour or so.

Place the other side frame in position and add the wheels, checking that both axles are square and true before applying the solvent. The wheels must turn freely and the frames must be square. Allow the parts to cure overnight.

Extra bogie fittings, such as cross-members, brake gear, footsteps and coupling mounts can now be installed. I had trouble fitting some of the brake blocks to these Ratio bogies, as they needed trimming in order to clear the wheels. Note also the plastic bolster pin – not an ideal way of mounting the bogies to the underframe.

to help the vehicle cope with curves and turnouts. Excessive side-play is undesirable, however, as it can lead to sloppy running. A basic rule of thumb is to align the frames to the point where the wheels begin to rotate freely, with no discernible feeling of inertia (about 0.5–1.0mm of sideways movement is usually adequate in 'OO' gauge).

Placing the vehicle or individual bogie onto a sheet of glass will reveal if the axles are perfectly concentric. Any rocking suggests that the frames are not quite aligned. For this reason I always assemble my chassis and bogies 'on the glass', holding the frames and wheels in place and checking performance before any glue is applied. One frame is then fixed to the floor or stretcher and the testing repeated before the opposite frame is also glued in position. More testing follows while the parts can still be adjusted. When all is well, the assembly is left to cure.

The means of attaching the bogies to the chassis differs from kit to kit. The Ratio kit featured in this chapter is rather odd in that the bogies feature a friction-fit plastic pin arrangement, which is far from satisfactory. A blob of adhesive is inevitably required to prevent the parts coming adrift whenever the carriage is lifted off the track and there can be a tendency towards wobbling while in motion.

Thankfully, a simple nut and bolt arrangement is more common, with the nut either being captive within the bodyshell or fixed from beneath the bogie. Either way, as we're unable to tighten the nut securely, in order to allow the bogie free movement, the fasteners must be prevented from working loose. A drop of Loctite thread sealant does the trick, applied precisely with a cocktail stick or fine brush.

Another consideration for bogies is the amount of clearance between the wheel flanges and the underside of the carriage floor. The bogie must be able to swing on its bolster without the wheels catching on any protuberance such as coupling mounts and solebars, allowing the vehicle to cope with the tightest curve radii on your layout. If insufficient clearance exists, try a slightly smaller set of wheels, or add a shim (brass washers, for instance) between the bogie and bolster.

Furthermore, this freedom of movement must not compromise the correct ride height of the vehicle, ensuring that buffers and rooflines of adjacent vehicles are consistent and as correct to scale as possible.

A superior bogie mounting can be created with a small brass bolt, nut and washer.

ROOF DOWN OR FLOOR UP?

One of the main issues that I have with the majority of plastic kits is the lack of facility for dismantling the finished model. Whereas RTR models allow for the roof and/or body to be opened up at leisure, by means of clips, screws or bolts, plastic coach kits are usually designed around a sealed shell.

Some kits are designed for interior access via the roof and these offer something of a double-edged sword: the convenience of easy dismantling coming at the risk of a visible joint between the sides and ends, although some careful fettling can often get the roof sitting neatly in position. Furthermore, adding a strip of guttering that hangs beneath the lower edge of the roof by a fraction can also act as a concealing device.

Maintaining access to the interior is always welcome, allowing for repairs to loose parts, especially glazing and passengers, that typically come

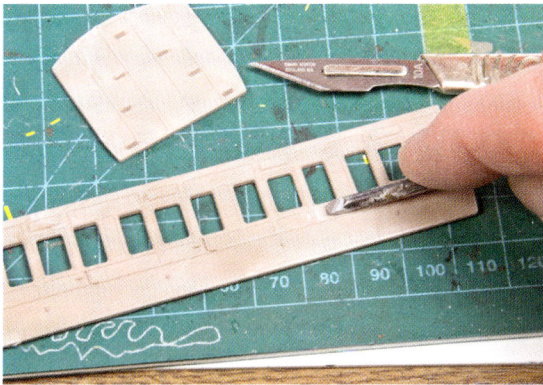

Making modifications or repairs to the body is easier before assembly, when the parts can be treated separately. Replacing moulded handrails and door furniture is a prime example and a small screwdriver ground to a sharp point will act like a chisel to reach into tricky recesses.

Although most kits offer little in the way of post-assembly dismantling options, my preferred practice is to bolt the body to the underframe. Layers of thick plastic card, reinforced by plastic angle, will act as a mounting point.

A simple alignment and assembly jig will keep the body square while the adhesive is applied and allow for hands-free assembly, leaving you to concentrate on ensuring that everything is correctly aligned.

A bolt-on body arrangement allows the roof to be fixed to the body sides and ends at an early stage, creating a strong and sturdy structure. With the body and roof glued up, clamp the assembly temporarily around the underframe to keep it perfectly formed.

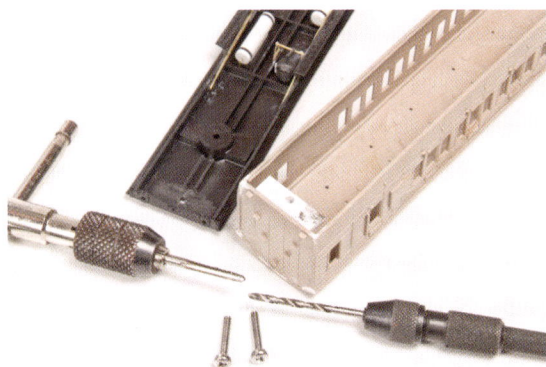

With the body joints completely dry, the location of the mounting points can be marked, drilled and tapped to suit the mounting bolts.

With the basics of assembly out of the way, the art of finessing the vehicle can begin. Firstly, any gaps or imperfections can be treated with a filling agent. Perfect Plastic Putty is great for small fissures and can be smoothed with a damp swab before it cures, thus minimizing the amount of sanding later.

It is easy to fall into the (expensive) habit of replacing moulded fittings with cast metal parts from other sources, but with a little careful attention, the original parts may be salvageable. These gaslight vents looked a little ropey on the sprue but after tidying up with files and abrasives, they'll do. A final brush over with thin liquid poly cement removes the last of the imperfections.

The main roof ventilators did need replacing, however, and the roof was further enhanced by 'plumbing in' the gaslights with fine brass wire. Once again, thin strips of insulation tape come in handy for the mounting brackets.

adrift over the years. In all but a handful of cases, however, this will require some degree of modification to the kit's components and build sequence. Planning such work from the outset is recommended, as making structural alterations later in the build will be difficult.

The demand for extra, yet fundamental, work is why many experienced modellers gain reputations for not bothering to read a kit's instructions. I've

been guilty of this attitude on occasion, and such an approach does have many potential pitfalls. Indeed, it's far better to carefully study the supplied guidelines before drawing up your own plans for how your build will deviate.

Perhaps the bodyshell can be built permanently around the underframe, with the roof adapted to a bolt-on or friction fitting. Or maybe the roof, ends and sides will be formed and an arrangement for

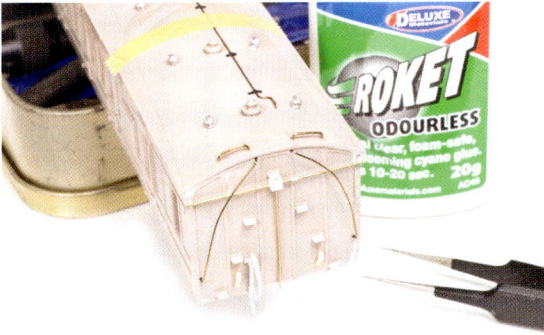

Brake end details consisting of emergency cord apparatus, handrails, lamp brackets and brake hoses add the finishing touch.

Improving plastic parts may be easier once they've been firmly installed. Buffers are a prime example: employ sanding sticks to remove any moulding seams and refine the heads to a more authentic profile.

securing this sub-assembly to the chassis created. We also have to bear in mind how the model will be painted and detailed, with ready access to the interior for fitting-out and glazing towards the end of the assembly.

I like to fabricate a set of mounting brackets from layers of plastic card, securely bound to the carriage ends. The mounting holes that have been in use to fix the underframe to the assembly jig are then employed to secure the body, the brackets being drilled and tapped with an appropriate thread. For 'OO' stuff, I commonly use M3 straight machine screws, with flat 'pan'-heads, negating the need for washers or countersinking. A 2.5mm drill bit forms the pilot hole before the thread is tapped carefully through the thick plastic brackets.

Admittedly, plastic – especially styrene – is not the best material to hold a thread. However, I've found that, as long as the bolts are tightened to a modest amount of torque (finger-tight only), then the method suits my needs perfectly. The model is not assembled and dismantled incessantly; rather a single trial fitting is enough before final assembly is effected, following painting and finishing. The only occasions where dismantling is then necessary is for occasional repairs, usually if a passenger has come adrift.

Besides, we shouldn't be relying on the bolts to close up any gaps between the body and under-frame, as the parts should fit together perfectly from the offing. Take your time throughout the preparation and assembly stages, fettling the parts until everything fits snugly and securely.

INTERIORS

Seldom does a plastic carriage kit also include parts to fit out the interior and, if it does, it's likely to be a very basic affair. It's not hard to source an array of

Not many kits include parts for the interior, but there are plenty of separate kits and components to cater for most prototypes. Lengths of bench-type seating are offered by Ratio, simply cut to length to suit your model. Use a razor saw in a mitre box to get the cuts clean and square.

Form an interior floor, partitions and bulkheads from plastic card, with the latter being shaped to match the inner profile of the roof. Mount all of the bulkheads together in a vice and shape them at the same time for convenience and consistency.

Mark out the spacing of the interior fittings carefully as the seats and partitions will have to align correctly with the window apertures. The ends of these bench seats will be visible, so the gaps have been filled and will be sanded smooth once the putty has dried.

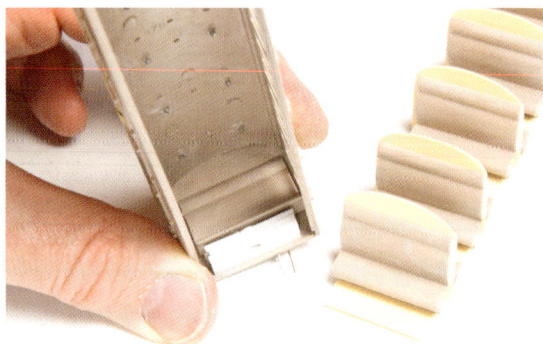

To cope with the body mounting brackets at each end, seats have been trimmed to fit and will be fixed into the body separately after painting and glazing.

A WEIGHTY ISSUE

Now is a good opportunity to consider how much extra ballast will be needed to ensure your plastic carriage runs reliably. As with RTR stock, plastic alone doesn't provide enough bulk to keep it on the rails and, unless your kit is supplied with a strip of metal for extra ballast, another solution will have to be found. Thin strips of steel or lead sheet inserted between the floor and the interior will be fairly un-obtrusive, although it's vital that the weight is evenly distributed across the whole carriage, preferably sited so as to give the vehicle a low centre of gravity.

Alternatively, if you're planning on replacing much of the underframe detail with cast metal components, along with a fully occupied passenger compartment using metal figures, there may be no need for much extra weight. The use of lead shot or Liquid Gravity requires the loose material to be piled in a void and sealed with adhesive, which isn't always as easy a job on a carriage as it is with a freight vehicle. The stresses of heavy weights and large amounts of adhesive, which is likely to shrink during curing, can also have a detrimental effect on long, thin components, such as a carriage floor unit, potentially causing it to warp or twist.

necessary parts, however. An economic option is to fabricate your own floors, bulkheads and partitions from plastic card, shaped to suit the inner profile of the roof. Adequate clearance in terms of height and width will be required, taking into account the glazing material to be employed and the position of the floor in relation to any extra weight that may be installed.

It is vital that the interior is assembled with due accuracy, ensuring that the banks of seating and par-titions align with the windows and doors, as per the real thing.

The National Model Railroad Association (NMRA) of America has set out a range of specifications for carriage weights across various scales, and it may be worth cross-checking these recommended practices (RP-20.1) as a helpful guide. Being aimed at US modellers, there are no listings for 'OO' gauge, although the 'HO' specs would not be too dissimilar.

I can't admit to diligently following these rules myself. Indeed, they were only recently brought to my attention by a couple of *Model Rail* readers following a feature on rolling stock weights. But they're certainly very useful as a rough guide. To avoid any potential problems, I have always aimed to ensure that each vehicle in any set rake is of a consistent mass. What is to be avoided at all costs is the running of vehicles that are notably heavier or lighter than each other, as derailments will be likely on curves and points. Excessive weight adds to the amount of friction on the axles, as well as causing potential strain on the locomotive, especially on curved or inclined track.

As a general rule, I'll aim for a gross weight of around 140g for a typical, predominantly plastic 'OO' gauge bogie carriage of around 60ft in scale

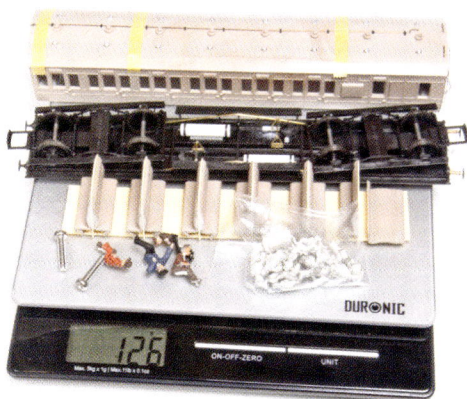

Weight is important for reliable running, especially where plastic vehicles are concerned. Extra weight must be installed, with thin lead sheet being an ideal, pliable medium. Scraps of metal are also useful, while Liquid Gravity from Deluxe Material is a non-toxic alternative to lead shot. Capable of filling small apertures and hollows, the fine pellets can be secured with adhesive.

Fix metal weights to the underframe with epoxy adhesive, distributing the mass as evenly as possible, preferably between the bogies.

It is possible to gauge the final weight of a plastic kit before it is complete by placing all of the intended components onto a set of weighing scales. By including the allotted group of passengers and even the body fixing bolts, an accurate gross weight can be calculated.

With a little extra effort and improvisation, the Ratio kit can produce a high-fidelity model. At the brake end, I substituted the kit's buffers for a set of long brass shanks, although the original plastic heads were employed, suitably thinned with abrasives and mounted on brass wire.

length. This is close to what a detailed and popu-lated RTR carriage weighs in at, meaning that my kit-built and RTR stock can run together with no issues in terms of ride quality and coupling perform-ance. Similarly, for my 'N' gauge stock, I find that 50g is a suitable 'all in' mass for plastic kits and RTR bogie coaches.

With 'O' gauge, I do not have a layout large enough to run more than a couple of four-wheel vehicles, so the issue of weight is not so important, especially as the sheer size of larger scale models invariably sees them blessed with sufficient mass anyway. However, if you have the luxury of running long rakes of bogie stock in 7mm scale, RTR stock from the likes of Heljan or Lionheart trains range between 650 and 900g each, with all-metal vehicles tipping the scales at anything up to double that amount. Here, we get into the issue of what your locomotive can cope with, but ensuring that no single vehicle is drastically lighter or heavier than the rest of the rake will avoid most problems – a mantra that applies equally well to any scale.

PRE-FINISHED KITS

A quick mention of a different kind of plastic car-riage kit is worthwhile here, notably those in the 'OO' range of Southern Pride Models. An innovative solution at the time, a variety of BR MkI vehicles were produced in typical plastic kit form, yet with the carriage sides rendered in clear plastic with pre-finished (or semi-finished) vinyl overlays applied.

While they certainly gave the modeller a head start as far as the finishing process was concerned, the kits included plenty of small detail parts and a full set of interior fittings. Not without their foibles, these kits provided a great opportunity to recreate a wide range of BR MkI vehicles, including some of the more unusual catering, Travelling Post Office and other non-passenger-carrying variants. A brand new range of kits continues that ethos, albeit with a more multimedia approach, offering some exciting departmental vehicles in particular.

The only example of the original style of plastic kit that I've assembled is a MkI Pullman car, started over a decade ago and only recently completed. In an effort to improve realism, extra detailing parts were added from other sources. Having made a mess of the original carriage ends and vestibule areas (I forget how), I fitted a pair of Comet end sections made up of etched brass and white-metal parts.

This Southern Pride MkI Pullman kit came with partly finished vinyl overlays to ease the finishing process. However, I wasn't happy with the vestibule ends, so replaced them with modified metal parts from Comet. This may have improved the body, but it made fitting the roof difficult and the model then needed a full repaint.

While this modification improved the look of the carriage no end, it made fitting the roof difficult. The knock-on effect of this was to render the bolt-together nature of the body redundant, with a glued-up option being taken. Far from ideal in many ways, another hitch of my own making led to a need to repaint the whole carriage from scratch; clear proof that sometimes nothing seems to go to plan! In my defence, I refused to admit defeat and eventually the model was completed to a fairly decent standard.

Gluing a bodyshell together and thus sealing the interior is only recommended as a last resort, as any subsequent maintenance will be tricky. Yet, employing a PVA-type adhesive, applied at strategic points, creates the opportunity to break the bonds easily in future with a sharp blade. A bigger problem arises if there are any gaps between the body and roof that can be disguised only with filler, as was the case with my Southern Pride Pullman.

Although things turned out well in the end, some valuable lessons were learnt in the process. Given the opportunity of building one again, I'd do a lot of things completely differently.

OTHER CONSIDERATIONS

With the main fabric of the carriage now complete, the fitting of smaller parts can continue as required. As with the decisions regarding how the model is to be dismantled in future, more consideration has to go into when to add certain detail parts. Can everything be installed now, or will some parts get in the way of the masking or lining stages? Some moulded features may be ripe for replacement, especially fragile plastic fittings such as

footsteps and buffers. Why not replace them with the finer detailing parts we've already employed on RTR stock? Or even fabricate your own?

Fitting the new ends also required the roof to be modified. Through my own incompetence, I ended up having to secure it with adhesive – something I'm only prepared to do when all else fails. Glue 'n' Glaze was employed as there's no risk of damaging the painted finish or glazing and the bond can easily be broken in the future.

Applying filler to disguise an ill-fitting roof is also not an ideal solution, as it ought to be fettled as accurately as possible. But if, like me, you make a mistake, it can come to the rescue. Acrylic putties can be applied via a syringe for precision and a damp swab will smooth it out with less need for abrasives. The finish will need touching up, though (see Chapter 14).

CHAPTER SIX

RESIN & LASER-CUT KITS

Although metal and plastic are the media that instantly spring to mind when discussing model railway kits, there are other viable materials to consider.

RESIN

Polyurethane resin is a lightweight material, most often employed in 'short run' kit or component manufacture where only small batches of parts are created. It can be moulded to a high level of detail without the need for expensive machinery. Indeed, creating your own cast resin components is not too difficult, as will be demonstrated later in this chapter.

The resin itself is formed from two separate ingredients, rather like epoxy adhesive or putty. The resin component must be mixed thoroughly with a hardening compound before the fluid is poured into a mould. Working time can be very short and it takes skill to achieve good results, especially on larger or complicated objects. As a consequence, there are some great resin kits and bits out there, but quality is by no means universal.

It is not unusual to be faced with hours of cleaning up excess material before assembly can begin, although the softness of the resin does make the job easy. On the other hand, it's very easy to unwittingly take away too much material. A little practice soon furnishes the modeller with an appreciation of how the resin behaves.

Surface flaws and trapped air bubbles are the most common pitfall, but as long as these imperfections do not occur at crucial locations, such as around window frames or along joint faces, they're easy enough to cure with filler. I've been faced with a few resin kits where the material hasn't penetrated into the mould correctly, leaving carriage sides tapering off into nothingness at the ends. Having to fabricate whole new sections and reinforce joints with heavy-duty car filler isn't much fun, and leads one to ponder whether building the model from scratch would have been easier.

If you're in doubt about a kit's merits, ask to check the contents before purchase. This is usually possible if buying the kit in person, but mail order

Resin parts are increasingly to be found in multimedia kits. The material is also employed to create one-piece bodyshells, often designed to sit on a particular RTR chassis.

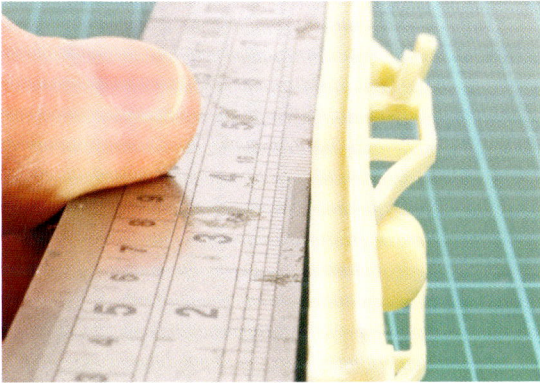

Resin underframes, especially for bogie stock, are seldom reliable. Some kits even feature brass rods cast into the resin frames, but with little success. The best kits feature simple etched brass floor pans.

Resin bogies can be acceptable, but brass axle bearings are recommended for reliable running and longevity.

renders it unlikely. Keeping an eye on the model railway press for product reviews or feature build articles, which may prove invaluable, or ask around at a club or web forum for other modellers' experiences. My personal recommendations for a number of resin kit and component manufacturers are listed in the Appendix.

In terms of carriages, most resin kit makers who know their trade will offer the bodyshell cast as a single component. Individual sides and ends, in 'OO' gauge and smaller, are often best avoided. Similarly, chassis and carriage floors are, in my opinion, not suited to rendering in resin. Such parts demand a level of integrity that goes beyond the limitations of this material. Instead, an etched brass floor may be provided or, more commonly, a RTR plastic underframe is either supplied or specified by a kit's instructions.

Bogies cast in resin are acceptable, but again much depends on the expertise of the kit designer. The material's weaknesses mean that items like footsteps become prone to breakage and a lack of mechanical strength can result in the side frames being cast in overly thick sections that may spoil the appearance. Additionally, fitting metal pinpoint axles directly into resin bearing holes may offer a low-friction interface, but the material may soon begin to wear, leaving excess play in the axles. With

this in mind, it's preferable to fit brass bearings into the bogie frames. Although more expensive, the best kits often incorporate brass bogie frames, complemented by cosmetic resin overlays.

One final advantage of resin – to the kit manufacturer at least – is the low cost, especially compared to the soaring costs of metals and plastics. However, from the customer's position, we end up having to pay slightly more for the labour-intensive production process and the fact that even the most expertly produced moulds have only a short working life. The nature of resin casting means that the moulds degrade rapidly, caused by the heat generated during the resin's solidification process. This explains why resin is preferred by smaller manufacturers, where demand is likely to be limited.

WORKING WITH RESIN

For large components, such as bodyshells, the first and most vital task is to give them a thorough clean. All resin parts are inevitably contaminated by a releasing agent, applied to ease their removal from the moulds. Unless completely removed, paint, filler and adhesives will struggle to bond with the surface. Special cleaning solutions are available, such as Silicone Buster from Finescale Model World, although a good scrub in warm water with an abrasive cleaner can also be effective.

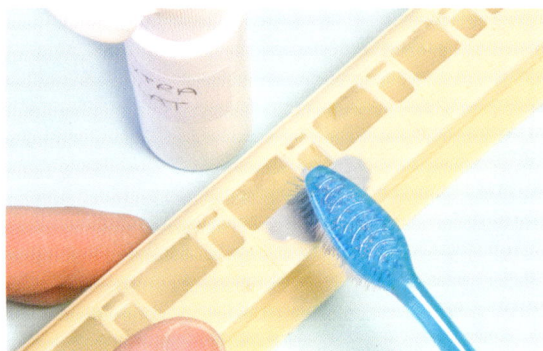

All resin parts carry traces of silicone and a thorough clean and degrease is essential before applying adhesives or paints. Special cleaners are available, such as Silicone Buster from Finescale Model World. I prefer abrasive cleaning compounds that polish the surface at the same time.

Depending on the quality of the moulds, resin components can boast a high degree of relief. Be prepared to undertake plenty of cleaning up before assembly can begin.

After fettling away the waste material, take the time to study the surface and look out for any notable imperfections. It's not always easy to spot scratches or rough areas, as the pale resin renders most of these blemishes invisible. Therefore, it's often worth applying a preliminary coat of grey primer simply as an aid to getting the surface dressed at this early stage. Waiting until fine details have been added before priming will make any subsequent remedial work far more difficult.

Having applied this 'proving' coat of primer, preferably via an aerosol or airbrush, filler can be spread where needed and the surface rubbed down with fine abrasives, using water as a lubricant. Once the component has been cleaned and dried, a further coat of grey primer can follow to reveal whether the surface is perfect. If not, a repeat of the filling and sanding is required. It's worth stressing the importance of thoroughness at this stage: the time spent on getting things right from the outset will be rewarded with a higher quality finish.

Always wear a facemask when cutting, filing or sanding any resin components. The fine dust created can be hazardous and cleaning up afterwards must also be undertaken thoroughly and carefully, wiping down work surfaces with a damp cloth and vacuuming away the dust at regular intervals.

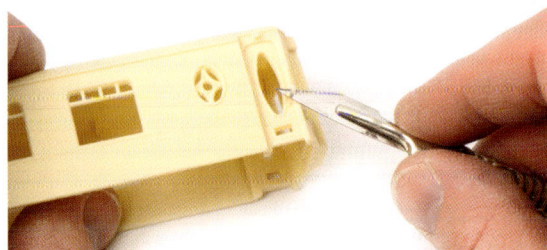

Because resin is soft, it's easy to modify moulded details, especially handrails, filler pipes, door handles and roof vents. Just take care not to remove too much material, working gently and patiently.

Recessed door and panel seams may appear shallow and poorly defined on some resin models. They can be re-scribed with a profile cutter, as produced by Tamiya and Olfa.

Once the initial preparation is out of the way, decisions can be made about improving or replacing some of the resin parts, especially smaller details. As has been stated, resin's inherent softness makes its use for exposed items like buffers and intricate items like brake gear and other underframe fittings rather fraught. Instead, try sourcing replacement parts (or perhaps fabricate your own fittings) in plastic or metal.

In extreme circumstances, either due to deficiencies in the kit or as a result of accidental damage, there may be a need to repair broken or missing parts. Areas around carriage windows are common victims, where it may be necessary to apply some epoxy putty and reshape the aperture or frame profile with files and abrasives. Splicing-in areas of plastic card or strip can also take care of holes, dents or missing relief. If parts are twisted or warped, they may be salvageable by soaking in very hot water (not boiling) and gently manipulating back to the required shape.

TOP: *A light spray coat of grey primer at an early stage acts as a proving medium, helping to identify surface imperfections.*

MIDDLE: *Apply filler where needed and rub down any rough spots before cleaning and priming the model once again. Don't be surprised if this has to be repeated several times before a perfect finish is achieved.*

BOTTOM: *Once the surface appears flawless, rub down the primer again with ultra-fine abrasives, lubricated with clean water, for a super-smooth finish.*

BONDING RESIN PARTS

Despite polyurethane resin being a form of plastic, it cannot be bonded with the poly cements that featured in previous chapters. These adhesives work to break down the chemical bonds of the material, allowing the two parts to fuse together, but resin requires a 'mechanical' type of adhesive. Both epoxy and cyano formulas are suitable, depending on the size and type of components being installed. Epoxy excels with large, heavy parts where a degree of repositioning may be required. Cyano glues, mean-

while, are recommended for smaller fittings. Both adhesives will also work well when bonding other materials to resin, such as brass, nickel silver, white-metal and plastic.

The gap-filling properties of epoxy are also welcome where the joint faces are not positive. Indeed, as alignment of the whole is of paramount importance, ensuring that the vehicle is to scale over the main dimensions, sometimes parts may not come together tightly. In such cases, some form of internal strengthening may be required to bridge

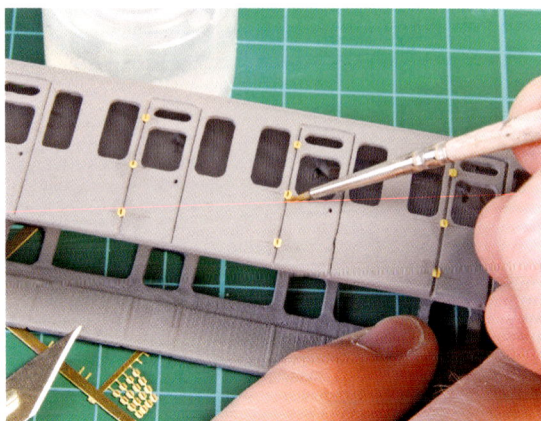

Start adding the fine details such as etched door hinges, secured with clear acrylic varnish or Johnson Klear.

Fold and fix etched door handles into suitable holes drilled with a hand vice (avoid power drills as the resin is too soft). Here, I'm also adding 10 × 10 thou' plastic above the doors to act as rain strips. Cyano is the ideal adhesive for these delicate tasks.

Handrails, roof vents and lamp brackets start to bring the resin body to life. A final layer of primer then leaves the model ready for the livery coats.

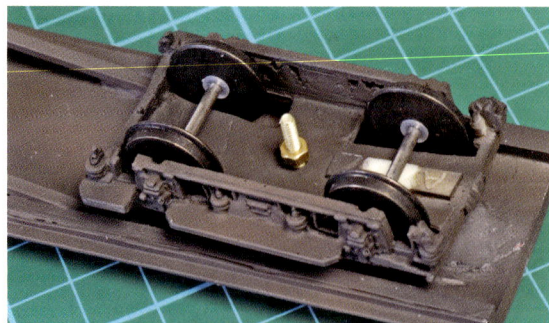

Resin bogies can be installed in the same way as those on plastic kits, with nuts and bolts. Check the ride height and add shims to the bolsters if necessary. Upon final assembly, add a drop of Loctite to the bolt threads.

MAKE YOUR OWN RESIN CASTINGS

This 'quick start' guide is offered as a way of demonstrating how to go about duplicating parts for a conversion, detailing or scratch-building project. Cold-cure polyurethane resin casting is described primarily because it is a relatively straightforward and cheap method, with little required in the way of tools or equipment.

In essence, all you need is a 'master' object to copy, whether it be a modified component from a kit or RTR model, or something crafted wholly by yourself. It can be in virtually any material, as the mould-making process uses no nasty chemicals or heat. As for the nature of the object, it can be anything from a brake cylinder to an entire carriage body, although the latter is something for the more experienced resin caster.

The casting technique is not complicated, but it does take time to get to know how best to construct your moulds. The key is getting the liquid resin to flow freely into the mould, reaching every nook and cranny, before the material starts to solidify. Once the two-pack resin compound has been mixed, working time is very short – usually just a few minutes – before the material struggles to flow evenly. Getting everything set up correctly before the chemicals are mixed is vital as there's no time to mess around. Any rushing or struggling will result in miscast parts, with trapped air bubbles being the most common cause of failure.

A typical resin casting kit includes a two-part resin compound, silicone rubber mould-making compound, release agent, mixing cups and instructions.

Masters

Creating the master demands care and it is important that the component is finished to a high standard, or any imperfections will be translated to the castings. As we have discussed, resin has strengths and weaknesses that must be considered while creating the master. It is not suited for very thin components, for example, or those subject to mechanical wear. Parts expected to retain a high degree of resistance to twisting or impact forces are also best avoided, unless it's feasible to cast in thicker sections. Buffers are fine in 4mm scale and upwards, as long as they're not expected to interact with other vehicles, if employing Kadee or tension lock-style couplings, for example. In its favour, resin is able to replicate an impressive level of surface detail, helped by the use of silicone rubber in the mould-making process, although much inevitably depends on the quality of the master and the mould.

Metal, plastic and even wood can be successfully employed and I prefer to treat the finished master to a few coats of primer from an aerosol. This is then rubbed down and polished to a glass-like finish, with any glue joints tidied as neatly as possible. If the castings are destined to require drilling-out, guide marks can be added with the tip of a sharp punch or scriber. Shaping of solid parts can be achieved with knife, files and abrasives, while round or cylindrical parts can be fashioned with the aid of plastic or metal rod, or even wooden dowels, with any shaping carried out with the part mounted in a drill press. All manner of 'found' objects could be pressed into creating masters, such

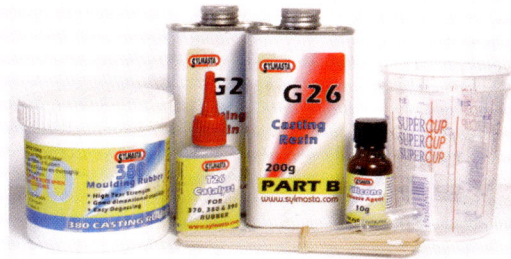

(continued overleaf)

as spare parts from kits or wound steel guitar strings (ideal for mimicking springs). Furthermore, sculpting masters from modellers' clay or epoxy putty allows textured objects to be created, such as curtains or upholstery.

Mould Making

Once complete, the master is employed to create a flexible two-part mould. A small casting box, a few centimetres larger than the object in all directions, can be assembled from Lego bricks, wood or thick plastic card. The box needs to be sturdy enough to withstand the pressure of the compressed mould medium, in this instance Plasticine.

The master is then immersed about halfway into the Plasticine and, after applying a coat of releasing agent, the silicone rubber is mixed and poured into the box. When cured, the box is upturned and the Plasticine removed, ready for the second part of the mould to be created. Effective feed channels for the liquid resin are vital, as is the need for registration points that will allow the two halves of the mould to be accurately aligned.

For simple, solid objects, the process is not too taxing, with the master arranged in the mould in such a way that the resin can flow into the open spaces cleanly and any delicate areas protected from the risk of breakage while the mould is being opened. For hollow forms, such as complete bodyshells, the master is best arranged to form an inner and outer mould.

With the mould set up and prepared with a further coating of releasing agent, the two-part resin compound is mixed and poured into the feed channels. The chemical reaction created when the resin elements are mixed generates an impressive degree of heat, helping the resin to cure quickly. This heat does have the unfortunate habit of degrading the rubber mould, so only a limited number of castings can be made before reproduction quality begins to suffer. Much depends on the size and shape of the mould, but an average lifespan is in the region of fifty to one hundred castings.

The mould ought to be left until the resin has hardened completely (usually thirty minutes but check the instructions). Any disturbance of the moulds will translate into broken or misshaped castings, so don't be tempted to peek inside too soon. Dismantling the mould gently should see the cast component easily removed, thanks to the silicone release agent. There's bound to be waste material to remove, not least the feed gates and the parts must be cleansed thoroughly before any adhesives or paints are applied.

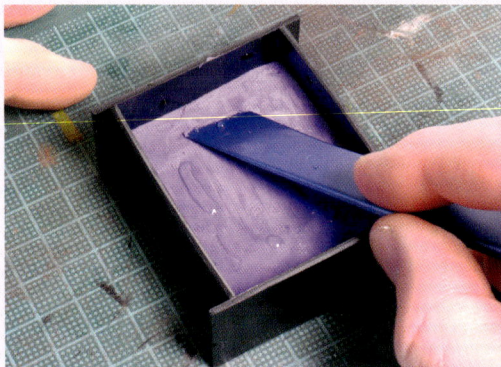

A simple casting box can be formed from thick plastic card or Lego bricks. Half fill the box with Plasticine, flattening and smoothing the upper surface with a damp spatula.

Press the master halfway into the Plasticine and form registration holes in each of the four corners with the handle of a paintbrush. Apply a thin coating of the silicone release agent, over the Plasticine, master and the edges of the box.

Mix the silicone rubber and catalyst fluid in the prescribed dosages and pour gently into the mould. Level off and allow it to cure overnight.

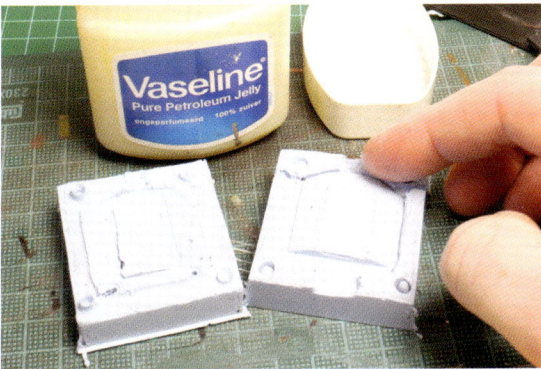

Upturn the casting box and remove the Plasticine, leaving the master embedded in the rubber. Create filling channels with more Plasticine to allow the resin to penetrate the mould. Brush on more releasing agent, followed by the rubber compound, again leaving overnight to cure.

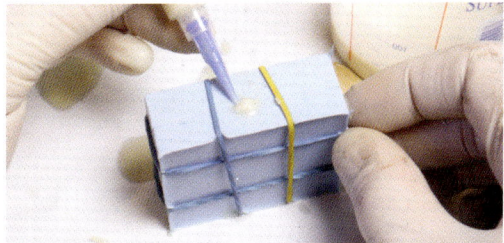

Remove the sides of the box, open up the two halves of the mould and remove the master. Note how 'pegs' have formed in the corners, which will ensure perfect alignment of the mould. Brush releasing agent onto the faces of the mould and a little Vaseline onto the outer mating faces.

Clamp the two halves together and mix the resin compound with the hardener, as instructed. Inject the resin into the mould from each channel using a syringe, until the fluid seeps out of each entry point. Stand the mould flat and allow to cure for at least thirty minutes.

Gently break open the mould and remove the casting. There's bound to be plenty of excess material to be trimmed away and the part will need a thorough clean before installation.

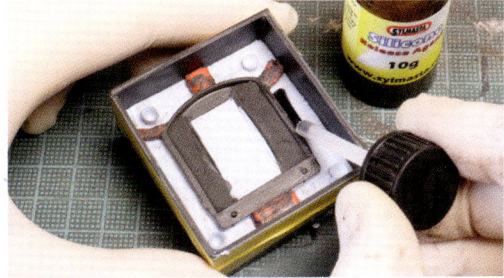

For detailing, conversion and scratch-building projects, resin casting allows multiple parts to be created from a single master, significantly reducing the amount of work necessary. It is also a simple way of replacing missing parts, as was the case with this RTR coach.

any gaps and produce a reliable bond. Plastic or brass angle is a good example for use at corners, with the epoxy adhesive filling the joint. Once fully cured, it can be sanded flush and any gaps addressed with filler. Thick, gel-type cyano can also achieve similar results, especially if mixed with a little talcum powder and, when cured, can be sanded smooth. However, working time is reduced drastically, making careful alignment more difficult.

LASER-CUT PLASTICS

Laser-cut plastic kits and components utilize specialist materials with specific properties, such as Mylar or Rowmark. Mylar is a flexible, polyester-based material that is perfectly suited to the creation of intricate detail overlays. However, it can be tricky to bond and employing cyano or epoxy glue in some instances is unwelcome, so the option of self-adhesive components is highly recommended. Rowmark is a tougher, less flexible plastic that can be bonded with strong poly-cement-type solvents, such as Plast-i-Weld.

The laser cutting process often causes a raised burr around the edge of each component, necessitating some careful abrading before assembly. Indeed,

this preparation will be vital if the kit is designed around a tab-and-slot method of construction.

Working solely with sheet material has the potential to create uniform, lifeless models, even when multiple layers are employed. However, a little creative thinking can quickly solve this problem. Rounding-over edges with abrasives is one option, while adding texture before assembly or during the final weathering stages is another.

Having said that, there's no reason why a well-designed set of laser-cut components can't prove highly realistic. A quick trawl through the website of York Modelmaking, for instance, reveals some truly marvellous instances of miniature plastic engineering. Anything from girder viaducts to signal boxes has been rendered in kit form, with plenty of rolling stock projects too. Indeed, a range of vans and carriages manufactured on behalf of the Broad Gauge Society (see Useful Addresses) is a good example of using cutting-edge technology to provide kits and materials for modellers with 'niche' interests, without the tooling costs associated with moulding or casting.

Moreover, scratch-builders or those wanting to modify kits and RTR models can commission the likes of York Modelmaking to design and produce

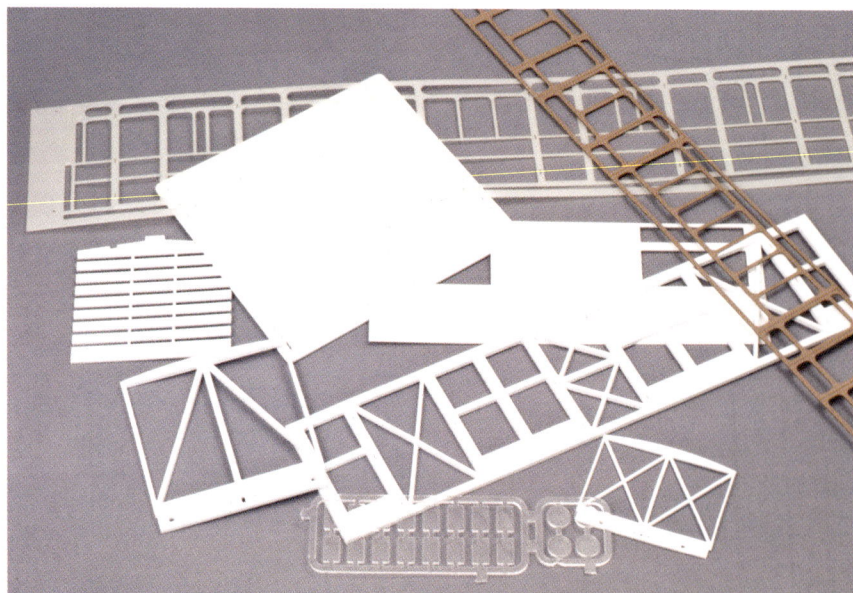

These are just a few examples of what York Modelmaking can produce in laser-cut plastic. Intricate panel overlays, engraved components or complete kits are possible in a range of materials, either off-the-shelf or produced to your own specifications. Door seams, hinge locations, window apertures and frames, planks and vents are all reproduced as necessary.

new bodywork, interiors or even laser-cut glazing, in a range of materials and sizes. Panelled vehicles are especially difficult to scratch-build but laser-cut overlays, with a strong self-adhesive backing, remove the need for hours of monotonous work. Any scale can be catered for, with modern sheet materials (such as Mylar) available in a range of thicknesses down to just 350 microns (0.35mm), while still offering a high resistance to tearing or buckling.

Furthermore, it's not only plastic that can be laser-cut: wood, paper and card can also be rendered thus, as we shall see in the following chapter.

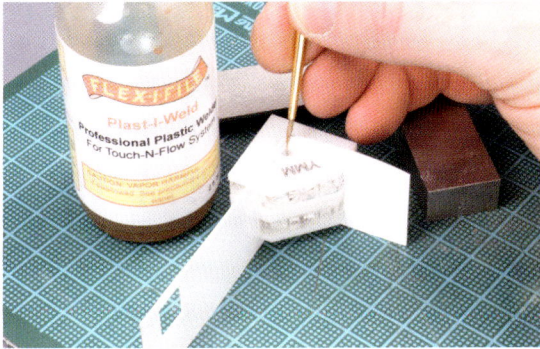

Laser-cut plastic can appear a little 'flat', especially when recreating timber-built vehicles. However, some texture can be added before assembly by rubbing with coarse abrasives or a steel brush. Keep all strokes in line with the likely direction of any wood grain on the prototype. This also acts to remove the inevitable raised burrs around every edge, caused by the cutting process. A sharp scriber will clear panel lines that the abrading is likely to clog.

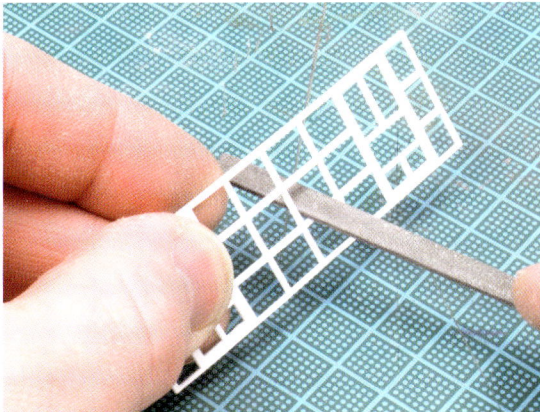

Strong poly cement is essential when joining laser-cut plastic parts, such as Slater's Mek Pak, Flex-i-File's Plast-i-Weld or Deluxe Materials' Plastic Magic. These Magnetic Mates clamps, also from York Modelmaking, are great for holding parts securely while gluing.

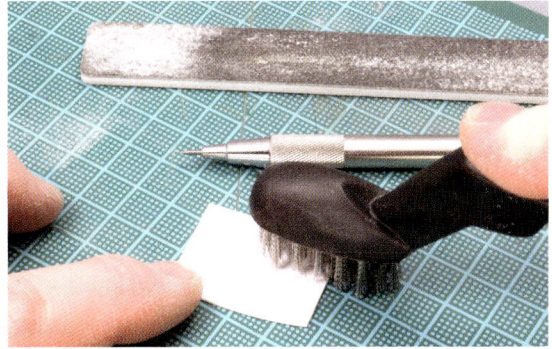

Correct alignment and square corners are essential, with few of the positive locating aids to be found on injection-moulded plastic kits. Work on a flat surface, such as a piece of glass, to keep the assembly true.

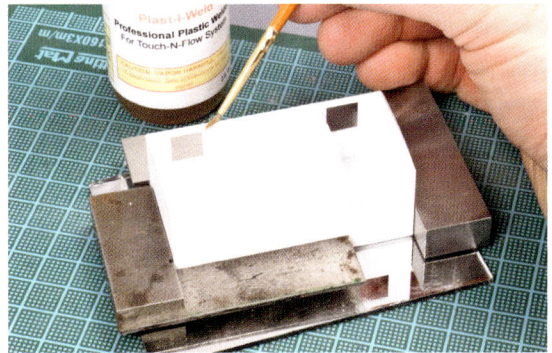

Laminating brings extra relief to laser-cut components, especially panel-sided stock. By filing the outer edges of the overlay, the slight chamfering or curving of the real thing can be replicated. This can be laborious but well worth the effort.

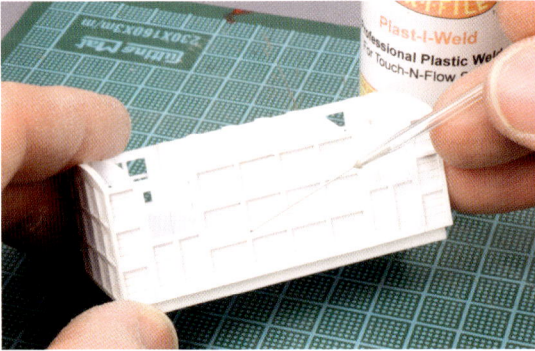

It is vital to fix the overlays securely without any excess adhesive spoiling the effect. A precision applicator, such as this Touch 'n' Flow from Flex-i-File, gets the right amount of liquid cement exactly where it's needed.

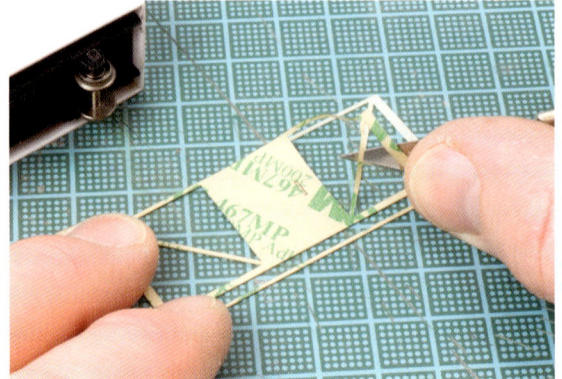

Some laser-cut overlays, especially those rendered in Mylar, may feature self-adhesive backing, making assembly even easier. I do find that a little drop of cyano glue at the corners is sometimes necessary, though. Subsequent layers of primer and paint will help ensure a durable long-term bond.

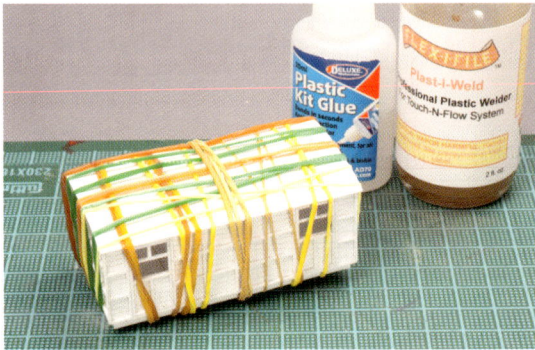

Roofs will need forming to the correct profile before assembly. Immerse in hot water and shape to an approximation of the desired curvature by wrapping it around a bottle or can. Fix in place as soon as possible to prevent the plastic reverting to its flat state, clamping securely while the cement cures.

The layering approach works equally well with laser-cut underframes.

For durability, etched or cast metal components may be desired for the underframe, especially for axleguards and brake gear. Suitable underframe parts for broad-gauge stock in 4mm and 7mm scales are available from Bill Bedford and Dart Castings.

CHAPTER SEVEN

WOOD-BASED MATERIALS & 3D PRINTING

Continuing developments in computer-aided design and manufacture has seen the rise of 3D printing, stereo lithography and rapid prototyping. As the cost of equipment and software falls, so these space-age processes have come within the reach of the humble modelling 'cottage' industry.

The use of wood-based materials has recently re-emerged, thanks also to new manufacturing technologies. Computer-controlled, laser-cut wood components offer many advantages to the coach builder, most obviously in terms of recreating the texture of the real thing; something that even the best plastic, metal or resin kits struggle to capture.

Plywood, a manufactured board created from several thin layers of natural timber, is an ideal modelling medium. Each layer (or 'ply') has the orientation of the grain set at opposing angles, providing a stronger, more reliable platform and laser-cutting processes now allow for the material to be formed into intricate shapes. Medium Density Fibreboard (MDF) is also suited to laser-cutting, offering a similar strength and warp resistance to plywood. It may lack any hint of realistic grain, but MDF does possess a slightly textured surface, which may or may not be desirable. The issue of scale is important here, as the grain of the timber ought not to be too intrusive to the eye, especially in anything 'OO' gauge or smaller. Indeed, the majority of wood-based kits in production today generally cater for 7mm scale and above.

Card is also employed in some quarters, either die-cut or laser-cut, and a combination of these materials can be found in specialist rolling stock kits. Parliamentary Trains, a firm who concentrate on nineteenth-century railway subjects, has employed laser-cut wood and card in some of its early kits, albeit mostly of freight subjects. IP Engineering is another company worth investigating, especially if larger, 'garden scale' railways are your passion, while York Modelmaking also offers a bespoke laser-cutting service in wood, card and paper (see Useful Addresses).

WORKING WITH WOOD

If you're tempted to employ the fruits of nature in your carriages, wood-based products can be joined with a range of adhesives. Penetrating glues, such as PVA and aliphatic resin, are especially good for plywood, veneers and thin strip wood as they allow plenty of working time. However, they're designed to sink deep into the wood's grain, making it impermeable to oil- or water-based stains and potentially causing a patchy appearance – not a welcome factor if a natural wood finish is desired.

Epoxy glues are highly effective with wood, MDF or card, as are cyano-type adhesives, although I'd suggest choosing slower-setting formulas to allow for accurate positioning of parts. Equally, the thinner, faster-setting types may be absorbed into the material before the bond can be made, resulting in a weakened joint.

It makes good sense to colour the bare timber components before assembly. Stains are easy to use and there is a wide variety of shades to choose from. Mixing your own colours is possible, provided the individual stains are compatible (use the same brand and formula wherever possible), practising on scrap material beforehand to perfect the colour. Oil-based stains are, in my experience, the most versatile despite their long drying times. Subsequent layers of glue, paint and varnish will not affect the finish, whereas water-based stains can be somewhat fickle.

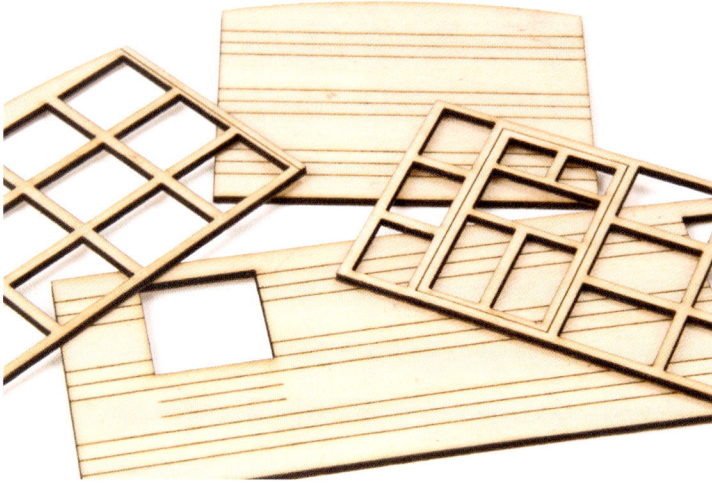

LEFT: *Laser-cut wood kits and components offer a unique sense of realism. After all, nothing can reproduce wood like the real thing. Fine-grade plywood offers strength and integrity but it needs to be treated with care.*

BELOW: *If the prototype sported a natural wood finish, it is best to treat the material before assembly. Oil-based stains are ideal and colours can be inter-mixed to achieve the desired shade.*

Furthermore, experimenting with wood stain finishes can create some dramatic results, with fading and distressing possible, using abrasives. Avoiding a uniform shade also helps add definition and relief to surfaces, especially on planked or panelled vehicles, where slightly different stains can be brushed on in strategic locations.

Working wood demands only basic tools and equipment, with a stout knife and straight edge often being enough. For larger parts (more than 3mm thick) a fine-toothed razor saw and mini-mitre box are recommended. To prevent the material

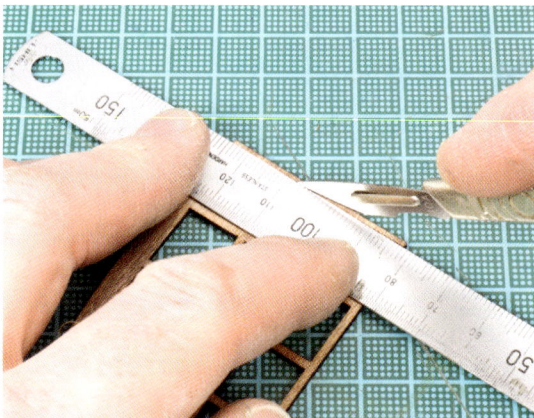

Cutting timber components requires care. If using a knife, fit a fresh blade and make numerous light passes, working against a straight edge.

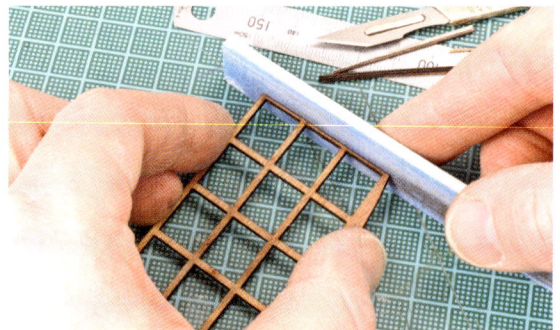

Ensure all edges are square and tidy before assembly. Abrade with a flat file or sanding pad, checking against a set square. Sanding the edges also helps remove carbon deposits from the laser-cutting process, helping the glue to penetrate the joint more effectively.

splitting, especially when working across or against the grain, we must work only with the sharpest tools.

As with all kit components, ensuring straight, square joint faces is essential and a good, close fit is always preferable if using a penetrating adhesive. If the parts don't tally up well, try gap-filling glue, such as epoxy or a thicker grade of PVA, although the unsightly gap will be apparent unless it can be filled and painted over. Ill-fitting parts also introduce structural weakness, so some recourse to hidden internal strengthening brackets may be required.

The use of glues with longer drying times makes for a more leisurely assembly experience, but the need to restrain the parts for long periods shouldn't be underestimated. An assembly jig will be a great help. It needn't be anything fancy, just an offcut of thick plywood or MDF with uprights attached, set at a right angle. The main bodyshell components will then have a reliable surface against which to be clamped while gluing up. Fine pins, tape and hobby clamps will keep the parts secure and York Modelmaking's nifty Magnetic Mates clamps, seen to good effect in the previous chapter, will also be useful.

A handy tip to stop any stray adhesive bonding the model to the jig is to spray the surface with a layer of dry lubricant, such as PTFE (as sold in hardware stores to lubricate saws and woodwork machinery). Alternatively, and more economically, rubbing the jig with a candlestick will achieve the same results. I've also used brown parcel tape to line a jig, although this can be awkward to remove afterwards. Basically, the idea is to form a barrier to prevent the glue from penetrating into the timber jig, without depositing any unwanted residues onto the model's surface.

If filling is necessary, many hobby fillers are compatible with timber, such as Revell's Plasto and Milliput. Coloured wood fillers are also available from DIY stores and craft outlets, many of which can be stained to match the surrounding timber. Alternatively, sand or file an offcut of the same wood and collect the fine dust. This can be mixed with a small amount of thin PVA glue to form a paste

that will be a very close match to the surrounding material. Not being porous, due to the adhesive, it'll be difficult to colour with stain. In which instance, some work with a palette of paints can help disguise the affected area.

Miniature plywood, although tough and resilient, can be shaped readily by soaking in hot water. After an hour or so, the parts can be wrapped around a suitable former such as a length of copper pipe or paint tin. Aim to form the part into a tighter radius

Apply the minimum of glue to the joints, preferably with a precision applicator, and clamp the parts securely in the jig. Look out for any distortion, clamping the parts along their full length wherever possible.

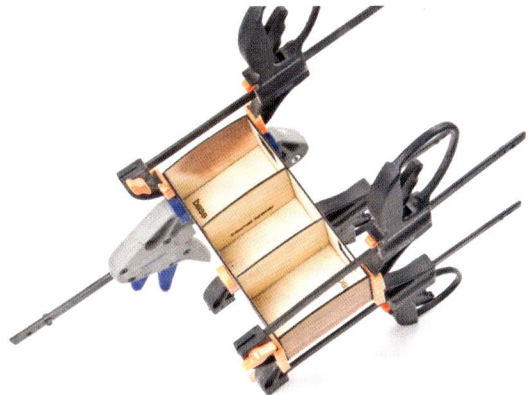

Allow the first half of the bodyshell to cure overnight before adding the other side and end, clamping in the jig or with lightweight sash clamps. Check the corners again and allow to dry thoroughly before removing the clamps.

than will be eventually required to allow for 'spring-ing' back once the wood has cooled, dried and been released from the mould. Once shaped (and dry), fix the part in place as soon as possible, clamping securely until the glue has cured completely.

Wood's pliability when wet is a clue also to its vulnerability to damp and humid conditions. Careful storage of the kit before and after assembly is important, with parts likely to warp or twist unless treated sympathetically. As the reliability of an item of rolling stock depends on the concentricity of its axles, a twisted body is likely also to pull the chassis and wheels out of true.

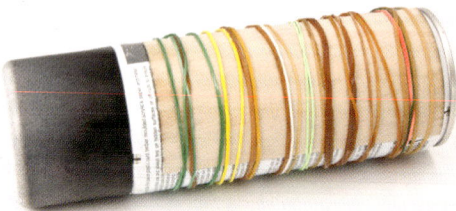

The exterior framing of this York Modelmaking kit is made up of separate laser-cut plywood overlays. Apply the glue sparingly before clamping up, wiping away immediately any that has squeezed out with a damp swab.

The roof is also rendered from laser-cut ply, but must be soaked in hot water for an hour or so prior to shaping. Choose a former of a smaller diameter than the roof's eventual profile. This aerosol can proved ideal and a host of rubber bands supported the wood while it dried.

Install the roof as soon as the timber is dry. Again, rubber bands offer the perfect clamping solution.

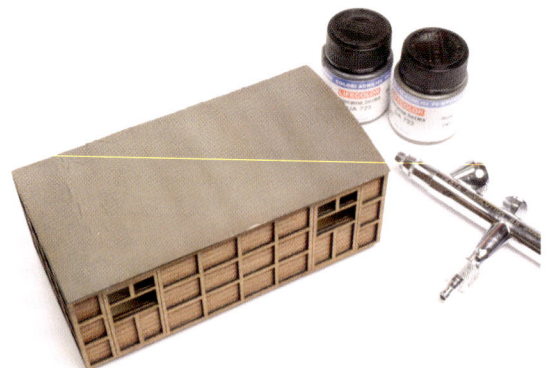

To replicate the traditional stretched canvas covering, a sheet of paper was fixed to the roof, having brushed on a thin layer of PVA glue. Once dry, the paper was trimmed flush with the edges.

Some interesting effects can be created when the roof is painted, particularly when employing acrylic paints. The high water content of Lifecolor acrylics, for example, encourages the roof covering to 'ripple' realistically.

3D PRINTING

Given that 3D printing was generally unknown a decade ago, the dramatic rise of the technology now means that a number of model railway retailers offer 3D printing services. Yes, retailers, not just specialist kit and component makers. Hatton's of Liverpool is one such example, with a design and production service currently available across a range of materials and processes.

When compact discs appeared in the 1980s, they seemed like something from the realms of science fiction and the cost was substantial. However, once the concept took off, prices soon plummeted and CD players are now as 'cheap as chips'. We're not at that point with 3D printing yet, but the costs have come down dramatically in the past few years. More importantly, in that time, the rise in the quality of printed components has been steadily increasing.

The development of the materials employed has also improved matters, up to a point. The earliest offerings may have looked spectacular at first glance, but they were incredibly difficult to work with, especially at the painting stage. Although things have improved, 3D printed parts can still offer a deceptively labour-intensive option. Plenty of work is required to get the surfaces ready for painting and the parts will require very careful handling at all times. However, these drawbacks are balanced against the fact that these kits require less in the way of general assembly work.

Furthermore, the limitations of the current materials raise an important question. For me, it's the assembling of kits that brings me the most joy and I'm sure I'm not alone in that feeling. Replacing the hours spent preparing and bonding individual parts with hours of sanding, filling and burnishing doesn't always appeal. This attitude may be coloured, however, by having just spent an entire weekend preparing a 3D printed bodyshell; at no point was I moved to think that this medium was the answer to a modeller's prayers.

Joking and current material limitations aside, it's looking increasingly clear that 3D printing technology will have a significant impact on the model railway hobby (in fact, it may well affect many facets of modern life). As far as kit manufacture is concerned, there are no expensive tooling or mould-making costs or even the need for any manufacturing facilities. All that's required is a set of computer-generated (CAD) scale drawings, which are then emailed to a remote 3D printing facility or sent to the designer's own desktop printing machine. Because there are no moulds or tooling to set up, any quantity of components can be produced, from one to one thousand.

The relatively low cost allows an unlimited number of prototypes to be produced and tested, with the CAD drawings tweaked accordingly, before the products are ready for the market. Hornby and other RTR manufacturers now regularly employ 3D printing and stereo lithography to create their initial prototypes, having realized the effectiveness of this approach.

Constant improvements in the technology also allow makers to keep their products up to date and, with rapid turnaround times, there's seldom any need to keep parts in stock, as they can be made to order. The printing machines themselves are also now more affordable (relatively speaking) and will no doubt continue to fall in price. In 2015 the desktop Makerbot Replicator, for example, was retailing at around £1,000 while the smaller Printrbot was around half that price.

WORKING WITH 3D PRINTED PARTS

At the time of writing, most 3D printed kits and components are being offered in two types of material. White Strong Flexible (WSF) is the more common and cheaper version, being resilient and pliable but unable to take very fine detail. The rough surface texture can be challenging, with much remedial work necessary before painting. Frosted Ultra Detail (FUD) is a slightly translucent medium that is more brittle and expensive, but it can be rendered in more intricate shapes with less in the way of unwanted surface texture.

FUD components, in particular, usually arrive with a waxy covering that must be removed before any assembly work commences. Buffing the surface

THE FUTURE OF MODEL KITS?

How does the process actually work? Once the printer has received its instructions, it begins by spraying a fine jet of an acrylic-based photopolymer. Upon exposure to light, the polymer hardens, allowing the construction of the object to continue in separate layers. It is this layered approach that leads most 3D printed components to retain a 'stepped' texture across their surface, which must be removed by the modeller before the kit can be finished.

Where an object requires hollow areas, or the inclusion of open apertures, a temporary framework is 'printed' before the rest of the object is formed around it. Once complete, the temporary frame is easily snapped away. Large, solid objects are often built up with a semi-hollow, honeycomb internal structure, providing great strength with greater economy and less weight.

There are a number of 3D printing services available to modellers, some of which will even take care of all the necessary CAD artwork, should there be something you'd like manufacturing that isn't otherwise available. As I complete this manuscript, I've just learned that Precision Labels is launching its own 3D printing service, offering some of the highest-quality production standards on small-scale components. What's more, the company can also create replicas of existing objects, using a laser-scanning machine, so if you've scratch-built or converted a carriage model and don't fancy repeating the trick, you can send it off and have as many copies made as you like, providing the subject will fit into the scanning machine.

There are myriad small-scale producers of kits and components plying their 3D wares via web portals such as Shapeways, who host the retail space as well as the actual manufacturing facilities. This is yet another medium that has opened doors for modellers with interests not catered for in the mainstream RTR or kit market. Accordingly, those with a yearning for narrow gauge, Irish or pre-1920s railway subjects now have much more scope for indulging their obsessions.

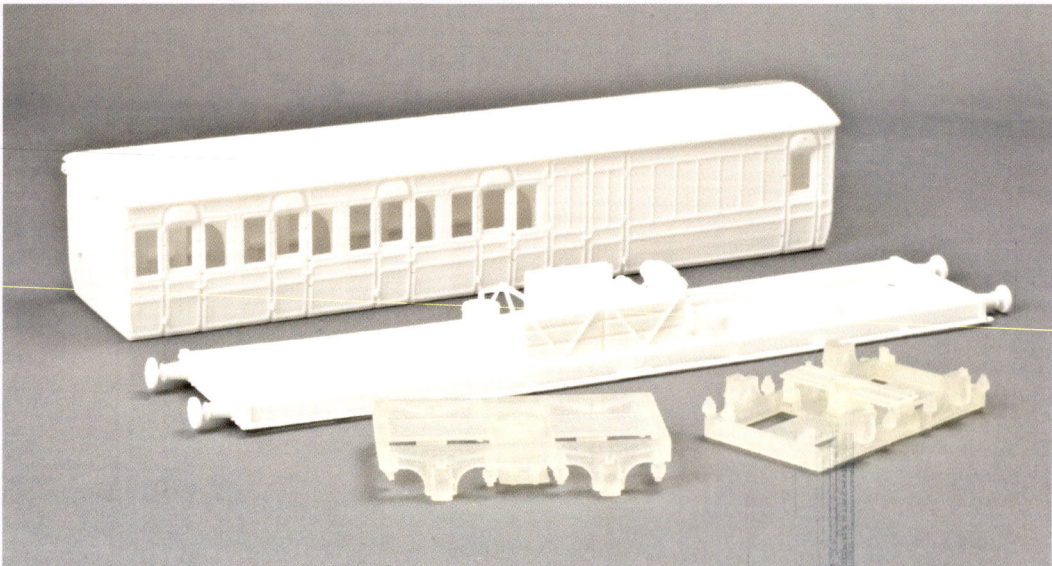

A typical 3D printed 'kit': a one-piece body and chassis, rendered in WSF material, with a pair of bogies in the more refined, but brittle, FUD polymer. This 'OO' gauge Metropolitan Railway carriage, designed by mattwicksbluebell, was obtained via the Shapeways online portal.

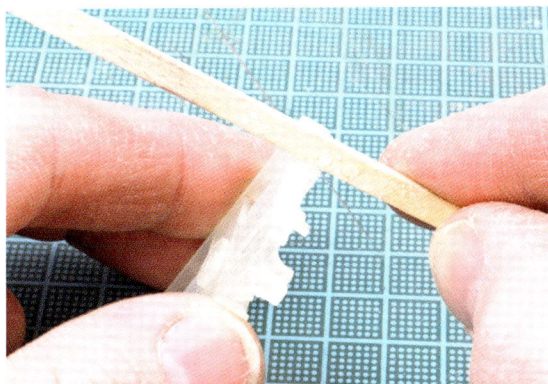

Files and abrasives are pretty useless on 3D printed parts and a wooden burnishing tool is far more effective. Coffee stirrers are ideal for removing the waxy residues left behind on FUD-rendered parts.

By shaping the tip of the wooden stirrer, the tool will also be effective for burnishing the relief on WSF components. It took a good few hours to smooth the surface of this carriage, before cleansing the parts in warm water and mild detergent.

Liquid filling agents work well, but the harsh thinners involved may damage the material. Therefore a couple of light coats of aerosol primer were applied before brushing on several coats of Mr Surfacer 1000. Each layer must be left to dry overnight before continuing.

To hide the prominent marks on the roof, modelling putty can be smeared on, built up over a couple of layers.

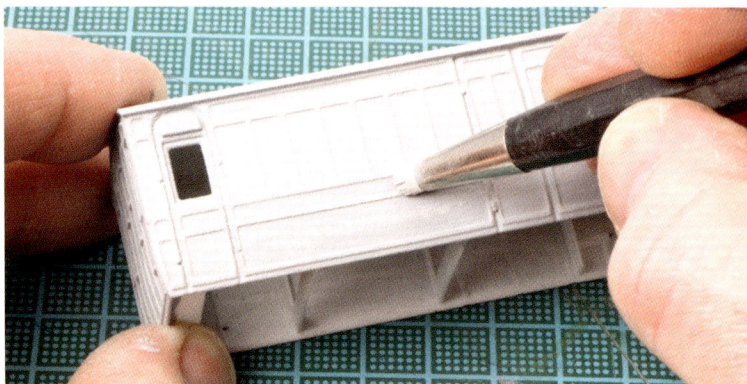

Once the surfacing agent has cured, a glass-fibre scratch brush effectively removes any lumps, bumps and brush marks.

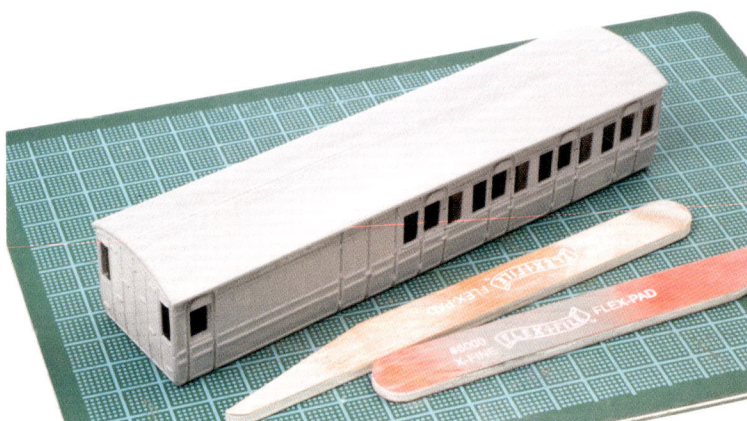

Take the time to abrade the bodyshell thoroughly, working through the grades until it's as smooth and blemish-free as possible. Then treat the body to a thorough scrub in plenty of clean water.

with a wooden spatula – of the type commonly provided with takeaway tea or coffee – can be remarkably effective and less invasive than working with abrasives. Chamfering the tip of the spatula to allow it better access into recesses and around raised details creates a very useful tool.

Where parts are designed to clip together, a prior immersion in warm water will add a little temporary flexibility to FUD-rendered components. Whatever medium is employed, a thorough wash in mild detergent, accompanied by a light scrubbing with an old toothbrush, will shift surface contaminants without damaging any delicate detail.

Models supplied in WSF format require much more in terms of remedial work and, in a similar manner to working with resin, preliminary proving coats of primer are recommended. The bare material is incredibly difficult to abrade with files or abrasives, so layers of primer (and a liquid filling

agent such as Mr Surfacer) provide an intermediate layer that can be abraded effectively.

Where WSF scores highly is in providing the bare essentials in terms of the overall vehicle outline, at relatively little cost and without the labour associated with scratch-building or complex conversion work. From this foundation, fine detail such as door hinges, handles, handrails, pipes, ventilators and various other adornments can be added, including raised rivets where appropriate.

3D printed carriage kits share a number of similarities with resin kits. They're usually rendered in the form of a single bodyshell, perhaps with a separate roof and underframe. Bogies are also available, as are a wide range of smaller components like carriage ends, ventilators and underframe fittings that may be of use in conversion projects.

Bonding also follows the same tenets required by resin kits, employing epoxy or cyano glue for the best results. Unless they're purely cosmetic, pro-truding parts like buffers or intricate underframe trussing are often best replaced with metal alterna-tives. Indeed, it should be borne in mind that resin and 3D printed models are inevitably more delicate than mainstream plastic or metal kit-built vehicles, and must be handled and stored accordingly.

One other point to mention is the sensitivity of some 3D printed materials to oils and solvents. Avoid employing white spirit, enamel or lacquer thinners directly onto either WSF or FUD rendered parts, although cellulose and oil-based paints and primers are compatible when applied in very thin layers. Care must also be taken when lubricating any moving parts as mineral oils may also damage the material. A useful alternative is PTFE dry powder lubricant, as produced by Labelle.

Having primed and painted the bogies, a soak in warm water will soften the brittle FUD material enough to accept a set of pinpoint axles. The DCCconcepts axle reamer clears out debris from the bearings and ensures free running.

Take great care with the bogies, as the fine detail is easily damaged. Gently slot the axles into place and check that they turn freely. Test on a sheet of glass to discern whether the axles are aligned correctly. Lubricate the bearings with Labelle's 134 PTFE-based powder.

Retaining the bogies is simple, using small brass nuts, bolts and washers. A drop of Loctite on the thread will prevent the nut working loose over time. Just check that the bogie has plenty of free movement.

Due to the amount of filling and sanding involved to get the parts smooth, addition of the smaller details must wait. With the handrails, roof vents and underframe fittings in place, the model is ready for a final primer coat prior to the livery being applied.

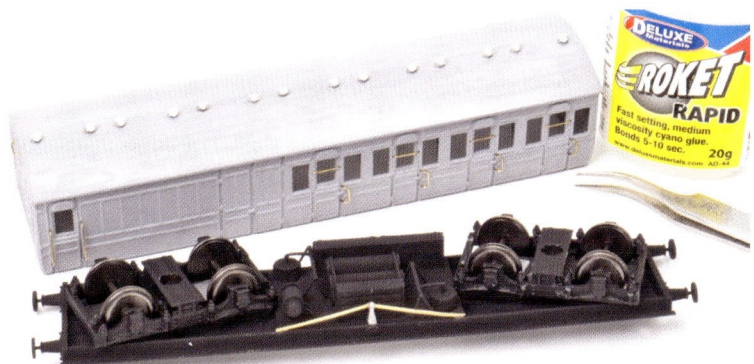

CHAPTER EIGHT

CONVERSIONS

From a commercial point of view, it's little wonder that some of the more obscure carriage types have not been made available in RTR form. Gaps remain, however, even among some of the more mainstream designs, such was the variation in the fleets of the pre- and post-nationalized railway companies. More modern vehicles, on the other hand, are regularly being refurbished or modified, making it hard for RTR manufacturers to maintain an up-to-the-minute range of models.

This situation leaves us with the option of modifying existing models in order to recreate something a little different. It may only be a minor deviation, such as altering the layout of the windows and sealing up the odd doorway. Alternatively, it may mean carving up most of the vehicle, or even cutting and combining multiple models to produce a single carriage.

An ever-changing selection of conversion kits for specific prototypes has been available for some time, ranging from side overlays for a not-too-dissimilar RTR coach body, to entire replacement bodyshells. There is also an option of printed, self-adhesive vinyls for 2mm and 4mm RTR stock, which can be especially effective for modern, flat-sided subjects in complex modern livery schemes.

There are plenty of other prototypes that aren't covered by conversion kits, leaving us to take more of a 'Do It Yourself' approach, using whatever existing kits, RTR models or separate components that we can find. This subject can blur into the realms of scratch-building, so the following pages will concentrate on projects using RTR models and kits as the main source.

Carriages cascaded into departmental use remain popular subjects, across most eras. Archaic rolling stock, lingering on as workers' accommodation, tool van or barrier vehicle, make for an interesting addition to a layout. These may only require the plating over of the odd window or removal of the gangways, along with a new livery.

Complete conversion kits exist for a variety of RTR models, especially in 'OO' gauge, including most of the necessary parts. In some cases, an entire replacement bodyshell may be available, such as this Keen Systems resin casting designed to fit atop the older style of Hornby Pullman chassis. A wide range of ancillary parts is available from the same source, allowing for a comprehensive rebuilding project.

A simple introduction to conversion projects is provided by self-adhesive vinyl overlays. Popular among 'N' gauge modellers, similar packages are available in 'OO', such as these overlays from Amsies.

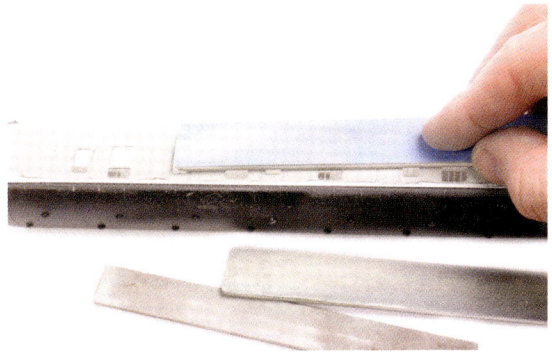

Before the vinyls can be applied, all raised relief must be removed from the carriage sides. The body will then need a thorough wash and dry.

More contemporary subjects may include Network Rail's test train stock, a motley selection of aged BR Mk1, 2 and 3 vehicles, equipped with all manner of technical equipment and usually hauled by traction of a similar vintage.

Catering cars appeared in a great many varieties. One-offs and tailor-made vehicles for specific express services, or mid-life conversions into 'Mini Buffets', are other options. The vast numbers of non-gangway suburban coaches, which were once a common sight in and around major conurbations, also offer possible conversion subjects, with existing RTR models seldom offering the full range of prototypes.

Modellers of Irish Railways will also benefit from conversion work, with only a small range of RTR models currently available. Plenty of components and replacement sides can be obtained, along with the necessary paints and transfers, to convert existing British outline vehicles.

A representative selection of conversion projects is offered in this chapter, with the various techniques and processes relevant to each described in detail. As mentioned, the possibilities are endless, so I've chosen subjects that offer specific challenges, along with a few easier options for those less intrepid modellers.

Don't forget that the interiors may also require modification, with the level of authenticity being dictated by how visible the innards will be. Choosing the right donor model is also important, with the aim of making the project as straightforward as possible. Careful prototype research will reveal RTR models or kits with the closest dimensions and profile.

EASY RTR CONVERSIONS

Probably the quickest and simplest means of conversion work is to employ pre-printed and pre-cut vinyl overlays from the likes of Amsies and Electra Railway Graphics. Without the need for extensive surgery or the hassle of repainting, vinyl can produce some surprisingly effective results, especially in the smaller scales. Some careful preparation is still demanded, with the need to remove all raised detail from the carriage sides. It may also be beneficial to blank off any unwanted window apertures in order that the overlays sit correctly on the surface. The work doesn't have to be to too high a standard, however, as the vinyl is thick enough to eradicate any minor blemishes.

What is important is that the shell is cleaned thoroughly to ensure a strong, resilient bond. The lack of relief can be overcome by installing extra details, such as handrails and door hinges, with the new materials touched-in with the appropriate shades of paint. A little judicious weathering will

Peel away part of the backing and position the vinyl overlay against one end of the carriage, pressing it down along the length. Work gradually to avoid air bubbles or creases and ensure that it sits flat against the gutter strip.

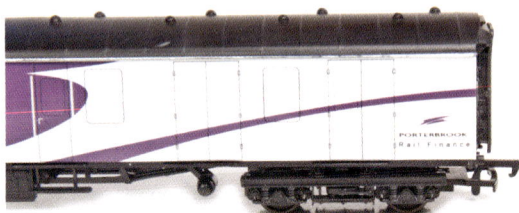

This simple, albeit superficial conversion can be effected rapidly but, in reality, this barrier coach would also need extensive modifications to the underframe, ends and gangways.

A more authentic option for a similar barrier vehicle is to fashion blanking plates from 5 thou' plastic card. The raised window beading has been flattened before the plates are fixed with liquid poly cement, applied from the inside.

Other modifications to this Lima Mk2 included blanking off the gangways.

mask any discrepancies and a sealing coat of varnish is recommended.

A more authentic approach would be to blank off the windows, with the new panels sitting either flush or slightly proud of the surface, according to the prototype. If they're to be flush, recourse to an internal backing and model filler will prove effective. If the plating demands separate raised panels to be installed, then thin sheet metal or plastic can be employed.

Cutting out the wafer-thin plastic or brass sheet demands care and patience, ensuring that the edges are straight and square and the corners rounded over consistently. Creating a set of templates is recommended, using them as a guide during final shaping.

The Lima model represents a Mk2B, but the prototype was a Mk2A, so the doors had to be re-scribed with an Olfa cutter.

New hinges were added from 10 × 20 thou' plastic strip, although the door handles had been removed on the prototype. Such conversions are a great way of breathing life into an old and unloved model.

Where windows are plated flush with the outside, a different approach is required. Either plastic sheet is fettled to sit within the aperture or a larger piece is fixed to the interior to act as a base for layers of model putty. Build up the filler in multiple layers.

Allow the filler to cure completely before abrading it flush. It may take a few attempts to get the filler flat and blemish free.

ADDING AND TAKING AWAY

Sticking with the theme of non-passenger-carrying stock, other attractive conversion prospects include modifications carried out to the ends of parcel vehicles in the later BR epoch. Older, pre-war carriages soldiered on well into the 1980s, albeit in pretty poor condition (cosmetically at least) with many having their gangways removed. Long since redundant, the connections were plated over, thus providing fewer fixtures in need of regular maintenance. Conversely, around the same time, a number of Mk1 general utility vans (GUVs) had gangways installed, allowing them to run with standard Mk1 BG vans, especially in newspaper trains.

Camping coaches were a popular source of holidays at scenic locations, providing a new lease of life for otherwise obsolete carriage stock. As well

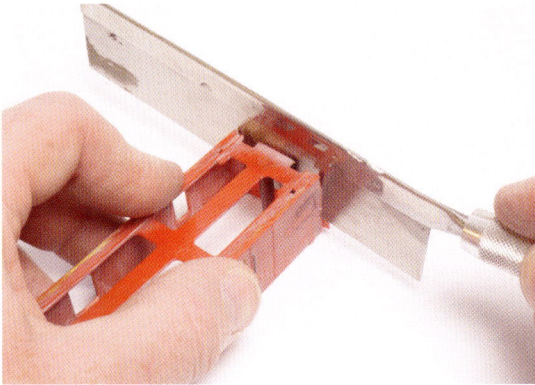

A more involved project is this newspaper van, converted from a Bachmann Mk1 GUV. A number of vans were modified with gangways and toilets to allow for mobile sorting operations in the 1980s. The model's slab ends have to be cut away very carefully with a razor saw.

Replacement Mk1 bow ends were sourced from the scrap box (probably from the Comet range) and installed with thick cyano glue. Plastic shims ensure that the ends sat square and vertical in relation to the sides. The underframe was temporarily refitted to act as a guide for the ends.

Once the glue had hardened, the corners were filed flush and the gaps filled. The toilet window was marked out with the help of an etched scribing template from LionRoar models.

A drill removed most of the waste before a sharp blade opened up the aperture within the scribed lines.

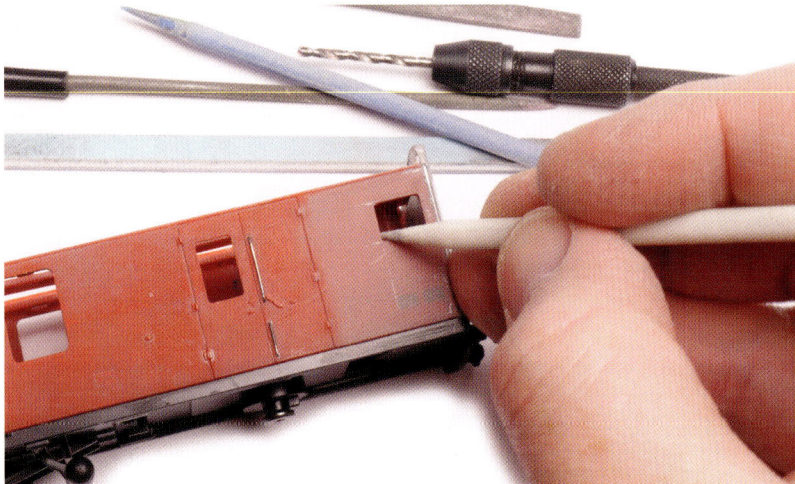

Files, sanding sticks and needles gradually took the material back to the scribed lines, working patiently and checking with the set square to ensure that the opening was straight and true.

With the body and ends tidied up, the finer details can be added, including the new gangways, roof gutter strips and water-tank filling gear. The revised roof vent layout was also copied.

The height and position of the gangways was checked by coupling up with other Mk1 stock.

as a completely remodelled interior, allowing for kitchen, lounge and sleeping facilities, the exterior was also modified. Underframe fittings were altered, including the removal of battery boxes and vacuum brake apparatus, while gangways and doors were plated over and roof ventilators rearranged.

Moving back to the twenty-first century, a number of modifications were made to Mk4 stock during the tenure of Great North Eastern Railway (GNER) on the East Coast route. Dubbed the 'Mallard' project, alterations were made to the passenger and catering

vehicles, with some windows plated over, additional vents added to the roofs and WiFi domes installed atop the Driving Van Trailers (DVTs).

Although the work was carried out back in 2004, Hornby's Mk4 range is still offered in the original guise. The 'Mallard' conversion involves plenty of work across the whole rake of carriages, resulting in the need for a full repaint. Interiors were also slightly altered to provide better access for wheelchairs. At the time, GNER and HSBC – the owners of the actual fleet – provided me with copies of the

A typical steam-age conversion idea is a camping coach. Once a common sight in sidings of picturesque railway outposts, redundant coaching stock was modified, with gangways and brake gear removed. Adventurous modellers may want to tackle the revised interiors, complete with bunk beds, kitchen and living accommodation. Suitable transfers are available from Fox.

original working plans, which proved a great help. Such documents are not usually available to the public (proof of the benefits of working in the media), but spending time on the platforms of an East Coast mainline station and a few journeys on the real stock will reveal the important modifications, still extant in 2015, despite the various franchise changes.

While this work is being carried out, it's worth correcting another error in the Hornby model: the gangway-less end of the Second Class coach marshalled immediately behind the locomotive. Replacement resin ends are available from Keen Systems and the model must be treated with a saw and files to remove the unwanted material. This can be a tricky operation, especially as the original end and roof are moulded integrally with the glazing. The brittle clear plastic makes it all too easy to crack or split the roof (as I did), so retaining the shell securely and cutting patiently with a sharp-toothed razor saw is essential.

Surgery was required to correct a Mk4 carriage, as the 'loco' end of coach B lacks a gangway. Hornby's rather primitive models are not easy to work with, as the roof and ends are formed from the same brittle plastic as the glazing. The resin replacement and underframe fairing, from Keen Systems, are best fitted to the carriage body and the roof modified for a close fit.

Other vehicles in the Mk4 rake also demanded major modification, including the buffet car. A number of the windows were blanked out, although I purposely didn't make the surface perfect as the real things show distinct undulations where the steel has been welded over the apertures. The interior also had to be modified.

In the days before the smoking ban, GNER installed extra roof vents for the smoking compartments. These were fabricated from plastic card, working from the original plans supplied by GNER and HSBC.

BRASS OVERLAYS

A more refined approach to modifying the sides of a carriage is to install etched brass overlays. A RTR model of suitable size and profile is chosen as a close match to the prototype and the overlays, as produced by the likes of Hurst Models, Bill Bedford or Comet, are shaped and fixed in place.

The degree of modification to the original body moulding depends on the prototype being portrayed, but this method offers up the opportunity to model specific vehicles within a broader range of stock, such as rarer BR Mk1 catering or service vehicles. They also offer a route to improving RTR models that may not be up to some modellers' exacting standards, with the sides from entire metal kits often being offered separately.

Shaping the metal parts is not always easy, although it's likely that they'll be following the existing profile of the RTR model on which they're designed to fit. Working gradually with a steel rod on a soft surface, such as a couple of PC mouse mats or a bed of tissue paper, and checking against the model's profile will prove helpful. If a steel rod isn't to hand, a length of wooden dowelling can be employed.

The technique of rolling brass is not too different from rolling out pastry with a rolling pin, with a firm but even pressure required to ensure that the shaping is affected across the whole length. Additionally, it's important to keep the rod parallel with the edge of the sides.

If the material is resisting your ministrations, try heating the brass over a flame until it turns a uniform pinkish shade. This process is called annealing and is a way of rendering the metal more malleable. Allow the material to cool naturally before continuing your shaping efforts. The intricacies of metalwork are covered in greater detail in Chapters 10 and 11.

Etched brass overlays provide an excellent means of transforming RTR models. For modellers of the Irish scene, Hurst Models can provide a range of overlays to convert BR Mk2 and Mk3 stock.

Before the overlays can be installed, the sides of the RTR model must be flattened and slots cut to give clearance for the new window apertures. Clamp a straight edge to the side and use a profile cutter or stout knife to gradually cut through the plastic.

A fine razor saw will cut into the corners more effectively than a knife.

The slot needs to be a few millimetres wider than the height of each window to allow for a strip of clear glazing to be inserted behind the etched sides.

The overlays may need shaping to suit the vehicle's profile. Rolling over a soft surface with a metal rod will encourage the brass to curl slightly. Keep the rod parallel to the sides and check against the RTR shell as you go until the desired shape is created.

Test fit the sides before committing to glue. Drilling out the handrail or other mounting holes now will help with alignment while gluing up.

Epoxy is the best adhesive for fixing overlays, spread over the brass with a cocktail stick. Clamp up the sides and double check the alignment by adding the handrails into the holes. The wire will prevent the sides slipping out of position while the glue sets.

Allow 24 hours for the epoxy to cure before treating the other side of the carriage in the same way. Once the clamps are removed, the brass sides and the corners of the carriage can be tidied up with sanding pads, working through the grades until the material glimmers.

Note how the slots in the plastic bodyshell will allow the clear styrene glazing material to sit just behind the thin brass sides. Clean out any deposits of glue from the recess.

A coat of grey primer will 'prove' the surface, highlighting any imperfections that can be treated with filler and abrasives.

CONVERTING KITS

Using a kit as the basis for a conversion project is just as viable as employing RTR products. It all depends on the prototype and the options available in your chosen scale. Plastic kits are probably the easiest to modify, the material being readily cut, shaped and joined. The ability to work with individual parts laid out flat is also a real boon.

It is to be hoped this chapter has offered a glimpse into the exciting world of conversion work. There's probably an entire book's worth of possible ventures, even within one particular modelling epoch. A little improvisation, careful choice of a donor model and detailed prototype research will prove to be the most vital ingredients for success.

Only once the sides have been sanded and deemed perfect should the delicate details be added. Etched hinges and toilet window vents are installed using Johnson Klear as an invisible adhesive.

Having converted the exterior of the carriage, the interior is also likely to demand alterations. This Mk1 suburban lavatory composite interior took quite a bit of remodelling. The original Bachmann moulding was hacked around and the remnants reorganized on a plastic card floor, with etched brass partitions from Comet Models.

CHAPTER NINE

COUPLINGS, GANGWAYS, LIGHTS & POWER

At the risk of stating the blindingly obvious, the couplings between our carriages are a vital feature and their efficacy will dictate how reliably a train will operate, and how realistic it will appear. There are plenty of off-the-shelf and bespoke options available, to suit any scale, with some offering authentic close-coupling between vehicles that automatically push themselves further apart when a curve is encountered.

Some couplings are designed to be semi-permanent, for use within carriage rakes that aren't intended for dividing on the layout. Others may allow for easy shunting, while others still may even offer electrical conductivity between vehicles, with interior and exterior lighting in mind.

Gangways linking carriages are equally important and they have a very close relationship with the couplings. Working gangways eliminate the 'daylight' between vehicles and depend on the use of appropriate couplings that will not hinder the free movement of each vehicle. Again, a variety of kits and ready-made units are available, mostly tailored to suit specific vehicle types, with the degree of realism often directly related to the price and amount of time required in assembly.

Working interior lights are not everyone's cup of tea, but if you've put hours of work into detailing the inside of a carriage – or if your locomotives and scenery boast working lamps – then it makes sense to create a consistent appearance across your layout. Where many lighting units disappoint is in overly bright or flickering illumination, but modern 'power store' and DCC options eradicate such problems. Furthermore, the use of LEDs allows the type and intensity of light to be tailored more effectively.

Such adornments require a power source: the most common examples take power from the rails, while other units offer a self-contained option, complete with miniature batteries.

All of these subjects are covered in this chapter, with a variety of couplings, gangways and lighting units showcased.

COUPLING UP

For 4mm scale modellers, RTR products of UK outline are still offered with the tension lock coupling system. Dating back to the 1960s, it may have been refined over the years, but it remains something of an anachronism in the twenty-first century. That said, it's a very effective system where the un-prototypical appearance is tempered somewhat by its ability to cope with short radius curves and complex track layouts. Bachmann, in particular, provide interchangeable semi-permanent coupling bars with a number of carriage types, moulded to replicate brake and heating hoses linking each vehicle. Perfect for marshalling coaches into fixed rakes, they look highly effective and offer reliable performance.

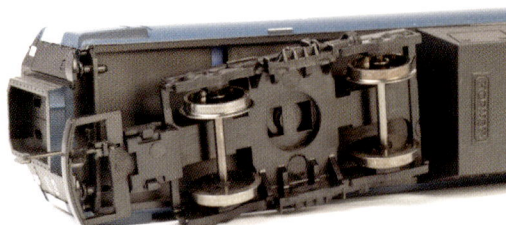

Archaic tension lock couplings are still the standard fitting for 'OO' gauge RTR models. This Hornby Mk3 is typical of the older, larger style, fixed directly to the bogie.

Older 'OO' stock, with larger tension locks, or those not equipped with automatic close-coupling systems, are limited in terms of appearance, with a larger gap between vehicles being inevitable. Such carriages can be upgraded with close-coupling kits, as will be described in due course. Fixed-axle carriages, especially those with a long wheelbase, produce a prodigious amount of lateral swing when entering a curve and coping with this can prove challenging.

For modellers in 'N' gauge, the ubiquitous Rapido coupler also boasts a long pedigree, with an equally unrealistic appearance overridden by performance and ease of use. Even with the archaic Rapido couplings, the latest designs of 2mm stock now tend to feature pivoting auto-coupler units in a similar fashion to those installed in 4mm scale models. This allows the gaps between vehicles to be drastically reduced while running on straight sections of track. A prime example is Farish's newly retooled BR Mk1 and Mk2 stock, which now feature a respectable gap between cars of around 2mm, although this can be reduced with the fitting of alternative drop-in couplings such as Dapol's Easi Shunt knuckle couplers. Compared to the 6mm gap between vehicles of the older style of Farish Mk1s, this is some improvement.

In order to attain some degree of standardization in the RTR market, the NEM-type coupling was introduced, ostensibly to match a set of specifications set out by European and US model railway associations. This has certainly helped matters as far as models designed in the new millennium are concerned, with fewer compatibility issues between different manufacturers, although there are still inconsistencies. The interchangeability of the NEM standard pocket, however, allows for simple customization, with a wide range of couplers available as simple slot-in replacements. Kadee knuckle couplers with NEM tails are particularly useful, offering easy operation and a more prototypical appearance for post-BR carriage types.

While 4mm scale users enjoy plenty of choice, there are far fewer alternative couplers available for 'N' gauge. Kadees are offered for 2mm scale under the Micro Trains banner and operate in a very similar manner, with operation by means of handheld or under-track magnets. Dapol's magnetic Easi-Shunt knuckle couplers are an attractive proposition, being simple to install and available in various lengths. Dapol also offers NEM conversion kits for older 'N' gauge rolling stock.

The modern, NEM-style coupling system offers much more choice and a less obtrusive appearance. When used in conjunction with pivoting close-coupling units, the gap between vehicles can be closed significantly, without hindering performance.

Modellers in 'N' gauge now have greater choice, with the venerable Rapido unit complemented by a variety of magnetically operated knuckle couplers from Dapol and Micro Trains.

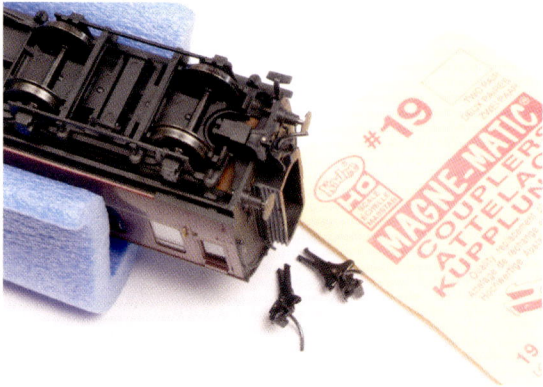

Kadee couplers are ideal for 'OO' coaching stock that boasts NEM sockets. Available in various lengths, a little trial and error is involved in finding the best choice to suit your own stock.

A height gauge is essential to ensure that the Kadees are set correctly.

A combination of alternative gangways (supplied with this Hornby model) and Kadees allow the gap between the vehicles to be almost eliminated. As the coach enters a curve, the pivoting coupling mounts push the cars apart to give adequate clearance.

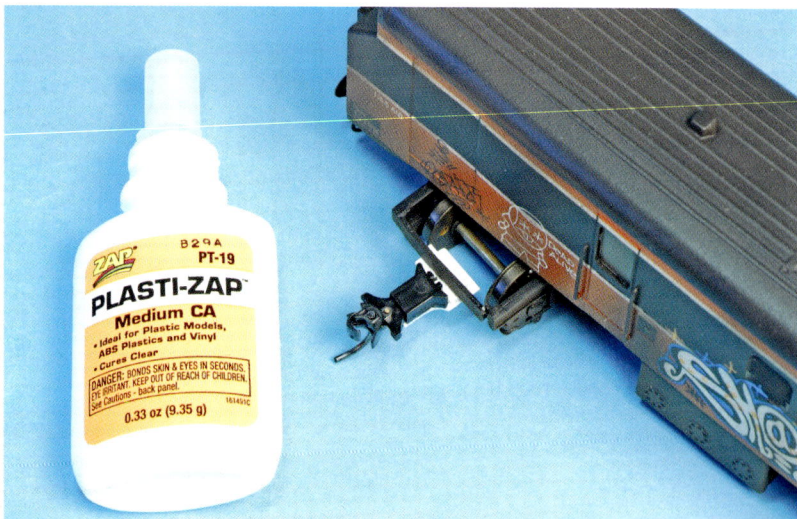

For stock without auto-coupler units or NEM pockets, alternative mounting solutions are needed. Kit-built models can be particularly demanding, with some recourse to improvisation likely. In this case, coupling mounts have been fabricated from plastic strip, sheet and angle, ensuring that the Kadees sit at the proscribed height. The mounts fit to the base and rear of the bogie frames for maximum strength.

COUPLINGS FOR KITS

The reliable use of knuckle couplers, especially those of the Kadee-style, is reliant upon the vehicles being weighted sufficiently. The issue of weight has been discussed in Chapter 5 and the need for a consistent mass across all similar carriages is of extra importance here. Indeed, study of the NMRA specifications regarding the size of the carriage and its optimum weight is recommended. Kadees are a US design, aimed at US prototype vehicles.

Given that US freight and passenger stock tends to be rather large and exclusively bogie-mounted, it's unreasonable to expect the couplings to operate perfectly on lightweight or short-wheelbase UK-outline coaching stock, especially those built from plastic or resin kits, without recourse to extra ballast. Having said that, I find that most Kadee-fitted 4mm scale RTR stock works fine without the need for extra weight, although the need for each vehicle to be of a similar mass remains.

Carriage kits, especially in 3mm and 4mm scale, seldom provide much in the way of effective coupling systems. There may be standardized brackets for tension lock units with NEM-compliant pocket mounts, if you're lucky, but working close-coupling units are conspicuous by their absence. This can create a challenge when running kit-built stock with modern RTR products. Kits in 7mm scale and above will usually provide a set of screw-link or three-link scale couplings, while 2mm kits are likely to be designed around the fitting of a set of Rapido-style units.

Luckily, there are plenty of sources for alternative couplings for kit-built stock, with the Keen close-coupling units in particular being an excellent option for 4mm scale. Designed primarily for upgrading older RTR stock, the Keen system can just as readily be factored into a plastic, resin or metal kit-building project. Symoba also offers a

Not all brand new models feature pivoting NEM couplings, a prime example being Hornby's recent LNER CCT van. For long wheelbase, fixed-axle vehicles, a pivoting coupling mount is essential, particularly when running with bogie stock. The original coupling mounts are shown being milled away to leave a flat surface.

NEM coupling mounts are becoming more common in plastic kits, especially 'OO' gauge kits of fixed-axle prototypes. They're also available as separate accessories, from the likes of Parkside Dundas.

A Symoba NEM pivoting coupling mount set is to be installed. A choice of pockets is provided to help set the couplings at the correct height and any NEM-tailed device simply clips into the pocket.

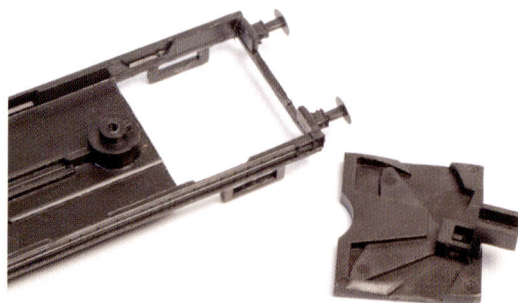

Fix the pivoting base to the underframe, aligned exactly with the vehicle's longitudinal centre line. Push the mounting pocket onto the shaft and set its height with the Symoba gauge before bonding with liquid poly cement. The excess material is then cut away from the shaft.

Keen Systems offer a retrofit solution for bogie stock not already fitted with pivoting close coupling units. Full instructions are provided and ease of installation depends on the model in question. This Bachmann Bulleid coach demands the cutting of an aperture at each end of the chassis.

Slot your choice of NEM coupling into the pockets. With Kadees, adding a shim of 10thou' plastic strip gives a secure fit. Setting the couplings to project the desired length can sometimes be helped by fixing the pivoting unit slightly further back. Initial installation with double-sided tape will help while the optimum position is discovered, before final fixing with epoxy or liquid poly cement.

The Keen unit has to sit level with the underside of the carriage floor, so careful positioning was required while gluing with epoxy. Keep the glue away from the moving parts. Lubricating with Labelle 134 dry PTFE lubricating powder improves performance markedly (as it will for any RTR coupling units).

Along with a range of other detail upgrades, the Keen coupling units help bring the aged Bachmann Bulleid stock up to twenty-first-century specifications.

variety of NEM-compliant coupling and mounting products, including close-couplers that are handy for fixed-axle stock.

Because these retrofitted coupling units often require some modification to the underframe, it helps to decide on their fitment from as early a stage as possible. Indeed, thought should be given to standardizing couplings across your fleet, or at least those vehicles most likely to run together. For instance, carriages that remain coupled in fixed rakes can employ close-coupling units between each vehicle, while more versatile couplings are fitted to the outer end of the first and last carriage, allowing for easier connection to locomotives.

OTHER COUPLING OPTIONS

As always, there's the additional possibility of homemade and kit-built coupling options. A stiff wire hook and loop, formed to mimic the brake and steam heat pipes between cars (rather like Bachmann's RTR plastic connectors) are fine for running in fixed rakes on layouts with gentle curves. They may not be so great if the carriages are to be propelled as well as hauled, although careful shunting may be possible.

Despite not offering much of a visual improvement, the BK coupling system does provide a more effective alternative, as far as performance is concerned. PH Designs offers a range of etched brass couplers designed to fit into specific brands of 'OO' gauge stock (Lima, Bachmann and Hornby) that, at first glance, look identical to the original tension locks. However, they feature enlarged tails with a couple of etched holes through which a metal staple is inserted.

The point of this system is to allow for remote operation of the couplings via magnets beneath the track. The staple and coupling tail is attracted to the magnet and lifts the coupling arm, thus allowing the vehicle to be detached as the tension in the coupling is released. As far as drop-in improvements go, this is definitely worth a try, as it requires minimal modification to the rolling stock.

Where there's no demand for hands-free uncoupling, Bill Bedford's cast brass couplings offer a very realistic appearance and ease of installation. The heavy components are attached to one carriage via a nut and bolt, tightened to allow enough play for the coupling to swing freely from side to side. The other end features a vertical pin and this fits into a hole drilled into the underside of the adjacent carriage. While they allow free movement on curves and permit both hauling and propelling moves, there's no facility for hands-free operation or automatic close coupling. Therefore, setting the carriages at the right distance apart to prevent buffers or gangways snagging can result in fairly large gaps unless your layout boasts very few, or very gentle, curves. Available in screw coupling or buckeye form, the castings do look realistic, once painted, but they will work out quite expensive if you have a large number of carriages to treat.

Kadee-type couplers are available in 'N' gauge under the Micro Trains brand. Magnetically operated, the units pivot inside sealed boxes, ensuring plenty of lateral movement.

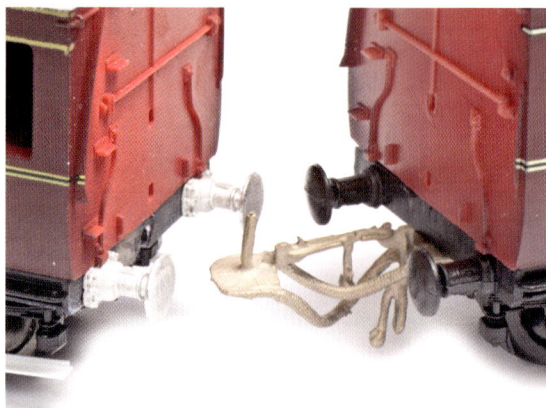

A novel coupling solution is this brass casting from Bill Bedford. Screwed to one vehicle and hooked behind the bufferbeam of the other, the coupling is free to pivot. Once painted it looks highly effective, although the gap between carriages remains fixed.

The Alex Jackson (AJ) system was pioneered in the 1950s by a well-known member of the Manchester Model Railway Society and has been employed on many a famous finescale 4mm scale layout. Consisting of an unobtrusive looped wire hook that can be controlled by electromagnets under the rails, it can appear fairly simple. Looks can be deceiving, however, and a high degree of precision is required for reliable operation. On the other hand, fitting requires little, if any, modification to the vehicle and operation is quiet and reliable once assembly and installation have been mastered. Consisting of little more than a length of spring steel wire (a 0.011in guitar 'E' string is a common choice), it is also a very cheap option.

Bending and assembly jigs, available from Dart Castings, make the job easier, although most adherents of the AJ system declare that it's much better suited to finescale 'EM/P4' rolling stock. More detailed information on the AJ coupling can be found on the Manchester Model Railway Society's webpage (see Useful Addresses).

The romantically named Spratt and Winkle (S&W) coupling system is another 'finer scale' option, for 2, 3, 4 and 7mm scales, again with the facility for magnetically controlled operation. Certainly more

discreet than RTR-style couplers, the etched hook and wire loop are still not particularly realistic. However, it does allow for cosmetic screw- or three-link couplings to be attached, which makes quite a difference visually.

Fitting the S&W system demands some degree of work on the vehicle's underframe and headstocks. The level of difficulty depends very much on the individual carriage. I must admit that I've only tried S&W couplings on fixed-axle stock (with great results), although I have seen them installed on bogie vehicles too. Whatever stock you're working on, this is not a coupling system suited to tight curves and short radius points.

As far as motive power is concerned, all the locomotives require is a straight wire fixed between the buffers on which the S&W coupling hooks can connect. As stock is shunted over a hidden magnet, the coupling mount pivots and disconnects.

SCALE COUPLINGS

For the ultimate in fidelity, you can't beat working 'scale' couplings. Three-link or screw-link couplings – as the prototype demands – certainly look the part, but require good eyesight and easy access to operate. For larger scales, they're not so difficult

The Spratt and Winkle system offers a more refined alternative to the tension lock principle. Remote operation is possible via magnets beneath the track. Practice is needed to get the assembly and installation right, but the system is great for fixed-axle stock in particular.

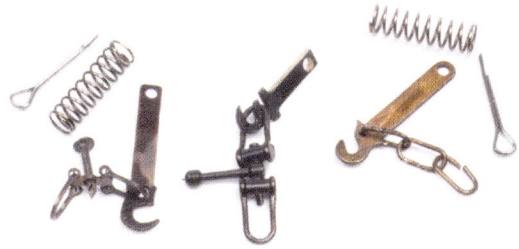

Three-link and screw-link scale couplings come in a variety of shapes and sizes, with a spring and split pin offering prototype-like operation. Sufficient space is required behind the bufferbeam to accommodate the equipment and the headstocks will need to be strong enough to withstand the pressure of the spring.

to deal with. For most of us, though, 4mm scale is about the limit, with 3mm at a push, yet I've seen 2mm finescale stock working perfectly with three-link couplings and looking terrific. Goodness knows how they can be operated without recourse to a magnifying glass.

For my 'OO' steam-age carriages, I like to employ scale couplings on branch-line carriages, as well as on the outer carriages of my express rakes. The main reasoning is that all of my locomotives are equipped with screw-links. Much depends on the individual kit or RTR model, but fitting working scale couplings can often take a fair bit of cutting, drilling and filing. They're also not cheap, especially the more realistic packages. Some economy can be gained by purchasing unassembled packs rather than the ready-to-fit sets and those offered in 4mm scale by Smiths and Romford/Jackson are my favoured options.

Although the drawhook is sprung, allowing a few millimetres of travel on each vehicle in order to absorb the hauling strain, the proximity of the buffers of adjacent carriages brings a risk of 'locking' on curves, especially during propelling movements. Sprung buffers help matters to a degree, but the use of scale couplings is not recommended for layouts with points or curves below third radius. The same goes for the AJ and Spratt and Winkle systems too.

GANGWAYS

The quest to fill the gap between gangways, while maintaining full operational control of the vehicle and its couplings, has seen a number of solutions developed over the decades, albeit of a broadly similar nature. Recent years have seen a few more modern options developed, most notably by Dapol, who showcased an excellent prototype system of working gangways for 'N' and (I think) 'OO'. However, at the time of writing, nothing has yet become of them.

Across the various scales, the most enduring type of working gangway is the paper 'bellows' type. These can be homemade affairs, cut from good-quality black art paper or thin card, or they may be supplied in kit form, with the parts marked out or already cut. Generic packs are fine in many respects but, for added realism, some makers offer specific profiles to match particular prototypes, with end plates and associated fittings like rain covers and bellows springs included.

We've already mentioned the idea of running coaches in semi-permanently coupled rakes and this applies equally to the type of gangways employed as it does to the choice of couplings. Vehicles at the outer end of each rake need not have working

York Modelmaking's laser-cut paper gangway connectors are simple to assemble. Plastic endplates are supplied, with various patterns available to suit a selection of 'OO' carriage types.

ABOVE: Scale link couplings look great, but they can be fiddly to operate, especially where gangways are present.

RIGHT: Once the paper bellows have been interlocked and compressed, the outer plastic covers are installed with a tiny amount of cyano glue, before the units are fixed to the carriage.

The laser-cut gangways really look the part, exerting just enough spring pressure to remain in contact without impeding performance.

An extra touch of class is offered by MJT, with the addition of etched brass gangway covers. The card 'bellows' are clearly marked out, ready for cutting with a sharp knife.

To complement the close-coupling units, Keen Systems also offer a range of working gangways. Consisting of a resin base, a sprung end cover fills the void and allows for free movement.

corridors (save for certain steam-age expresses to match corridor-fitted tenders), but rather a set of end plates over a retracted gangway.

It should be remembered that couplings and gangways are interdependent, with the choice of one often being influenced by the other. The coaches will have to be kept apart within certain limits, on straight and curved track, to allow particular gangway options to function properly. Conversely, a set of gangways that is compressed too tightly by the couplings may cause running problems. Experimentation is the key to success here, simply trying out different combinations to find what works best on your own layout and stock. Something else to consider is the opportunity that working gangways afford to fill the unsightly gap between coaches not fitted with close-coupling units.

For 4mm scale modellers, Keen Systems' floating end plates eschew the traditional bellows pattern in favour of injection-moulded plastic plates, retained with a spring inside plastic or resin gangway frames. The tension of the spring can be adjusted to allow more of the end plate to protrude, thus sealing the 'daylight gap' between different types of rolling stock. End plates and gangway frames are available in a variety of shapes to suit specific prototypes. Designed primarily to complement Keen's own close-coupling units, the 'floating' gangways can nevertheless be fitted to stock with similar existing couplings.

LIGHTING

Working interior lighting is becoming more of a common feature of RTR coaching stock, even those in the cheaper price brackets. Hornby's recent 'OO' Mk1 and Mk2D stock are good examples, both being released while this book was being produced and featuring simple LED light bars and power collection from the axles. They're not without their limitations, however, as a one-size-fits-all policy sees the lighting only reaching certain parts of some carriages, especially compartment or brake vehicles. Higher-grade RTR models, such as Pullman-style carriages, even feature working table lamps in many instances.

The use of capacitors within these RTR lighting circuits allows the power to be 'stored', thus keeping the interior illuminated for up to several minutes after the power to the track has been interrupted (when running on traditional analogue control). DCC users, meanwhile, have the benefit of the track always being live and the interiors being constantly lit. By fitting separate decoders, the interior lighting can be switched on or off via the main controller.

Lighting units are also freely available as aftermarket accessories in kit or ready-to-fit format. There's even the chance to choose between different types of light, to suit the brighter incandescence of modern strip lighting, or the softer glow of steam-age electric or gas-lit carriages.

Not too long ago, fitting carriage lighting could be a fiddly exercise, with bulky components and trailing wires to disguise within the interior. In addition there was the issue of collecting power from the rails without impairing the smooth running of the

axles. Happily, things are much easier nowadays, with plenty of off-the-shelf solutions available.

Pre-wired packages are the easiest to retrofit, with little soldering required. Even simpler are the self-contained, battery-powered options from Train-Tech. These ready-to-install units require minimal space and come in a choice of styles to suit modern (fluorescent) or traditional (filament bulb) lighting types. All you need to do is clip in the long-life battery and fix the lighting strip to the inside of the carriage roof with sticky pads, ensuring that the LEDs line up with any partitions or bulkheads (or trim the interior moulding accordingly) to ensure that all necessary parts of the carriage are illuminated. Operation is automatic, via a motion sensor, and the flicker-free lighting remains illuminated for long after the carriage has come to rest. There's even the facility to add a glowing or flashing tail lamp from the same circuit board (see Chapter 17).

Other lighting options consist of PCB strips, ready mounted with LEDs that can be trimmed to fit your carriage exactly, ensuring that all compartments are illuminated. For greater economy, lighting units offered in kit form are worth considering, as they also offer more facility for customization.

TOP: **While Farish's newer Mk1 stock is far superior in terms of detail and coupling equipment than their predecessors, the gap between the gangways can still be improved with a set of paper bellows or a slither of soft black foam.**

BOTTOM: **There's plenty of choice among bespoke carriage lighting kits from Train-Tech, DCCconcepts and DigiRails, some in pre-wired ready-to-fit format, or supplied as self-assembly kits.**

One of the simplest solutions is offered by Train-Tech, with self-contained circuits powered by long-life batteries, negating any need for power collection from the rails. A motion sensor automatically switches the lights on and powers down several minutes after coming to a halt. A choice of modern or traditional lighting effects is also available and they can also power a head or tail lamp.

Coating the inside of a plastic coach body with a few coats of black paint prevents light bleeding through the bodywork.

Train-Tech's traditional 'warm' glow lighting option is perfect for this Stanier carriage.

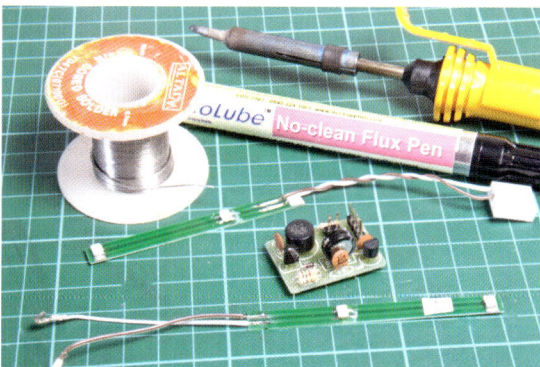

Self-assembly lighting circuits demand more time and effort. When soldering electrical parts, be sure to use a 'no-clean' flux. Marketed on eBay by Mike Carrington, this unit features a light store facility and is powered from the track supply (DC or DCC). The LED strips can be trimmed to suit the interior of a particular vehicle.

The lighting circuit needs a discreet location, such as a guard's compartment.

Some lighting circuits, especially those with large capacitors for storing the power, are invariably bulky. By installing the master circuit in a guard's or baggage compartment of one carriage, and employing conductive couplings between vehicles, smaller 'slave' lighting circuits can be installed and powered throughout the entire rake. A similar arrangement exists for digital control users, where a single decoder is installed in one carriage and power transmitted throughout the train.

POWER COLLECTION

Apart from battery-operated lighting systems, power will have to be taken from the running rails by means of wiper-style contacts, bearing on the axles or wheels. UK RTR models with working lights now regularly boast power collection via discreet copper pinpoint bearings, this having been a feature of Continental models for some time.

As with the lighting units themselves, there is plenty of choice among off-the-shelf pickup kits and components, as well as various homemade options. What is vital is that any collector bearing on the wheels or axles should not be introducing excessive friction, thus impairing free running of the vehicle.

The choice of wheels is also important. Plastic-centred types, as offered by Gibson, won't be much use. If the wiper pickups are to bear on the wheels themselves, then each bogie can collect both polarities, resulting in ultra-reliable operation. If the power is to be taken from the axles, however, then it's important to note which wheel is live and orientate the power leads accordingly. Make the job easier by employing DCCconcepts coach wheels that feature pre-fitted ultra-fine coiled pickups that rest on each axle. Simply soldering a wire to the pickup leads is all that's required and, by aligning the live and insulated wheels accordingly, both polarities can be absorbed from each bogie.

One of the tasks associated with lighting that I seldom enjoy is running wires from the bogie pickups into the carriage body. Again, there is the danger of impeding the free rotation of the bogies and the constant movement causes wear and tear on the wires and any nearby solder joints.

Routing the cables into the interior and keeping them out of view can also be tricky, although much depends on the nature of the individual carriage and its size. Modellers in 7mm scale, for instance, will seldom have any issues in this respect. Choosing the most slender multi-core wire that you can find will make the job a lot easier (single core wire is less flexible and more prone to breaking).

Another option is to install copper or phosphor-bronze bearing conductors, fixed to the carriage floor and upper surface of the bogie frame, as employed on some RTR products. As long as the two halves of each conductor stay in contact while the vehicle is in motion, there should be few continuity issues. A little electrolytic grease, such as Contralube 770 (www.newgateonline.com) keeps everything moving freely.

Whatever system is chosen, insulating the two polarities is important, especially for DCC users, where short circuits can be especially frustrating. Additionally, the need for clean wheels on all items of rolling stock is also fundamental.

The LED strips have been secured with double-sided sticky pads and yellow cellophane filters fixed with a few drops of PVA glue.

JOINED UP THINKING

Adding the extra dimension of working lighting helps to bring out the best in a detailed model carriage. Combined with working gangways and less intrusive automatic couplings, the overall effect can be impressive. It's not all about looks, though, and ensuring that the vehicles run reliably is of more importance to most layout operators.

Off-the-shelf wiper pickups can be obtained from Brelec, or fashioned from strips of phosphor bronze, shaped to bear against the wheel treads. Fit a pair to both bogies and employ fine, flexible wire to transmit power to the circuit board.

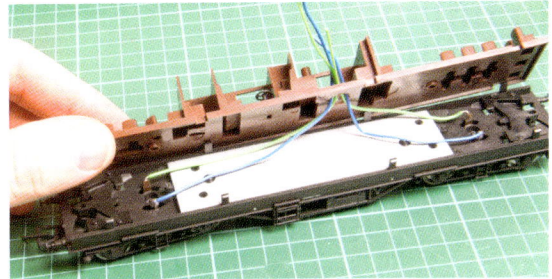

These DCCconcepts wheelsets are pre-fitted with friction-free power collectors wrapped around the axles. All we have to do is solder wires to the tails and secure the flex to the bogie to keep it out of the way. Check which wheel is insulated on the axle, to ensure that both polarities are collected from each bogie.

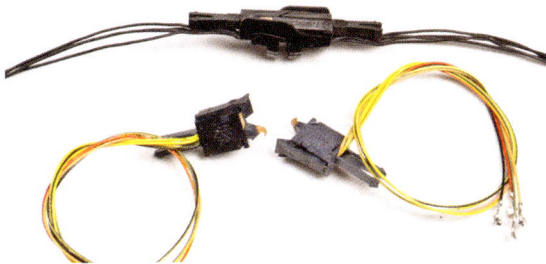

This Bachmann observation saloon features power collection gear on the bogies, albeit without any lighting equipment. Wires have been soldered to the power strips and a hole has been drilled into the kitchen compartment where the lighting circuit will be accommodated.

If running fixed rakes of carriages, there's no need for a circuit board and pickups on each vehicle, as the power can be transmitted throughout via conductive couplings. These NEM-tailed units are from Brelec and come with up to four separate power leads.

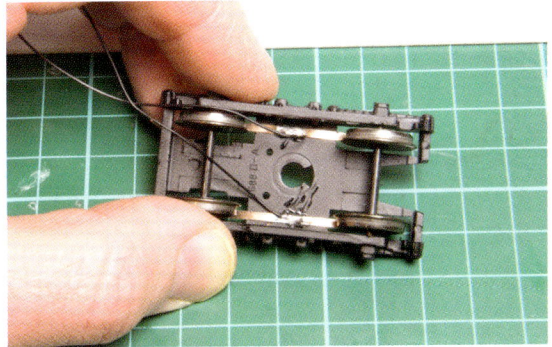

If you've put the effort into detailing the interior, you may as well illuminate it to show off your handiwork.

CHAPTER TEN

FOUNDATIONS IN METAL

There's something special about model carriages crafted from metal, both visually and in a tactile sense. The near-prototypical thickness of the carriage sides and the inherent mass create a certain presence that is hard to define.

The ruggedness of brass, nickel silver and whitemetal is also a point in their favour – so long as the solder joints have been made properly – and the extra weight is likely to improve the vehicle's running performance. The flipside to the weight issue is that a long train of metal carriages has the potential to overtax the locomotive, especially on inclines and curves.

Despite the growth in new materials technology and a slow decline in the numbers of modellers with the time and inclination, the number of available etched or cast metal carriage kits remains at a healthy level. Such kits may include all of the necessary parts to complete an entire carriage. Alternatively, other kits may be designed merely as 'component packs' featuring body sides and ends or even just an underframe, allowing the modeller to customize a kit or RTR model from another source.

Kit manufacturers have their own distinct building styles and foibles. Indeed, one of the joys of this hobby is the endless variety, even in fields where some uniformity would be expected. Pre-formed sides and roofs may or may not be provided as standard (although some makers will undertake the shaping required for a modest fee), with roofs providing a pertinent example. Some may be supplied as a flat etch to be rolled to shape, others may provide a pre-formed version of the same. Others still may supply a length of extruded aluminium that must be cut to the final size and shape, or maybe the kit will include a plastic moulding.

METAL FACTORS

Working with metal does offer certain challenges, but this shouldn't be seen as a discouraging factor. Indeed, it's the purpose of this chapter to explain the various techniques involved and explode certain myths about the difficulties surrounding shaping

Etched metal kits are predominantly rendered in either brass or nickel silver. The former material is easier to work with, but nickel silver offers a more durable, stiffer option that is especially suited to underframes.

and soldering etched components. Only a handful of special tools are required to get going, with a decent soldering iron and equipment costing about the same as some new RTR carriages.

Etched parts are likely to be complemented by white-metal or brass castings. The etched components themselves may also be in varying materials to suit their particular roles, with brass and nickel silver being the most common. Stainless steel has its uses, as does copper wire or strip. There may also be some plastic and resin parts. Knowledge is the key to success in any field and availing oneself with knowledge of each material's strength and weakness, as well as how to work and bond them, will prove highly beneficial.

The etching process allows a degree of surface relief to be created, as well as folding and locating guides. Mounting holes and slots may be ready-formed, but they are likely to need opening out to the required size before assembly.

ETCHED PARTS

By dipping sheets of metal into a bath filled with an acidic solution, any areas not treated with a resisting coating are eaten – or etched – away. Originally the chemical resistant coating was applied using photographic techniques, giving the process its traditional name of photo-etching. These days, computer-controlled printers transfer the artwork onto the metal, resulting in a cheaper and more convenient system.

Etching, or 'bathing', times vary, depending on the thickness of the metal. Limiting exposure creates 'half-etched' detail, where only a certain amount of metal is removed. This permits surface relief to be incorporated, such as rivet heads, seams and panels. Additionally, fold lines are also rendered in this way, allowing the components to be shaped easily and accurately.

Another use of half-etching is to create locations for the modeller to punch out rivet detail from the interior. A drawback of this method, however, is the creation of a ridge along the edges of components. This not only looks unsightly, but will also interfere with the fit of interconnecting parts. It is therefore vital to flatten the exposed edges with files before assembly.

In common with plastic and resin components, etched metal parts also retain residues from their production that will interfere with the bonding and painting processes. It is good practice to begin any metal project by cleaning up the etched sheets with abrasives and an alcohol-based cleaner.

CASTING

The most notable limitation of etched parts is their flatness, with the likes of buffers, ventilators and brake cylinders impossible to create in that format. Instead, white-metal or brass castings are employed, the latter by the laborious lost wax process.

As with many facets of kit making, much depends on the quality of the original moulds, but both of these materials, in the right hands, can be used to create superbly detailed components. All cast parts are likely to have excess material to be removed prior to assembly. Indeed, a high-class kit is usually identified by minimal amounts of 'flash'.

In contrast, older kits inevitably wear out, resulting in some pretty dubious castings. Decisions are needed in such instances whether to persevere with the bits in hand or to replace them with superior components from another source.

ALUMINIUM

Small numbers of coach kits have been offered in aluminium, some of which have featured the sides and roof as a single, pre-formed component. Created by punching out the relevant window and door apertures, the level of finesse is rather limited, especially compared to etched metal kits. Flush-sided stock is the usual subject for aluminium bodies, as replicating panelled sides is not easy in this format. Holes for roof ventilators, handrails and door handles have to be marked out and drilled, making for a time-consuming job.

Soldering aluminium is not easy and demands the use of particular fluxes and solders, although epoxy or contact adhesives are viable alternatives. Aluminium kits usually incorporate some form of composite construction, perhaps with an underframe of fibreboard, along with cast white-metal ends. Furthermore, numerous high-quality brass kits offer pre-formed aluminium roofs, such as MJT.

BRASS

Brass has been a popular material with model makers for a long time, which is no surprise given its workability and versatility. Commonly found in sheet, strip, wire or angle form, it can also be cast and turned readily. Formed mainly of copper and zinc, the metal is flexible and easily shaped into complex forms and is perfectly suited to soldering. The majority of etched metal kits and components are rendered in brass, in a variety of thicknesses.

COPPER

Copper is an excellent electrical conductor and is ideal for power collection and transmission. Soft and malleable, it can be soldered readily and hardened by hammering, if necessary. Copper is available in sheet, strip, tube, rod and angle form. It is perhaps most useful as a source of flexible wire for detailing work.

NICKEL SILVER

Nickel silver has a bright finish and is an amalgam of copper, nickel and zinc. Stiffer and a little harder to work than brass, shaping can be eased by heating (annealing). Slightly more expensive than brass, nickel silver is ideal where very thin, yet resilient, parts are required and it can be soldered easily.

A distinct bonus of nickel silver is its resistance to buckling when heated. Very thin brass distorts readily when hot, making accurate soldering work trying at times. However, substituting nickel silver for fine detail overlays or thin carriage sides offers many advantages.

STEEL/STAINLESS STEEL

Ordinary steel alloys are not likely to appear in any great quantity due to their weighty nature and susceptibility to corrosion. Soldering steel is possible, but it poses more of a challenge than brass or nickel silver. Etched stainless steel parts do crop up from time to time, however. Usually employed to mimic chrome or bright polished metalwork, this is a tough material that is difficult to shape, and even harder to repair if the parts are distorted.

A sharp set of cutting shears or a saw is needed to trim stainless steel parts from the fret and any accidental distortion is very difficult to remedy. Again, this material can be soldered but it requires a powerful (and expensive) iron and specific formulas of flux and solder.

WHITE-METAL

Something of an umbrella term, white-metal refers to a range of lead- or tin-based alloys that may also include quantities of antimony, cadmium, bismuth, copper and zinc. A dense, silvery material, white-metal alloys are designed to melt at lower temperatures (around 150°C), making them ideal for casting but tricky to solder to other metals. Athough its most common application is in detail castings, it can also be employed for larger structural components.

The quality of white-metal components can vary, depending on the purity of the alloy. Sometimes waste material may be added to the melting pot and any impurities will have annoying consequences, such as a rough surface texture or a resistance to paints and adhesives.

Relatively soft and pliable, white-metal can also be deceptively brittle, depending on the alloy's exact ingredients. For example, higher levels of lead make for a more flexible material, but the presence of such toxic materials means that white-metal must be used with great care. Always wash your hands after handling white-metal parts.

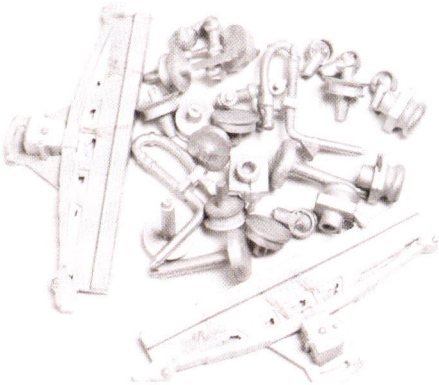

Chunkier parts, such as detail fittings, buffers and chassis components, are better served by casting. These white-metal castings are typical of what can be expected, with the inevitable areas of excess material that will need tidying up.

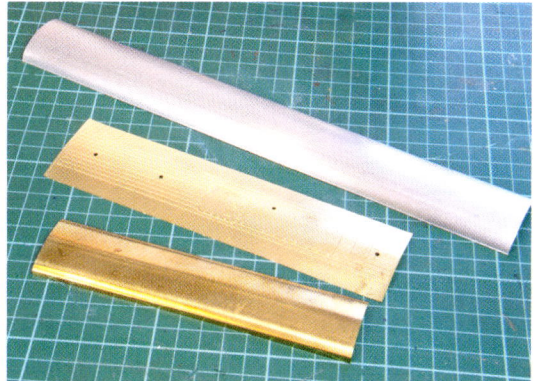

If you are lucky, carriage roofs may be supplied pre-formed, but you should be prepared to have to roll your own. A further option is extruded aluminium section, supplied in 'blank' form that will have to be cut to the desired length.

A mixed-media approach to kit manufacture, as offered by this Southern Pride package, reduces the amount of soldering necessary. The pre-formed metal components, featuring tab-and-slot assembly, together with injection-moulded plastic and resin parts, makes for a quick and less complex building project.

Gently heating the material beforehand will help if white-metal parts need reshaping. Modifying components is easy enough, but saw blades and files will clog easily with particles of the soft material. A stiff wire brush will keep your tools working effectively.

GETTING STARTED

Removing etched components from the surrounding fret comes with the ever-present risk of damage, something that can be hard to remedy, especially when working with nickel silver. The parts may also be sharp, so watch your fingertips. Where possible, use a set of good-quality, sharp metal shears to cut away the parts as they're required, leaving a small stub of waste material to be filed flush. If shears are unable to reach around the fret, try cutting away waste material to give the jaws better access. Small metal shears are available for just this purpose and are more convenient for smaller parts than are regular cutters.

All metal parts should be cleaned before assembly. A rub-over with abrasive pads before any parts are cut from the fret is a quick and easy solution.

Abrade both sides of each fret and wipe away the debris and any remaining residues with isopropyl alcohol (IPA).

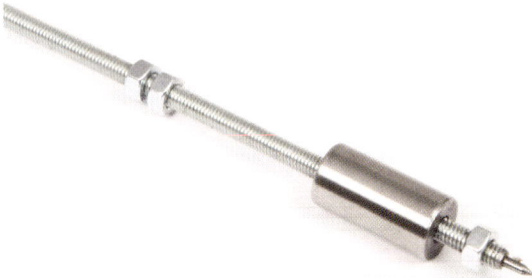

Punching out rivet detail is also easier while the parts are still attached to the fret. A scriber or centre punch will do the job, but this Gravity Riveter (from Eileen's Emporium) ensures quicker, more consistent results. The weight is dropped down the shaft, from the desired height, exerting even pressure on the tip.

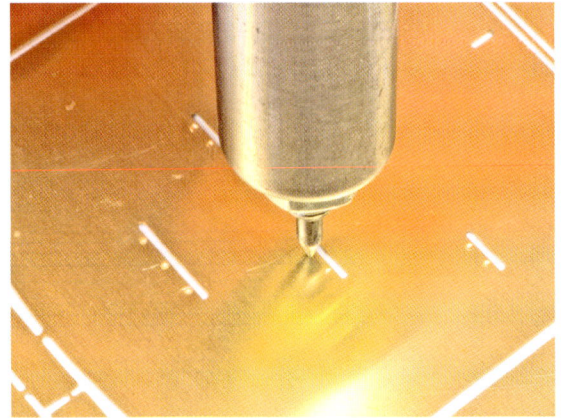

Work on a hard surface, such as plywood, to avoid the parts being distorted. And be careful not to pierce the metal.

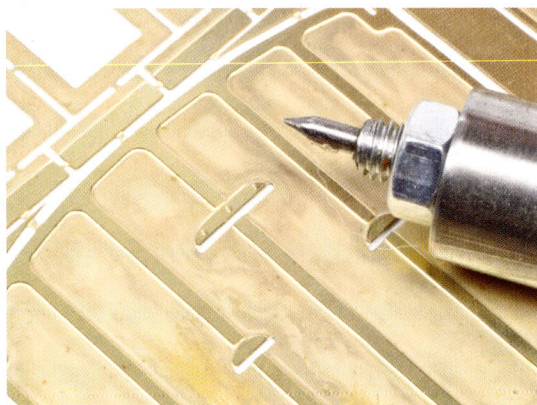

Ideally the rivets should appear even and crisp.

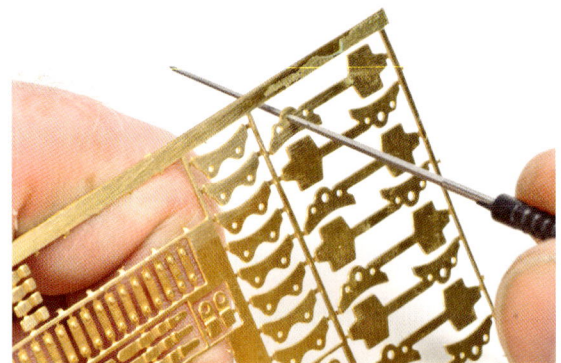

Etched holes and slots must be fettled to the correct size. Reamers are preferred to drill bits, offering far greater accuracy.

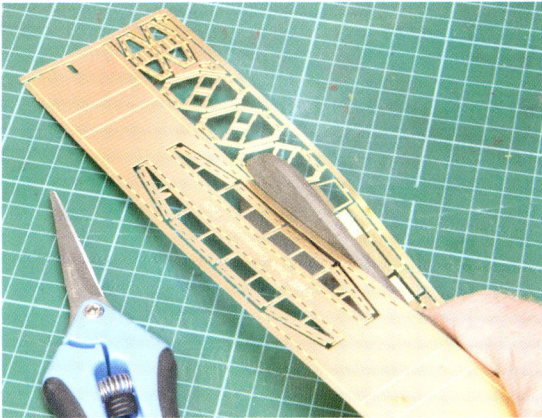

Separate the parts from the fret with a good-quality set of shears. DCCconcepts and Xuron offer tools specifically for etched metal, although I prefer my big shears in most cases, as they are better at ensuring a straight cut close up to the edge of the component. If the shears won't reach between the fret, try a Stanley knife, with the metal held over a sheet of plywood.

To avoid distorting smaller parts, don't try to cut the tangs flush with the component's edges in the first instance. It's much safer to mount the part in a vice and dress the edges flat with a file. All etched parts will need fettling anyway, to remove the ridge caused by the multi-stage etching process.

A stout blade or a punching tool is a viable alternative, working over a sheet of timber (plywood or MDF). Much depends on the thickness of the metal and, if you're still having trouble or you deem the components at risk of distortion, try cutting through the tangs with a jeweller's piercing saw, supporting the etched fret securely at all times.

Metal castings are usually supplied loose, with any waste material being removed with a set of end-cutters and files. Cast brass parts, in particular, may still be attached to a large 'runner' and each component will need cutting free. The tough metal is not easy to snip through, so a piercing saw or cutting disc mounted in a mini-drill may be required.

Moving from needle files to fine abrasive strips will remove all tool marks for a super-smooth finish. Be prepared, however, for further cleaning. Tarnishing of the metal surfaces will appear from exposure to the atmosphere, chemical fluxes and from the natural oils secreted by our skin, all of which will hinder the soldering process. Indeed, maintaining a high state of cleanliness is a must from this stage forward.

SHAPING METAL

Taking a series of flat metal parts and creating a three-dimensional object is one of the most rewarding facets of metal kit building, especially when there may be some intricate shapes or elegant curves to replicate. Although many parts will be employed in their flat state, built up concentrically to form a basic shell, there is naturally a demand for certain crucial parts to be folded or rolled. Carriage roofs, ends, underframe components and solebars are obvious examples and, while kits aim to make the shaping process as easy as possible, there are certain challenges involved.

We've already mentioned the presence of half-etched folding lines, which, as a general rule, usually lie on the *inside* of the fold. The etched cavity allows the metal to fold easily back onto itself without distorting. Indeed, when done correctly, the fold should take on a knife-edge neatness that is crucial for the overall appearance as well as the location of subsequent components. However, parts designed to fold back upon themselves in order to double their thickness or to create intricate shapes will have the half-etched line on the *outside* of the fold; another reason why careful study of the instructions is vital.

Forming these folds demands care but it can be far less complicated than one may suppose. Bespoke tools, such as one of the fantastic Hold 'n' Folds (as seen in Chapter 4), are worth every penny, allowing for consistently perfect and speedy results. Moreover, the formation of complex folds, on parts big and small, is difficult to achieve without such a device. Lengths of steel or aluminium angle set in a regular bench vice can be highly effective, especially

Check the instructions to confirm on what side the half-etched folding guide ought to be. Folding is possible in a vice, between blocks of wood or metal 'bending bars'. Apply even pressure across the length of the fold and check with a set square to achieve the correct angle.

for larger parts, but they can be somewhat cumbersome in other instances. Good quality pliers with smooth inner jaws can do a passable job of shaping small components, but will struggle to achieve a high standard of finesse.

The properties of the material in use are important factors to consider before any shaping takes place. The excellent working characteristics of brass make it a favourite of kit builders and folding into tight, clean angles requires little effort, as long as the kit has been designed and etched to a good standard. It's worth reiterating the importance of checking the instructions at regular stages, as the metal will be at risk of snapping if the folds are bent back and forth more than once or twice. This may not prove a terminal disaster, though, as the parts can be soldered back together, but hours of extra work can be avoided by simply double-checking each stage before the metal is shaped.

Shaping nickel silver or thick brass demands more physical effort, with an accompanying risk of uneven folds and possible distortion. Things aren't so bad as long as plenty of material, on both sides of the fold, is available for clamping and levering. When this isn't the case or the parts require folding in a variety of directions, some extra help is required. Annealing, whereby the metal is heated over a flame until it takes on a uniform pink-orange appearance, results in the material becoming more pliable. Thicker

A Hold 'n' Fold offers far more versatility and consistent results, especially when dealing with intricately shaped parts.

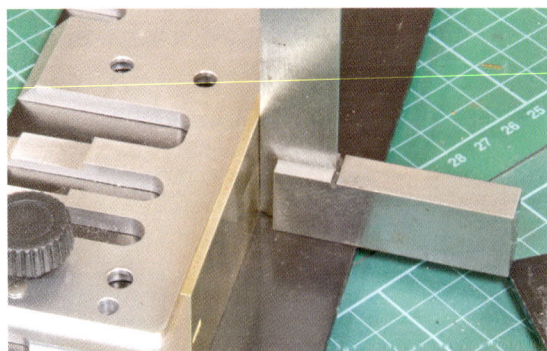

Hold 'n' Folds offer a better platform for checking angles and ensuring that key components, such as chassis members, are formed perfectly straight and true.

material, whether it be brass or nickel silver, will need heating for longer periods or the process repeated a couple of times. Never quench the hot metal in water, as it must be left to cool naturally.

Creating curved profiles effectively requires only a rudimentary array of equipment: a couple of PC mouse mats and metal rods and tubes of varying diameter. The mouse mats, with the soft foam backing uppermost, provide support for the metal components, while dispersing evenly the forces from the rolling process. The diameter of the rolling rod or tube will dictate the resulting curvature of the component: smaller rods create tight curves; larger diameter rods produce a gentler profile.

With the part laid on the mats, the rod is simply rolled over with a moderate amount of hand pressure. Depending on the thickness and malleability of the metal, the part will soon begin to curl and, as more pressure is applied, a greater curvature is created. A little practice will provide an appreciation of how different materials, pressure and the rod's size affect the process. Otherwise, it's a technique that is quick to master.

Recently I came across some lengths of painted steel tube in a DIY store, offered in various diameters, aimed primarily at creating hanging rods for wardrobe interiors. Cut up into appropriate lengths, these have proved ideal for rolling metal parts, with the highly polished surface removing the risk of any lumps and bumps being transferred from the rods to the brass sheet. Similarly, hardwood dowel can be effective for brass, though less so with nickel silver. In both cases, more physical effort is required than with metal tube or rod.

What offers a greater challenge is creating a series of differing profiles on the same component. Roofs with compound curves or body sides with pronounced tumblehomes are perfect examples. In these cases, there's usually a gentle curve across much of the surface before it segues into a much tighter radius at the outer edges. Varying the diameter of rolling rods and careful clamping can be combined to create the required shape, but it can take a few hours of gentle manipulation, checking constantly against a template to ensure a consistent profile is achieved across the whole of the component. Thankfully, most metal kits come with pre-formed roofs or body sides, which takes care of what can be the trickiest part of the whole building process. Moreover, there have been times when I've adapted a plastic roof from a RTR model in place of the kit's etched component, primarily as a time-saving option.

If the material is resisting the ministrations of your rolling rod, due to the thickness or stiffness of the metal, the annealing process comes to our aid.

If you are struggling to bend or shape the metal, annealing can help, rendering the metal more pliable without compromising its strength. Use a mini-blowtorch to heat the metal evenly until it turns a uniform orange/pink colour, then leave to cool.

Forming curved profiles is surprisingly simple: all that is required is a couple of computer mouse mats and various diameters of metal rod or tube.

With the component placed face down on the mouse mats, align the rod or tube parallel with the edge of the metal and begin rolling, applying firm and even pressure.

Keep checking the profile of the metal. The smaller the diameter of rod and the greater pressure is applied, the tighter the curvature will be. Practising on plain sheet brass is highly recommended.

Forming compound profiles can be tricky, but employing various diameters of rod and combining the rolling process with the use of a vice or Hold 'n' Fold will help. This roof was particularly awkward, as the edges had to transition into flat vertical sections. The Hold 'n' Fold was essential in helping to form the brass over the rod, with pressure exerted with a steel bar from the outside.

The various radii and flat sections were eventually achieved, although it took time to get it right. Annealing the brass beforehand made a big difference.

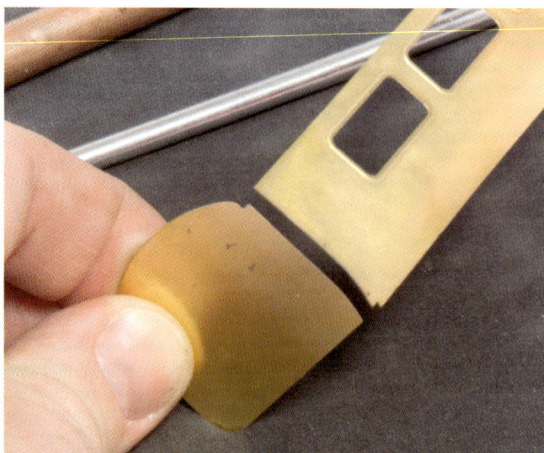

Forming carriage side profiles follows the same principle, using the ends as a guide. Be sure to keep the rolling rods parallel to the edges of the metal sides as the shape must appear consistent along the carriage's length.

It is far better to spend a few minutes heating up the metal to make it more pliable than persevering and potentially disfiguring the components. Annealing does not degrade the material, but it does leave a heavily tarnished surface that must be cleaned thoroughly before soldering, gluing or painting.

The same shaping processes can be pressed into action if any etched parts have been damaged or twisted. Working on a flat metal surface, such as a mini-anvil, and drawing a piece of flat steel bar over the surface should iron out many of the kinks. Beware of damaging half-etched relief with excessive pressure, however. Very thin parts can be flattened by rolling a steel rod over the rear face, with just enough pressure to cancel out the existing curvature. Work over a hard surface, such as a cutting mat or sheet of plywood.

Thicker parts that demand reshaping may benefit from annealing or a little light tapping with a hammer on the anvil. For small distortions, however, I usually find that a rub-over with a flat file will level the surface and any depressions can be remedied with epoxy putty or model filler after assembly. Once fully cured, the putty and surrounding material is sanded flush.

Shaping long components, such as solebars, body sides and roofs, will demand the use of a large Hold 'n' Fold or long sections of metal angle mounted in the jaws of a vice. The larger Hold 'n' Folds are not cheap, but they'll prove a worthy investment if you intend to build a number of kits. A long levering tool will also be required to exert even pressure along the full length of the component: working in stages is rarely successful.

SOLDERING

There remains something of a mystique around soldering but, as long as you follow a small number of important rules – and employ the right materials – then it's not actually that difficult. Vital tasks, such as 'tinning' the iron tip correctly, cleaning the surfaces thoroughly and applying the most appropriate type of flux are often overlooked by modellers, who then lament their lack of success.

Another common misconception is the perceived need to spend a fortune on equipment. At the time of writing, a high-quality, modestly powered soldering iron costs less than £30, with an iron stand, flux, solder and a couple of other useful tools taking the total outlay to around £60. Compared to the cost of the average RTR 'OO' gauge carriage in 2015, that's pretty good value for money.

SOLDERING IRONS

Soldering irons are relatively simple devices, consisting of an element that is heated, usually by electrical means. The tip of the iron is then used to warm the workpiece and melt the solder. Soldering irons were originally heated up in a furnace, but mains-powered units offer the convenience and reliability of a constant operating temperature.

The power output of an iron is expressed in watts, although this does not directly influence the temperature of the tip. Rather, an iron's watt rating refers to the tool's capacity to maintain the heat in spite of the drain caused by contact with metal parts. Working on larger pieces of metal demands a more powerful iron, as it's crucial to disperse the heat quickly and efficiently over the whole jointing surface. Smaller scale work, on the other hand, demands that only a few square millimetres be heated at a time, allowing the use of an iron with a lower wattage.

For years, I've managed quite well with my 'OO' gauge work by using a 25-watt iron. However, a recent upgrade to a 50-watt Antex iron has made a significant improvement to both 4mm and 7mm scale jobs. As well as the facility to adjust the output, the extra power creates a slightly hotter tip (up to 450°C) but, more importantly, it heats the metal parts more quickly and effectively. This is great for creating the main fabric of the carriage, employing a high-temperature solder formula. Smaller details can then be installed with lower-temperature solder, having also reduced the iron's output, with little risk of weakening the previous bonds. This tailoring of working temperatures and solders will be explained in due course.

Soldering iron temperatures vary from tool to tool, with some being adjustable by way of a separate control unit, complete with a temperature readout, or simply by means of a variable resistor mounted on the iron handle (as with my new Antex 50-watt tool). Indeed, modellers with the ambition of working with a broad range of materials are encouraged to invest in an adjustable iron. Far cheaper than they used to be, they offer the possibility of tailoring the tool's operating temperature to suit the job in hand and allow one tool to be used for a whole range of tasks.

Temperature-controlled units differ in specification and those with a digital readout are more user-friendly than the traditional dial type. Indeed, having an instant visual reminder of the tip's temperature takes away much of the guesswork and allows you to work in full confidence, especially with white-metal components.

As well as mains-powered irons, portable devices are also available, running on batteries or butane gas. These are often a little harder to control in terms of setting the temperature, but the lack of a power cord is welcome when working remotely. Gas-powered mini-blowtorches, as demonstrated earlier in this chapter for annealing metal, can also be employed for soldering tasks, especially for the lamination of several layers of sheet material or when working on larger components.

RESISTANCE SOLDERING

Resistance soldering irons work in a different manner, creating an electrical circuit with the metal workpiece, in a similar fashion to arc welding. Offering a more efficient option, the electric current is only drawn when the iron is brought into contact with the joint and this also allows for a more localized transmission of heat. In theory, this carries less risk of re-melting previous solder bonds.

The power is often controlled by a foot-switch, freeing up one hand to administer the solder or hold the assembly still while you work, which can be a great benefit when your 'third hand' is not available. This convenience doesn't come cheaply, however. Being specialist tools, with only a small market, they're expensive and hard to come by. If I'm honest, given that the simple mains-powered iron can do the job perfectly well, I don't really see the point in resistance soldering. However, I wouldn't dream of dismissing the process out of hand. Indeed, I'm all for trying out different methods before settling on what suits the individual best and I know a few modellers who continually espouse the benefits of resistance soldering, looking at my simple tools with piteous eyes.

THE FUNDAMENTALS OF SOLDERING

The best place to start with this subject is by looking at your soldering iron. If you're starting with a new tool, remove the packaging and check that everything is as it should be by referring to the instruction manual. Before you power it up for the first

Soldering irons come in all shapes and sizes. Temperature-controlled irons are helpful, but not essential unless you intend to work with white-metal parts. Gas-powered irons and torches also have their uses, although a trusty mains-powered tool with a decent flat bit and 25–50W power output will do for most work in brass and nickel silver.

time, you must have a few other items to hand: a damp sponge, plus some regular 60/40 resin-cored solder (we'll look at solders in detail shortly). A stand for your iron is also desirable, keeping the tool secure between tasks without the risk of damage to work surfaces or yourself.

Once the power is switched on, the iron may begin emitting an unusual smell as the tip warms up. Wipe the tip on the damp sponge and, when it starts to sizzle, try melting a little solder onto the tip. It may need a little longer to reach operating temperature but, as soon as the solder begins to melt, draw the molten material around the tip, covering both sides and the end. Immediately rewipe the tip on the damp sponge, treating each face, until a shiny deposit is left on the tool. If there are any gaps or the solder has not adhered, simply repeat the process, allowing the tool to heat up again after being quenched on the wet sponge before melting the solder again.

Wiping the tip quickly over the cleaning sponge will finish the job and leave the tip gleaming with a bright silvery sheen. This may dull once the power is cut and the iron cools but, every time it is switched back on, the same routine should be observed to keep the tool in tip-top condition. Indeed, the cleaner the tip, the better it will transfer heat across the jointing surface and this 'tinning' process also provides protection against corrosive fluxes, which will otherwise shorten the working life of the tool.

It's important to adopt good habits from the outset: wiping the iron tip on the sponge before and after every soldered joint, then again at the end of a session as it cools down, should become part of your regular routine.

If the iron refuses to melt the solder, even when working at full temperature, give it a wipe with a tip-cleaning compound. These contain mildly abrasive materials and the heat of the iron liquefies the surface to create a fizzing bath that gives the tip a thorough cleansing. It really does pay to look after your soldering iron, as it does with any tool. Even switching it off if there's likely to be a delay between solder joints is likely to extend the life of the heating element as well as saving on the electricity bill.

No iron tip will last forever, and it's worth invest-ing in an iron that features replaceable tips. Some brands, such as Antex, offer interchangeable tips of different shapes and sizes to suit a variety of tasks.

WHAT IS SOLDERING?

Put simply, soldering is a means of bonding two metals by introducing a third metal – the solder – in a molten state. The type of solder can be tailored to suit the materials, as it must melt at a lower temperature than the components. The solder must also be able to penetrate the joint and fuse with each of the metal parts. To achieve reliable joints, the mating faces must be scrupulously cleaned and heated evenly to the required temperature. This is where a correctly prepared iron and the right formula of flux come into play.

Unfortunately, the heat from the soldering iron causes the metal's surface to tarnish once again, thus hindering the soldered bond. The purpose of the flux is to keep the surface clean, even while the heat is applied, encouraging the molten solder to flow freely into the joint. This benefit comes at a price, however, and the acidic nature of most leads to continued chemical attack. Unless the model is cleaned thoroughly after soldering, flux residues will lead to failed bonds and a ruined paint finish.

CHOOSING SOLDER

Solder is an alloy containing a variety of different materials suited to specific tasks. Most commonly formed of tin and lead, small quantities of bismuth, cadmium or silver may also be added for improved flow characteristics or to encourage optimal electrical conductivity. It is this mixture of ingredients that dictates the temperature at which the solder will melt, as well as its compatibility with specific materials.

I mentioned 'standard' 60/40 grade solder earlier, this being the most common type available and designed for a wide range of tasks such as electronics and small-scale brass or nickel silver work. The ratio 60/40 refers to the tin/lead content of the solder, with a higher amount of tin creating a stronger bond, while the lead is there to help the molten material flow at a lower temperature.

Lead-free solders are becoming more widespread, with copper and silver being popular alternative ingredients. Consequently, lead-free solders may demand a slightly higher melting temperature (up to 20°C higher). Specifications differ according to brand and formula, so checking the label before you buy is recommended.

Choosing the right solder is important and depends on the type and size of materials being joined. Other characteristics may also be desired, such as a lower working temperature, so that smaller detail parts can be installed without weakening previously soldered joints. Additionally, some solders contain elements that may react adversely with certain metals, while others contain a flux within the solder that may or may not prove corrosive. Therefore it helps to know as much about your solder as possible.

High-quality solders aimed at model making are branded with their melting temperatures (in degrees Celsius) by way of easily identifying their suitability. For instance, Carr's range includes 70, 145, 179, 183, 188, 224 and 243, covering a broad range of potential applications. Some of the lower temperature solders are best suited to detail work where the surface can be heated quickly with a cooler iron, while the 70°C version is aimed at white-metal work. Higher temperature solders are usually thicker and can be helpful when joining ill-fitting parts or when more material strength is required, although the iron will need to be powerful enough to heat the metal to a sufficient temperature.

This brings me to the issue of a solder's working range, whereby the alloy will melt at a certain temperature. Depending on the solder's ingredients, the molten material will solidify once the temperature drops to a certain point. For example, a solder may melt at 180°C before returning to a solid state at 170°C. This 10°C difference is what is known as the working range. Good-quality solders have a smaller working range, sometimes down to 2°C, meaning that the molten solder will solidify almost as soon as the iron is released from the joint. Others, with larger working ranges, will stay molten for longer, suggesting that the parts must be securely clamped during assembly.

Such fine-tuning of solder is only worthwhile if you are using a temperature-controlled iron. Moreover, it makes it all the more desirous to have a soldering station with some form of iron temperature indicator to get the tool at exactly the right heat setting.

FLUX

Just as choosing the right solder is important, so too is opting for the most appropriate flux. Available in liquid, paste and powder form, many are acid-based and must be neutralized, after the solder joints have been made, by washing in plenty of water and a suitable detergent. Another hazard of acid fluxes is the noxious fumes emitted when the surface is heated, making it vital to work in a well-ventilated area. Acid-free fluxes are now available that are much less hazardous and easier to clean away.

Flux formulas are tailored to suit specific metals and working temperatures, with liquids offering greater penetration into tight-fitting joints, while a thick paste or cream will stay put on vertical surfaces more readily. There are even water-based fluxes that do not require cleaning away after the soldered joint has been made, being intended primarily for electrical work.

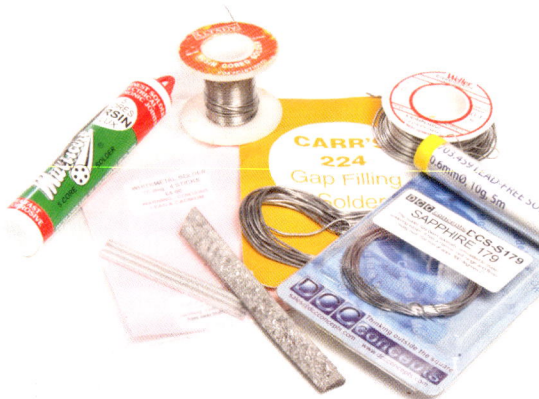

Solder formulas are tailored towards specific applications, such as electronic work or particular materials. Working temperatures also vary, which can be helpful, especially if operating an iron with variable heat settings.

SURFACE PREPARATION

Always check the fit of each component, mounting a 'dry run' and fettling away any excess material wherever necessary. Take the time to plan how the parts will be held in position while the soldering takes place, bearing in mind that the surfaces will get very hot very quickly.

When you are ready to make the bonds, it's imperative that the surfaces be cleaned of all traces of dirt or grease. A thorough scrub in a bath of diluted soda crystals or other household detergents should shift most residues, while isopropyl alcohol can be equally effective.

Brass is particularly liable to tarnishing upon exposure to air, with the problem being exacerbated when the material is heated up. Nickel silver is similar in this respect and, before each joint is made, it doesn't hurt to rub the area with a fibreglass scratch brush or abrasive pad.

MAKING SOLDER JOINTS

With the parts aligned and ready to be bonded, the iron can be switched on and allowed to reach operating temperature, cleaning and 'tinning' the tip if necessary.

Fluxes are a vital cog in the soldering process, ensuring that the surface is kept free of tarnish while the heat is applied and helping the molten solder to flow into the joint. Liquid and paste formulas are the most common, with acid-free versions offering a less toxic option.

A heatproof working surface, assembly jigs and clamps will be required for safe and accurate assembly. Skamolex board (Axminster Tools) is especially useful, while plywood and MDF will resist the high temperatures involved in soldering.

Apply flux to the joint with an old paintbrush and give the iron another wipe on the damp sponge, before melting a little solder onto the tip.

As the tool is placed onto the joint, the flux will fizz and spit before the solder starts to flow. Move the iron slowly along the joint to ensure that the solder is spread evenly. With thin material or very small parts, avoid potential distortion by heating the parts for a short time only. Remove the iron and wipe the tip on the sponge. If the joint needs more solder, simply repeat the process, adding fresh flux to the surface and melting more solder onto the iron's tip.

Soldered joints must be left to cool naturally and it usually takes a few seconds for the solder to solidify, although the metal may still be too hot to handle for a moment. Never quench the parts in water, although it's a good habit to wash each joint of flux residues as you go, saving time in the later stages.

If the hot solder refuses to adhere to the surface of one or both parts then the metal will need a thorough clean, preferably with a scratch brush. Another reason may be that the iron tip is not hot enough or that the iron is not powerful enough to heat the material sufficiently. Also, try adding a little more flux, checking that you're using the right formula to suit the materials and solder at hand – lead-free solders often require a special flux, for instance.

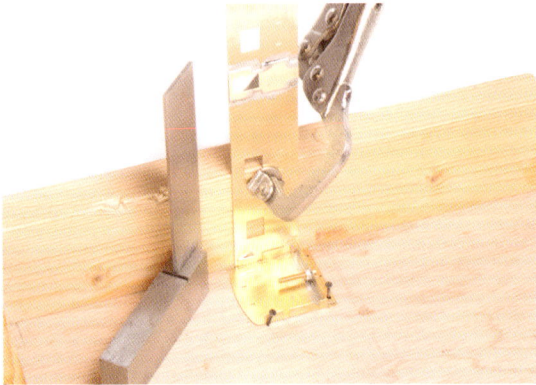

Keeping your iron in tip-top condition is essential. Preparing it correctly from new is also vital, 'tinning' the tip with a little solder as the tool is heated for the first time and wiping over a wet sponge at regular intervals.

Take the time to closely align and clamp the parts before making any bonds, checking with a set square and straight edge. Working with both hands free whenever possible makes life infinitely easier.

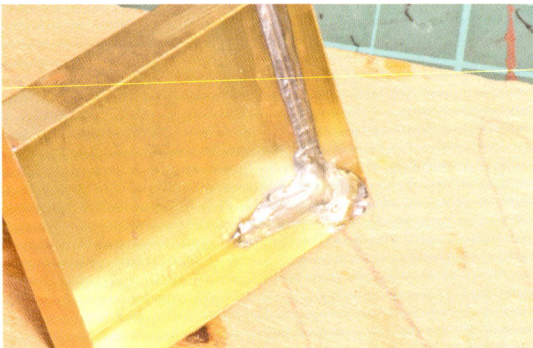

With the parts cleaned, aligned and clamped, brush on some flux, melt a little solder onto the iron's tip and place the tool against the joint. The flux will fizz and, after a second or two, the solder should begin flowing onto the surface. Remove the iron and allow the solder to cool before disturbing the parts.

Avoid big, unsightly lumps of solder such as this. Only a small amount is needed and such a heavy-handed approach may compromise the fit of subsequent parts.

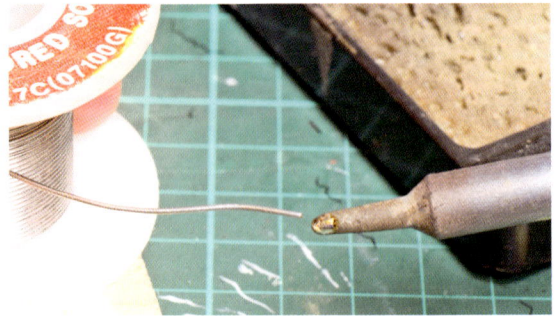

If the solder doesn't transfer easily to the surface, it could be for a number of reasons: the metal may need cleaning, the iron tip is dirty or not hot enough, or insufficient flux has been applied.

After making the initial 'tack' solder bond, recheck the alignment of the parts, add more flux, melt more solder onto the iron's tip and apply the tool to the metal. The molten solder should then flood into the joint. Move the iron along the whole joint to treat the entire area. A good joint should appear shiny, even as the solder cools.

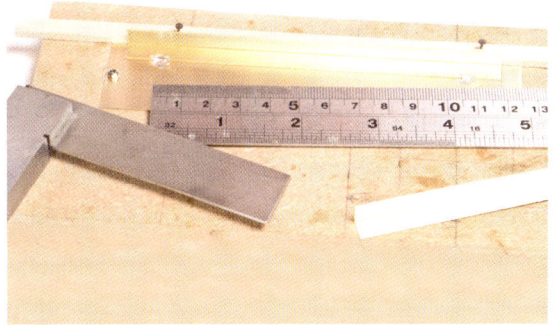

When dealing with longer parts, 'tack' each end initially and check alignment before adding more evenly spaced bonds.

Check again and, if happy, apply more flux and run the iron steadily along the entire joint, adding more solder if necessary until the whole length is evenly covered.

Practice really does make perfect where soldering is concerned and if you can lay your hands on plenty of scrap brass or nickel silver, even in the form of offcuts from the fret, you can try out the technique free from the worry of ruining expensive kit components.

Tidy the joints if necessary with needle files, abrasives or a scratch brush. Be careful not to remove too much of the solder, lest the joint be weakened.

Typical body assembly follows the pattern already outlined for other materials, with each side joined to an end before the two 'halves' are brought together. A simple assembly jig helps maintain correct alignment.

GLUING METAL

For myriad reasons, there are instances where soldering metal components may not be the best option. Perhaps there are previously soldered joints in the vicinity and a strong risk of loosening the parts by reheating, even when working at lower temperatures. Maybe the parts are too fiddly or there's insufficient space for the iron to work in. Or maybe you just don't fancy soldering in the first place.

Whatever the reasons, metals can be bonded effectively using adhesives, provided that all surfaces are spotlessly clean and there's sufficient surface area on which the glue can adhere. For instance, butt corner joints of thin sheet metal do not make for a reliable glue bond, no matter how much adhesive is smeared on. However, etched kits employing tab-and-slot construction are better suited to the use of adhesives, as are cast metal components, although the bonds will still be nowhere near as reliable as soldered joints.

Epoxy glues are recommended for use with all metals, especially load-bearing joints. It's worth trying a range of different grades: five-minute formulas are great for fixing smaller parts, while slower-setting epoxies provide longer working times to aid alignment and clamping.

Cyano glues are fine for adding fine details, where epoxy is too bulky or potentially messy. The generally brittle nature of cyano precludes its use for many structural applications, although gel-type formulas offer greater versatility.

It's vitally important that all of the soldering work is complete before employing glue. The model

Having erected the main structure with regular-grade solder, commonly with a working temperature of about 180°C, lower temperature solder, such as 145°C, can be used to attach smaller parts, lowering the risk of previous bonds being loosened. If the iron tip temperature can't be controlled, keeping the tool in contact with the metal for as short a time as possible should suffice.

You don't have to solder everything, as adhesives may be better suited to some tasks. However, only apply glues once all of the soldering is out of the way and the model has been thoroughly cleaned of flux residues. Epoxy and cyano glues are best for metal, the latter for smaller, detail parts only.

should also be thoroughly cleaned. Traces of flux will interfere with adhesives and, worse still, heating the metal will weaken any glued joints. Additionally, there's a risk of highly noxious fumes being released. In particular, cyano glues emit cyanide gas when heated and this is not something we want to be inhaling.

EXTRA CONSIDERATIONS

In contrast to kits formed mostly from plastic or resin, the need to add extra ballast to metal kits is extremely rare. I've mentioned before the benefits of maintaining a consistent weight across a rake of similar vehicles, and this applies equally to metal-rendered stock. The hauling capacity of your motive power must be considered, along with the gradients and curvature of your layout's track.

If you're concerned about whether your traction is up to the task, it may be possible to run a series of tests in advance. Certainly, if you've already built one metal carriage of a particular size and type, keeping a note of its final 'in service' weight is recommended. With this information, a rake of coaches and wagons totalling the expected weight of the entire train can be made up

and trialled on your layout. The tractive effort of your locos can be improved by installing a power-boosting magnetic system, such as Power-base by DCCconcepts. Such systems, however, must be considered at an early stage in a layout's construction, as they're designed to lie beneath the tracks.

Metal's ability to conduct electricity can be used to our advantage if installing power collection and lighting circuits, yet it can also prove problematic unless care is taken to insulate the wheels and axles to avoid short circuits. Underframe components, such as brake shoes and rodding, must also be installed with care, ensuring adequate clearance from the wheels and flanges, taking into account any side-play or movement from a compensation system.

Other hazards need to be borne in mind, such as being wary of sharp edges and the need to clean up thoroughly after fettling metal parts. The ingress of swarf or filings into bearings will cause excessive wear and pose a risk of short circuits in electrical components.

Now that all of this important theory is out of the way, we can delve into more of the details surrounding metal carriage construction.

CHAPTER ELEVEN

METALWORK IN PRACTICE

Having covered the basic processes behind metal kits and soldering in the previous chapter, we can now put this knowledge into practice. In keeping with my policy of demonstrating the most important practical processes, rather than specific carriage projects, a representative selection of kits is featured in this section. Illustrating the most typical assembly sequences and techniques that you are likely to encounter, each of the methods can be comfortably transferred to almost any kit.

I've purposely chosen some of the most modeller-friendly kits. These are products that I'd recommend highly to anyone making a start with metal. Modest features such as positive location aids for components are a small detail in the big scheme of things, but they can make the difference between projects being pleasurable or frustrating.

Rather than cram everything into one phase, I've shunted the subjects of roofs, bogies and fixed axle chassis into Chapter 12. Here we'll concentrate on getting the main fabric of the carriage shaped and assembled perfectly, as well as looking into the subject of soldering white-metal.

RTMS: 'READ THE MANUAL, STUPID!'

In the dim, distant past, one of my many temporary jobs was on an IT helpdesk and, as you can probably imagine, most of the queries could have been resolved if the user had simply read the instructions. Much does depend on the quality of the kit's reference material, but taking the time to study the step-by-step guidelines and familiarizing oneself with the parts and assembly sequence will make a world of difference. Ideally I always like to sit and read the material alongside prototype information and images, jotting down my own list of points and observations as to how the project should progress.

Gaining an idea of what goes where, as well as the how and why, should remove any guesswork once the practical work begins. There's always at least a 90 per cent chance that, when you're not certain where or how a part is meant to fit, any guess will soon be proved wrong and the parts will need dismantling. Trust me, I know!

Planning how the model will be modified, detailed and painted is also something to consider now, before anything has been stuck together. Perhaps the instructions will offer some guidance on this matter, but experience has shown that we all develop our own preferred ways of working and this is something that you will appreciate after building one or two vehicles yourself.

The recurring issue of interior access remains of importance, with kit makers varying how the bodyshell is to be erected. Some coach bodies are designed for access from the bottom, where the body and roof is bonded together from the outset, forming a resilient shell akin to many RTR models. The ends may incorporate mounting brackets with captive nuts, allowing the underframe to be bolted to the body. Although not universally employed, this system offers great convenience, with the innards being easily accessible in case of passengers, glazing or interior details coming adrift over the years.

If your kit is designed in a different format, perhaps it can be adapted to your own preferred assembly system. Either way, making such important decisions at the beginning of a project is strongly advised.

UNDERFRAMES

Metal underframes are probably my favourite area of carriage building and, if the kit permits, the point from which I prefer to begin. Although bodyshells bring their own satisfaction, manufacturing a working underframe has more of an air of miniature engineering about it, albeit a rather superficial one.

Etched brass and nickel silver chassis tend to follow very similar assembly sequences, with the large floor being stiffened by separate parts, themselves having to be formed to an 'L' or 'C' shape channel. Although the floor is likely to curl up slightly when removed from the fret, the fitting of the solebars immediately brings it back true; provided of course that they're assembled correctly.

Working on a flat reference surface is essential and fixing the floor and mainframes to a simple homemade jig will make the world of difference. Furthermore, in the case of certain 'universal' underframe kits that require trimming to the desired length prior to assembly, care must be taken not to distort the components. In these instances, half-etched lines should denote the different lengths and a heavy-duty set of metal shears or a hacksaw and files can be employed. The etched line will help guide the tool to a degree, but I like to use a set square to be sure that the cut is at an exact right angle.

Comet, MJT and Palatine Models make some fine underframes in 4mm scale, most of which are available as separate kits, allowing their use with RTR or scratch-built bodies if desired. Palatine's chassis are particularly good, with lots of care and attention going into the design of the parts and the instructions. It's the small things that always impress me and I particularly like the etched guides on the floor, showing exactly where all the underslung equipment should fit and which side of the coach the corridor should be. My favourite feature, though, is the half-etched recesses to give clearance to the wheel flanges, allowing a realistic gap between bogie and floor and the ability to fit the correct diameter of wheels.

Folding the solebars may be tricky, especially with small-scale parts. With so little metal to clamp in a vice and even less to lever with the bending bars or steel rule, there's a chance that the parts will be damaged. As mentioned previously, annealing the metal beforehand will be helpful, especially if working with nickel silver.

Once the main frames are assembled, the smaller details can be added. Methods of underframe trussing vary from kit to kit and between prototypes, but a couple of varieties are illustrated here. Other underframe equipment will likely be a mix of etched footboards, steps and brackets, complemented by cast boxes, cylinders, tanks and dynamos. As long as all soldering work is complete and the parts pre-washed, there's no reason why epoxy or thick

With this MJT BR Mk1 underframe, the solebars are integral to the main carriage floor and must be shaped carefully. A consistent, knife-edge fold is essential. Clamp the whole of the material securely in a large Hold 'n' Fold or bench vice and employ a stout steel bar as a lever.

A flat reference surface is vital to check that all is well as the parts are formed. The main trussing is also folded up from the floor pan, while transverse members are doubled-up and the angle sections folded over.

To keep everything straight and true during construction, the chassis has been fixed to a strip of 12mm MDF with a pair of pan-head screws. The parts are soldered securely, with a gap-filling solder employed for the laminated trussing members.

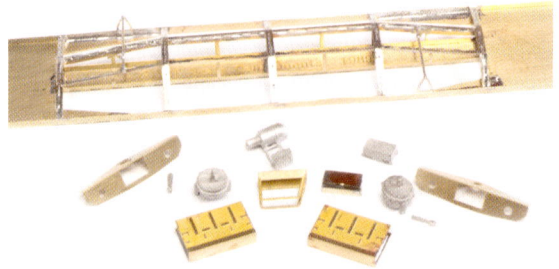

Once the gap-filling solder has cooled, the exposed faces of the trussing can be filed square and flush. The MJT kit also provides various underframe parts. However, most parts can't be fitted until a floor has been installed on the upper face of the chassis, either from sheet brass or plastic card.

Other kits offer an alternative approach. This Palatine Models chassis features separate solebars with tab-and-slot locating aids and, to help with the shaping, etched gaps along the fold line.

Once the solebars have been formed, they can be located readily into the slots on the floor and soldered. The etched fold-relief gaps can then be filled with solder, using plenty of flux to help the molten material flow along the recess.

Again, the floor is mounted on an MDF base but, due to the protruding tabs of the solebars, some brass shims are added to give adequate clearance.

cyano glue can't be employed for most of this work, especially where some of the parts are plastic or resin castings. However, if the parts are formed from white-metal, then low-temperature soldering will offer a more durable bond.

RIGHT: **This Palatine chassis proved a joy to construct. Locating instructions are half-etched into the floor, so there's no excuse for sticking parts in the wrong place.**

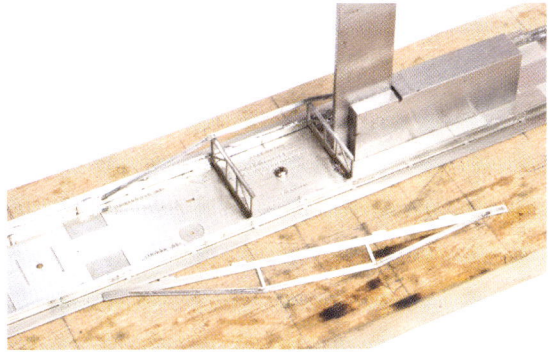

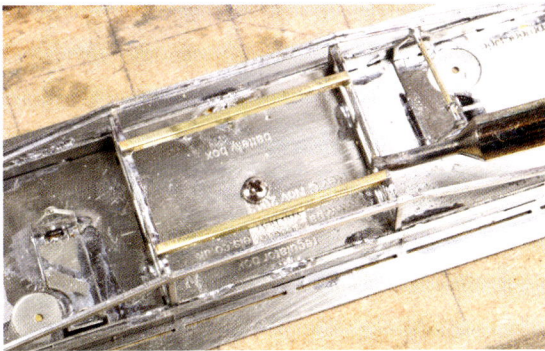

Extra lengths of brass angle are required to finish off the trussing, although I used 1mm square tubing instead. With the initial stages of assembly undertaken with 179°C solder and the iron set at 400°C, smaller details were added with 145°C solder and the iron turned down to 300°C, lessening the risk of previous joints being disturbed.

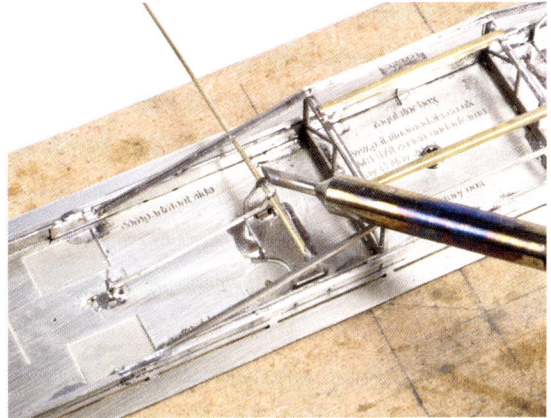

Brake hangers and rods are also provided by Palatine, with brass wire soldered in place and trimmed in situ. Resin battery boxes and vacuum cylinders are supplied, but these will be installed with epoxy later.

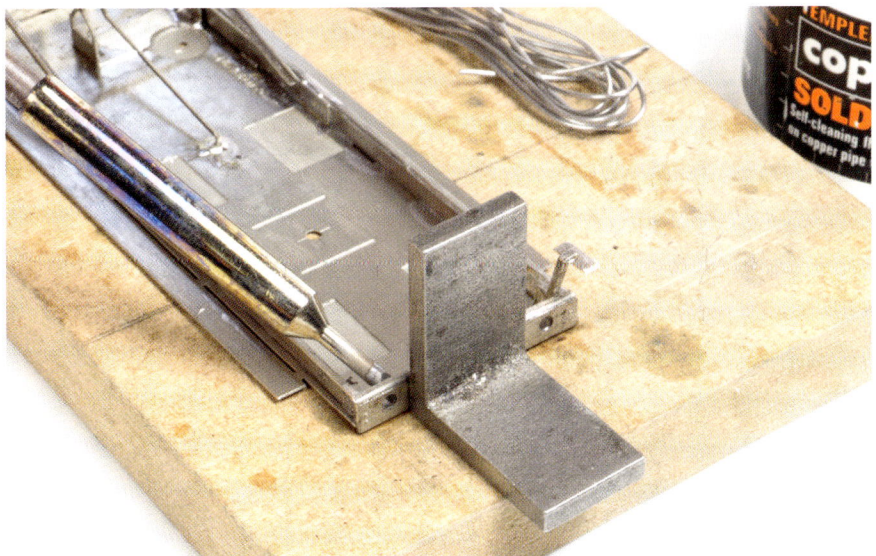

Both solebars should be perfectly aligned, but, if not, dress them level and square before adding the headstocks, checking that they are centred and sitting at the correct angle.

SOLDERING WHITE-METAL

The ingredients that make up the various white-metal alloys all boast relatively low melting temperatures and, although the basic techniques involved in soldering are similar to those already discussed, there is a need for a specialist approach.

For starters, the soldering iron will need to be set at a much lower temperature, ideally by means of a controllable power output. There are instances where the temperature can be lowered or raised, depending on the size of the components or whether white-metal is being joined to another material, such as brass or nickel silver. Therefore, having a single tool that can adapt to the needs of each joint will prove economical and convenient.

Temperature-controlled irons are much easier and cheaper to obtain these days, with digital readouts revealing the exact temperature of the bit at any given time. Separate power regulators are also available, taking the place of a standard iron's mains plug, or irons may be fitted with a simple dial control on the tool itself. Each offers a cheaper, though less versatile, option when compared to a fancy soldering station. As popular brands of 'low-melt' solder will liquefy at 70°C, an iron that can be set to a temperature of 100°C or less will be useful for very small or intricate work. However, such tools can be more expensive.

My own soldering station has a minimum setting of 150°C and, as I often use 100°C solder for white-metal work, especially on larger 'OO' gauge or 'O' gauge parts, it has served me well. Besides, for very small components, especially detailing embellishments, I prefer to use glue anyway. A handy test to see if your iron is set low enough is to bring the tip into contact with a scrap of the same white-metal, such as a sizable offcut of flash. If the metal melts, the tool is too hot.

White-metal's constituents also demand the use of specific flux formulas. Cleanliness is also of paramount importance, as it is with any form of soldering. White-metal components usually contain a residual coating from the casting process, as well as a naturally occurring tarnish, all of which must be removed before each part is

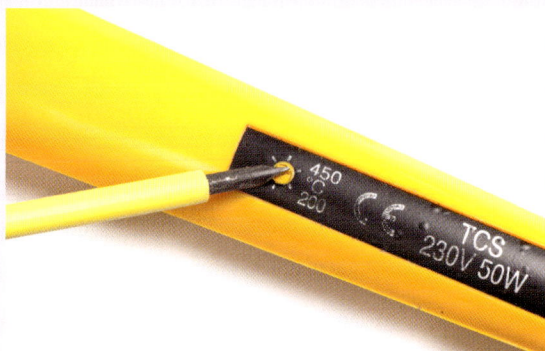

Antex offers a few soldering irons that can be controlled via a small potentiometer on the handle, such as this TCS50W. An updated version has since appeared, featuring a small digital readout allowing for more accurate adjustments. The lowest 200°C setting is fine for work on larger white-metal components, but must be used with care.

bonded. Rubbing with a file, abrasives or a scratch brush will immediately create a lovely, shiny surface. As soon as this starts to dull, whether by excessive handling or aborted solder joints, it will need re-abrading to restore the shine before any successful bonds can be made.

'Tinning' white-metal parts before joining them together may prove a little more time-consuming, but the higher probability of success makes it worthwhile. This approach also means that, when the joints are being made, the iron need not be in contact with the metal for too long, thus reducing any risks of damage. Clamping the parts wherever possible is recommended, especially if working with an iron set at 100–150°C. Recalling what we discussed in the previous chapter about a solder's working range, waiting for the solder in a white-metal joint to cool to below 70°C or so will take anything up to

10–20 seconds. If holding the parts with your fingers, that time will seem like an eternity as the burning sensation reaches your nerve endings.

If the parts move at all during the cooling of the solder, the integrity of the joint will be compromised severely. Another factor to bear in mind is that, once melted and solidified, many low temperature solders will subsequently need a higher temperature to liquefy again. So, getting your joints correct in the first instance is desirable as increasing working temperatures with white-metal parts is always fraught with danger.

Greater accuracy can be achieved by forming a quick initial 'tack' solder bond between parts. Strength isn't important at this time, with the bond serving only to keep the parts together while checks are made for alignments and so on. If adjustments do need to be made, there is very little solder to re-melt. Once you're happy that everything is set up correctly, the bonds can be made properly and permanently.

Joining white-metal to brass is possible, provided that both parties have been correctly prepared. After cleaning the joint surfaces, 'tin' the white-metal face with low temperature solder and the brass surface with a more typical 60/40 solder, having turned the iron up to 300–400°C. The reason why the brass must be 'tinned' with ordinary solder is that some of the ingredients in 'low-melt' formulas can react against the brass (or the alloy's zinc content to be exact). This intermediate layer of solder resolves the issue.

Having set the iron back to around 100–150°C, bring the two parts together, clamping them securely if necessary and apply plenty of flux. Melt a little low temperature solder onto the iron's tip and begin heating the joint gently, until the white-metal solder softens and bonds to the 'tinned' brass surface.

(continued overleaf)

White-metal parts must be cleaned prior to soldering. Rub the jointing areas with a scratch brush and 'tin' with 70°C or 100°C solder. If joining to brass, 'tin' the latter with 145°C solder.

Bring the 'tinned' parts together and add more flux. Set the iron to around 200°C, load the tip with 100°C solder and apply the heat to the brass. The 'tinned' areas will soon melt and the joint will be made. Move the iron gently along the joint, but don't dwell longer than is necessary. Remove the heat and allow the surface to cool before repeating along the other side of the component.

Soldering white-metal fittings to brass or nickel silver underframes offers far greater strength than adhesives, but it takes a little practice. Solder bonds should appear bright and shiny. If it appears dull and grainy, then the parts have moved slightly while the solder was in a molten state. Add more flux and re-melt the joint.

The same process is also effective for white-metal–nickel silver bonds. Just remember, when working with a controllable iron, to make sure that the tip has cooled sufficiently before reverting to work with the white-metal. Believe me, it's all too easy to forget to make the adjustment, resulting in a pool of molten white-metal.

Cleaning the parts after soldering is just as vital with white-metal as with any other material. Flux residues must be neutralized and removed, preferably as soon as possible. I like to wash every joint as I go along, just to keep the workpiece, work area and my hands as clean as possible. A bowl of water (regularly refreshed) and a ready supply of swabs is all that's needed.

At the end of every work session, a more thorough cleanse is undertaken. A scrub with an abrasive detergent, followed by a soak in diluted soda crystals will shift any unwanted debris and residues. Finally, a thorough rinse in clean water removes the cleaning agents and the model can be set aside to dry before the project continues.

A great way of using up scrap brass fret is to create dynamo belts. Clean and 'tin' the white-metal and brass parts with 100°C and 145°C solders, respectively, apply plenty of flux and heat the joint from the outside (set the iron to around 150–175°C). This will 'sweat' the solder and form a strong bond. The ends of the belt can be trimmed to length once the bogie has been installed.

Joining white-metal parts to each other is simple enough, following the same basic tenets of clean surfaces, plenty of flux and the iron set at the correct temperature. For delicate items, such as this white-metal trussing, set the iron to a maximum of 150°C and employ 70°C or 100°C solder. Keep the hot tip in contact for the minimum amount of time – a few seconds should be enough.

BODY SIDES

Along with the roof, the sides of a carriage are the most visible and, therefore, must look the part. Flat-sided stock is not so difficult to construct, the bodyshell being little more than a rectangular box. Panelled or curved sides, however, take much more in the way of careful forming and bonding.

Before shaping or assembly work begins, consider whether any tasks would be easier to undertake now, while the sides can still be laid out flat on the workbench, such as marking and drilling holes for handrails and door handles, fitting separate drop-lights or ventilators to the window apertures, or maybe installing grilles on departmental vehicles.

Many etched kits omit small details, especially doorstops. These rubber projections prevent the opened doors from damaging the bodywork when fully opened and they're easy to replicate, by drilling holes, inserting brass wire of a suitable diameter and soldering from inside. The waste can be snipped away and the outer face filed to a uniform height. Hinges too, if omitted from the etch, can be easier to fit while the sides are laid flat.

This pre-assembly work isn't necessarily right for every project, as the extra surface relief may interfere with the clamping up of parts in a jig during assembly of the bodyshell (unless the jig is modified accordingly), hence the benefits of planning as much of the construction before leaping in with the soldering iron. If you'd prefer not to fit certain parts until

Pre-formed body components, such as this three-piece shell from a Southern Pride kit, take much of the hassle out of metal kit assembly. With only minimal folding work required, the tab-and-slot joints make for easy alignment.

Working in a simple assembly jig, the tabs can be 'tacked' gradually to the roof, checking alignment as you go. Once both sides are in position, the corner joints can also be made. Here, 179°C solder has been employed for the initial stages.

Although the instructions advised otherwise, I decided to run solder all along the outside of the joint between the sides and roof, in order to fill the gap. Plenty of flux was applied, working on an inch or so at a time. The iron was set at a slightly lower temperature, using 145°C solder, to preserve the previous bonds.

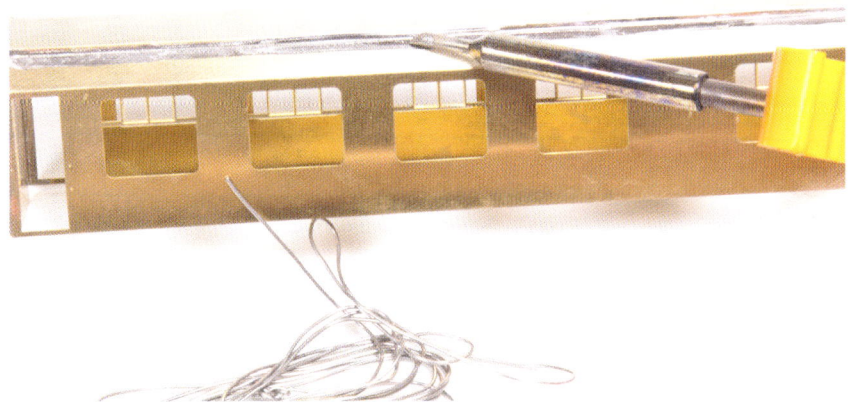

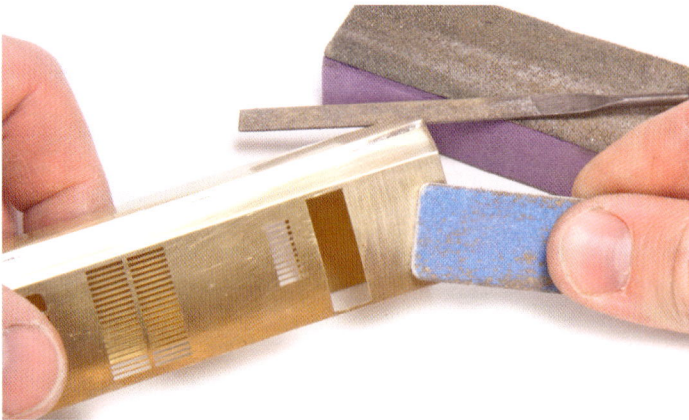

The solder was then filed and abraded, producing neat and seamless joints. The corner joints were also tidied up, being careful to keep the edges square. It is best to perform rough work like this before adding any smaller parts.

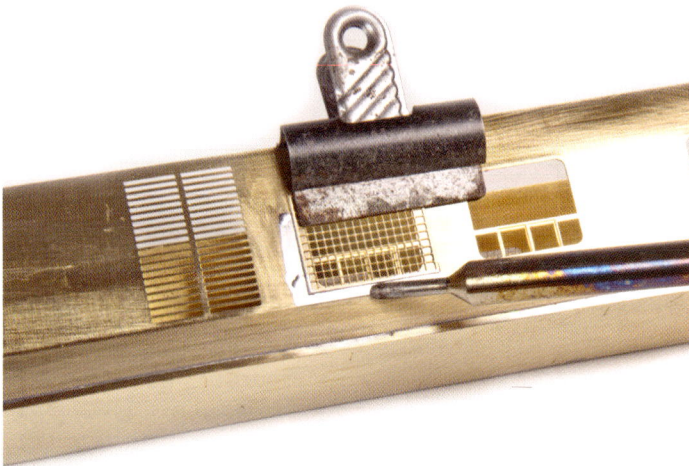

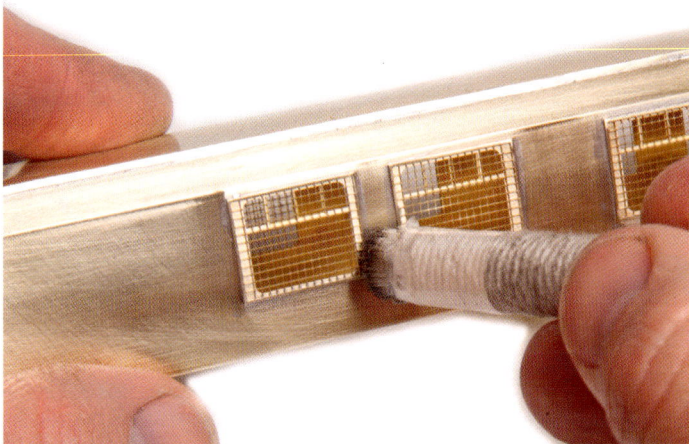

later, at least their mounting holes can be drilled or reamed out now, while the material is easier to work with. Also, don't forget that, unless the detail parts are set away from the corners, the soldered bonds may be at risk of re-melting when the body is fixed to the ends and roof.

It is occasionally necessary to scribe door seams into etched brass sides, especially on panelled stock. The task may also be required if existing seams have become clogged with solder. Having marked out the locations carefully, employ a good-quality, sharp scribing tool or profile cutter against a straight edge. Apply light pressure only, as it's easy for the tool to go astray, and make repeated strokes until the desired depth is achieved. A slight burr will appear either side of the recess and this can be flattened with an abrasive pad.

According to how a kit has been designed, the sides of panelled coaching stock will be rendered partly by half-etching the recessed areas, leaving the beaded edges to stand proud. For prototypes with a greater degree of relief, extra panels may need soldering to the main side etches.

MIDDLE: **External detail additions can now be installed. The window mesh had to be aligned and soldered carefully, being sure not to clog the fine mesh.**

BOTTOM: **The solder joints were tidied up with a fibreglass scratch brush and abrasives.**

This Connoisseur Models kit required the sides to be profiled to form a subtle tumblehome, with the rolling technique discussed in the previous chapter employed. As the brass was quite thick, I found that annealing the sides beforehand made the job a lot easier. When the profile matched that of the ends, the upper and lower brackets could be folded over, checking for squareness and trying not to undo the curved profile – this is where a Hold 'n' Fold justifies its cost.

Before the bodyshell is assembled, think about fitting parts while they can be accessed more readily. Window droplights are a prime example, clamped and soldered to the inside. Vary their positions for a bit of extra visual interest. Another common feature is door hinges that are folded up and secured into slots from the inside. These give a neater appearance to the exterior and are best installed at this stage.

For stock with curved sides, gently forming the required profile can be a challenge. If the kit is rendered in nickel silver or thicker brass, then recourse to annealing before shaping is recommended. Using the carriage ends as a template takes away any guesswork, checking regularly and working patiently and methodically until the correct shape is achieved across the whole of both sides. Consistency is highly important, as is the need for the profile to be concentric along the carriage's whole length.

CARRIAGE ENDS

As with the carriage sides, working on the ends before assembly may or may not prove beneficial. Again, simply marking out and drilling all necessary mounting holes for handrails, jumper cables and gangways at this point will ease the detailing task later.

If your kit is so designed, then now is the time to form the end brackets and secure the captive nuts

Now is also a good time to install any mounting brackets for the chassis. Captive nuts at each end are a simple but effective solution. 'Tin' the nut and bracket and hold everything in place with the bolt, having protected the threads with Vaseline, before making the solder bond with the aid of plenty of flux.

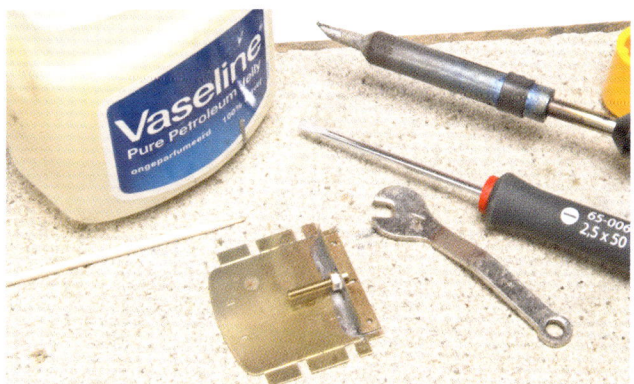

for the body-to-underframe mounts. These solder joints are critical, as the mechanical stress from tightening the bolts will break any inferior bonds. Clean both the carriage parts and the nuts themselves with a flat file and abrasives and use plenty of flux. Holding the nuts in position is easy enough: just screw them tight with the bolts. Keep molten solder out of the threads by adding a few drops of oil, candle wax or Vaseline onto the bolt before driving it home.

Some kits feature cast white-metal overlays for the ends and these will require flattening on the inside and fettling to ensure an exact fit. Add these once the main shell of the carriage has been assembled, either by low temperature solder or epoxy adhesive and fill any gaps with putty.

ASSEMBLING THE SHELL

Creating a simple jig to help join the carriage sides and ends will help get the parts aligned squarely. It will also allow the parts to be clamped securely, keeping both hands free to wield the soldering iron and to avoid burning your fingertips. Test-fitting everything will reveal if any parts require fettling and a few 'dry runs', with the parts clamped and checked, are a good idea. We need to be sure that nothing will move while the joints are made and the metal cools down, or 'dry' joints will result.

'Dry' solder joints are weak and likely to break under the lightest of loads. They can be discerned by the dull grey appearance of the cooled solder, which should ideally maintain a shiny, silvery outlook.

As the parts will get hot during soldering, the assembly jig will need to be heat resistant, as will the clamps. Heatproof board, such as Skamolex (from Axminster Tools) is handy, not least as you can drive pins into it to act as retaining clamps. Metal surfaces are best avoided, but blocks of thick plywood or MDF are ideal, preferably with a set of shoulders fixed at an exact right angle. The sides and ends can be readily clamped up, checked for alignment and the solder joints made with little fuss. More complex jigs are possible, but my simple version has suited my needs perfectly so far.

Take care when clamping, being sure not to distort or damage the soft metal by exerting too much pressure. Padding the jaws of the clamps with offcuts of cork or leather will offer some protection. Miniature steel G-clamps are great for the job, but the metal will act like a heat conductor, drawing away the energy and forcing the soldering iron to work harder to keep the brass or nickel silver at the correct temperature. Therefore, ensure that the clamps aren't too close to the site of the soldered joints.

Once one end has been married to one side, the other half of the shell can be likewise assembled before the four 'walls' are brought together. Keep checking that everything is square and true before each bond is made. After tidying up the edges of each corner joint, other fittings can be added at this stage while the interior is easily accessible, following the kit's instructions closely.

As we have seen already, the body can be built up one side and end at a time, with the two halves being brought together in a simple alignment jig. Tack the corners in order to check the angles and profile.

Once you are absolutely sure that the shell is square and true, apply plenty of flux and flood the corner joints with solder.

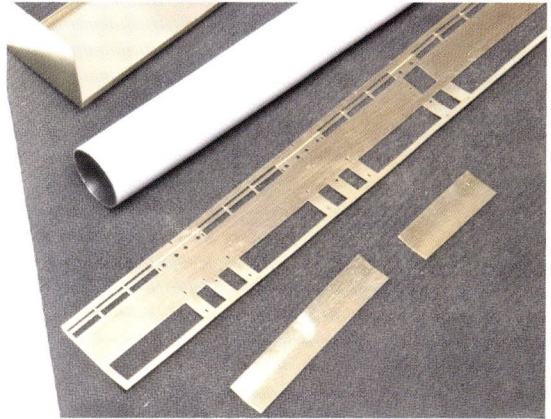

Laminated sides can be complicated if the layers require profiling individually. However, the process follows the usual rolling routine.

RIGHT: With kits such as this MJT product, it is best to fit one of the sides to the floor unit first, checking for correct alignment. The panels can then be soldered from the interior. Once again, employing a high temperature solder for the main structural bonds, followed by 145°C solder for the detail work, is good practice.

Check the profile and alignment of the panel overlays before 'tacking' into position. Check again before making the permanent bond. It will take time to treat both sides, ensuring that the panels are the right way up. Repeat the process with the other side.

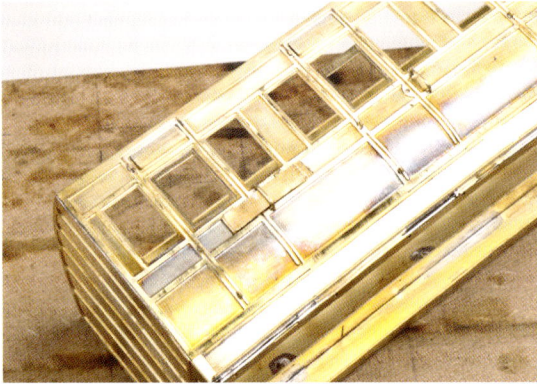

Ensure that handrails stand at a uniform height by inserting a shim of scrap fret material while soldering the wire to the inside of the carriage.

Small details can either be fixed with adhesives or solder. If employing solder, neater results can be obtained by making 'sweated' joints, whereby both faces are 'tinned'. The solder is then rubbed down lightly with abrasives to remove any lumps.

The 'tinned' areas are then cleaned and covered with more flux and the parts brought together. As they are heated, the solder will re-melt and form the bond without too much excess molten material oozing out, or so one hopes.

ABOVE: Where the prototype dictates, some kits feature white-metal castings for the ends, such as this bow-ended LNER coach. The castings can be either 'tinned' and soldered to the brass frame or fixed with epoxy.

LEFT: Other details can be installed at this point, including end fittings such as steps, lamp brackets and piping/conduits. Emergency brake gear can be formed with brass wire. Flatten the ends by heating and hammering lightly before dressing with a file to create a square edge.

CHAPTER TWELVE

ROOFS, BOGIES & FIXED AXLES

By way of rounding-off the subject of metal kit construction, this chapter looks into the assembly and installation of roofs, bogies and fixed-axle chassis. Sticking with a single material is not a necessity, so we'll also contemplate other options for these 'top-and-tail' tasks, with various factors determining choice, such as weight and cost.

The issue of compensation – adding working suspension systems – also features in this chapter, albeit rather briefly. Finescale modelling is too large a subject to cover within a single chapter, so what follows is merely an introduction to the means of improving the performance of your coaching stock, whatever scale or gauge that you're working in.

ROOFS

In my humble opinion, by far the most user-friendly carriage kits are those designed with a detachable underframe, allowing the roof to be fixed permanently to the body shell. This offers great support to the sides and ends, while also removing the risk of any unsightly gaps between the parts. Being as the roof is the most visible area of any scale model, such factors are of paramount importance, so it pays to get the roof fitted as neatly and accurately as possible.

Pre-formed roofs are a real boon, although some are supplied in standard lengths that will need trimming and/or shaping to match the body-shell, especially when a bow-ended vehicle is under construction. Be warned that the supplied profile doesn't always match the kit's ends exactly and some fine-tuning may be necessary. Even in such cases, the modeller is still offered a considerable head start compared to having to begin from scratch.

In nearly all cases, no matter how the roof has been rendered, it will also need to be marked out and drilled to accept the appropriate array of ven-

tilator hoods, water tank fillers and associated pipework. If you're lucky, the kit will include a paper template to aid the marking out. With luck this will be rendered to full size and can be cut and fixed temporarily to the metal roof with tape, while the locations are transferred with a scriber and punch. Alternatively, the paper can be fixed permanently with contact or epoxy adhesive, adding a more realistic texture to the smooth metal (as demonstrated in Chapter 4).

If no plans are provided, or they're not to full scale, some careful work with a ruler and set square is needed, ensuring that the vents are correctly aligned and spaced. By establishing an accurate longitudinal centre line in the first instance, the rest of the job will be pretty straightforward. Marking out dimensions onto a strip of masking tape on a flat surface, then using the tape as a flexible tape measure, is a handy remedy to the challenge of working on a curved surface. It's a long time since I was last in a branch of IKEA, but the Swedish home furnishings store used to provide customers with paper rulers, which are perfect for tasks such as this, as are fabric tape measures available from craft stores and haberdasheries.

Gutter strips and destination-board brackets may also be required, with some kits presenting etched components or suggesting their creation with metal strip or wire. Raised or recessed panel seams may be a distinctive feature of your prototype and thin strips of insulating tape or plastic will assist with the former, while a scribing tool offers a likely solution for the latter. Remember, though, that all of the soldering tasks must be complete before introducing plastics or adhesives to the carriage.

With sheet metal, marking and drilling is easier to perform before the material has been profiled, with the detail components added later, once the roof has been installed. Extruded aluminium or cast metal roofs have enough strength to withstand drilling without the risk of distortion. However, if sheet brass or nickel silver has already been formed, it must be supported with a shaped wooden block to absorb the pressure of the drill.

Once the roof is ready for permanent installation, it can be carefully positioned and clamped to the body wherever possible (masking tape will suffice), as the roof needs to be soldered carefully in stages, working from the inside. Start with a small 'tack' bond in the centre of the roof's width at one end, before re-checking the alignment and 'tacking' at the opposite end. Ensure that the overhang (if there's meant to be one) is equal on both sides and ends,

If the roof is supplied in sheet-metal form, it is easier to mark out and drill any mounting holes for rooftop equipment before shaping. A scriber and centre punch will help with accuracy, working over a block of wood to avoid distortion. Roll the roof to the desired profile, keeping the rod parallel to the sides.

If the roof is to be affixed permanently, position it carefully atop the body, checking for an equal overhang on all sides (where appropriate) before 'tack' soldering the centre of one end. Recheck the alignment and 'tack' the other end, followed by each corner, and continuing along each side.

Make a final check before running more solder into the end joints, aided by plenty of flux. This will help to fill any gaps and create a super-strong bond. A scratch brush, files and abrasives will clean up any excess solder that seeps through to the exterior.

double-checking that the roof's profile is correct, before adding further 'tack' bonds in each corner and then at regular points along each side in turn.

It is not uncommon to be faced with gaps at the roof join, especially in the corners. These can be left for now and remedied with filler once the remaining solder assembly is complete, or a gap-filling solder employed to make the joints in the first place. This material will usually demand a higher working temperature, with the attendant risk of loosening previously soldered bonds on the carriage body. Furthermore, the solder will likely require fettling from the outside anyway, so its use doesn't offer the perfect short cut in comparison with epoxy putty as a filling agent.

In certain situations, installation of the roof may have to wait until most of the painting is complete and the interior and glazing has been fitted; yet there must be no unsightly gaps between roof and body. Therefore, any fettling must be done at an early stage, with the parts trial-fitted before painting commences. If the kit offers no facility for a bolt-on roof, the component will have to be glued in place and, in order to improve adhesion, a little modification may be necessary.

Much depends on the kit in question, but sometimes I find it helpful to fit a small bracket of brass or plastic angle (soldered or glued accordingly) along the inner edge of the roof, spaced to provide a snug fit inside the carriage sides. The depth of the bracket is dictated by the space available between the top of the sides and the top of the window aperture, allowing a few millimetres on the inside for the glazing to be secured.

As well as serving to strengthen the thin metal sides, guarding against the inward bowing that regular handling is likely to cause, the brackets also eliminate any daylight between the body and roof. Finally, once the model is ready to be sealed up, the brackets provide a convenient platform for a light coating of PVA (I use Glue 'n' Glaze clear glazing adhesive) to affect a temporary, easily broken bond. Of course, if the roof sits snugly with just a friction fit into the body, that may well be sufficient, depending on your operating needs.

AN EASIER WAY?

Some of you may be wondering why fitting a roof to a metal kit sounds so complicated. Surely, it's just a glorified lid on a box-type structure. Believe me, I've pondered this on many occasions, as I've faced more issues with roof–body joints than any other coach-building factors, especially as I prefer to keep my coach innards freely accessible.

Adapting the roof for bolt-on assembly is not so difficult, but it can be a real hassle in some cases. As always, much depends on the design of the kit. The MJT LNER carriage featured in this and the previous chapter is a perfect example of a car interior that can only be accessed via the roof. But, with no readily offered facility for a demountable roof, the modeller is left to come up with his/her own solution.

In many cases, I prefer to create mounting brackets from brass strip, formed to fit discreetly at each end of the carriage and possessing a captive nut arrangement that is bolted to the floor from the underneath. It's a simple enough affair that has proven more than adequate for almost any type of carriage, with the only sticking point (pun intended) being how to fix the upper section to the underside of the roof.

The MJT LNER carriage illustrated here, with its separate curved castings at each end, provides just enough white-metal onto which the brass can be soldered. However, aluminium can be a real pain to solder, so if the brackets have to join this material, I'll always opt for an epoxy glue bond. Roughing up the aluminium with coarse abrasives will improve the adhesive's grip.

Whatever form your mounting brackets take, drill the corresponding holes in the carriage floor slightly oversized, allowing a little room for adjustment as the roof is attached. It's often wise to add a washer between the bolt and the floor, to even out the pressure as the fastenings are secured. Either way, the bolts must only be tightened enough to bring the roof and body together and must not be used to close up any gaps between ill-fitting parts. Overtightening risks distortion to the underframe

Sometimes a roof is rendered in other materials or, as with this Hurst Models kit, a modified Lima Mk I roof was specified. The RTR roof was trimmed and shaped to slot inside each end.

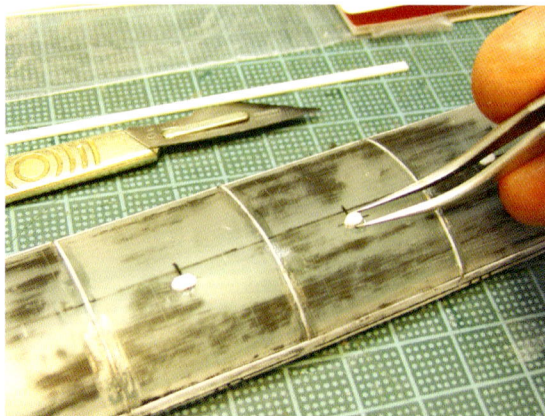

Having fettled the roof and ends to a near-perfect fit, the original roof fittings were replaced with scratch-built ventilators and raised beading, each being cut from plastic strip.

To ensure a snug interference fit within the brass shell, as well as offering the thin sides some extra strength, lengths of plastic strip were secured to the underside of the roof, spaced accurately so as not to distort the shell.

After painting and finishing, the roof proved a comfortable friction fit, with the toilet filling pipes also serving to keep the carriage intact. Inevitably a small gap remains at each end, but it shouldn't be too obvious.

Extruded aluminium sections are provided with MJT kits. They require cutting to the desired length (with a hacksaw in a mitre box) and, with this LNER coach, separate white-metal castings are needed to create the distinctive sloped ends.

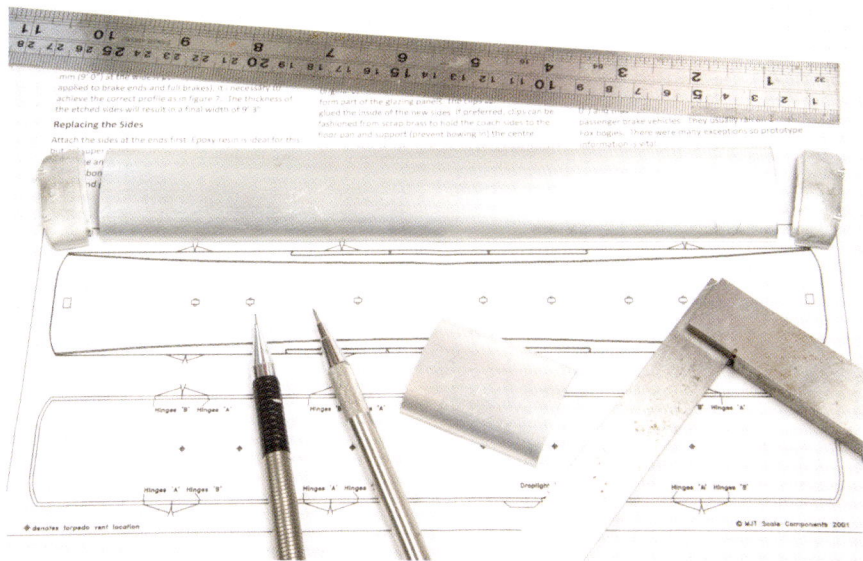

Having fixed the end castings with plenty of epoxy, the squeezed-out glue is smoothed over the top to fill any gaps. Once fully cured, the profile can be refined with files and abrasives. The locations of the vents are transferred from the supplied plans, punched and drilled out.

After a proving coat of grey primer, any blemishes in the roof surface are repaired before the vents are glued in position. Gutter strips are formed from thin strips of insulation tape and etched destination boards are fixed with Johnson Klear.

and roof, as well as damaging the mounting pillars, so be sure to fettle the roof and body to achieve a perfect fit beforehand.

Why don't kit makers offer a better solution in such instances? Rather than sit around moaning, however, I prefer to get on with the job and some potential remedies are outlined here, including the use of roofs salvaged from RTR models. If they're available cheaply and sport the correct profile, then why not make use of this time-saving – and weight-saving – option?

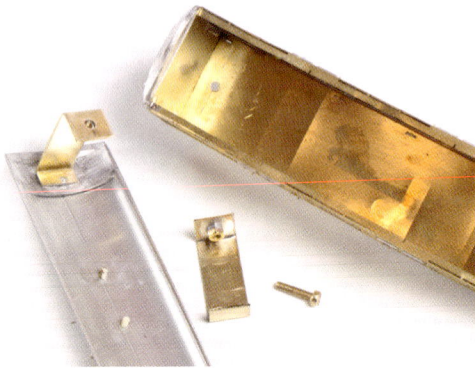

Improvised roof mounting brackets allow for ready interior access. Thick brass strip is ideal, folded so as to sit within the carriage ends and with nuts soldered to the lower brackets for bolting through holes in the floor. Here, the brackets have been soldered to the white-metal ends of the roof. Otherwise, epoxy glue would do the trick, especially when fixing to aluminium roofs.

RIGID BOGIES

As well as sourcing roofs and other bits and bobs from RTR models to supplement a metal kit, I'm also open to the possibility of employing plastic bogies (kits or RTR), albeit with some extra detail additions and refinements. A number of reasons have led to their use, either related to budget constraints, the desires of customers or the lack of suitable alternatives.

The need to make some weight savings has probably been the biggest reason, however. A typical pair of 'OO' gauge white-metal bogies will weigh in at a whopping 60g, as opposed to 30g for plastic equivalents. When coupled within a rake of predominantly plastic kit-built or RTR coaches, the heavier all-metal vehicle is likely to cause performance issues, especially on tight curves and points. Issues with the couplings may also arise due to the weight imbalance. As has already been mentioned, much depends on the demands of your own layout, rolling stock, traction and operating procedures.

As far as difficulty is concerned, there's not a great deal to worry about when building rigid (that is non-compensated) metal bogies. Following the same principles outlined back in Chapter 5, kits usually consist of a central frame, either as a main spreader-cum-bolster or as a fold-up arrangement that also incorporates the axle bearing points. All-white-metal bogie kits offer a hefty option, while brass or nickel silver frames are a more delicate

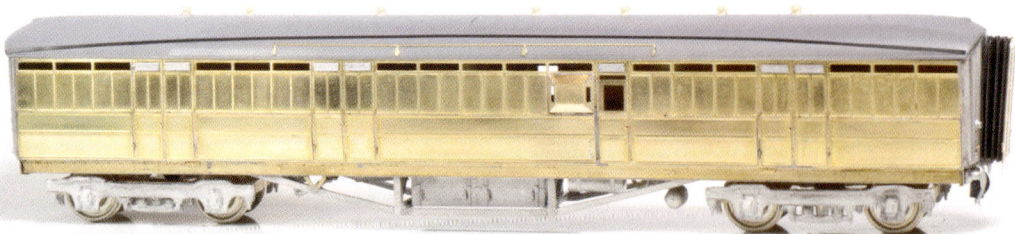

Fettle the roof for a perfect fit to the body and do not overtighten the mounting bolts, lest the brackets break away from the roof or the floor becomes distorted.

alternative, with detailed side overlays rendered in white-metal or, increasingly, resin.

Assembling bogies on a sheet of glass is recommended, helping to ensure that the axles and frames are square and true. The axles, wheels and flanges must have adequate clearance to turn freely without excess side-play. Being of an all-metal construction, there must be no danger of both wheels coming into contact with the frames. Insulating material is usually fitted between one wheel and the axle, so if the brake shoes or frame members are too close to the flanges, then both wheels will be energized, causing a short circuit in the track supply. Additionally, adequate clearance must be provided between the wheel flanges and the carriage floor and solebars, checking for free movement over the tightest curves on your layout.

All-white-metal bogie kits can be assembled with epoxy adhesive if desired, but low temperature solder will offer a far more resilient bond. Brass or nickel silver frames must be soldered, but white-metal overlays can either be glued or soldered according to taste. Before assembly commences, the pinpoint axle bearings must be installed. The mounting holes will likely require drilling or reaming out to the correct depth and diameter. Take care when working with a power drill in white-metal, as the heat created by the bit may damage the material. Set the drill to a slow speed if possible and add a drop of light oil to reduce friction.

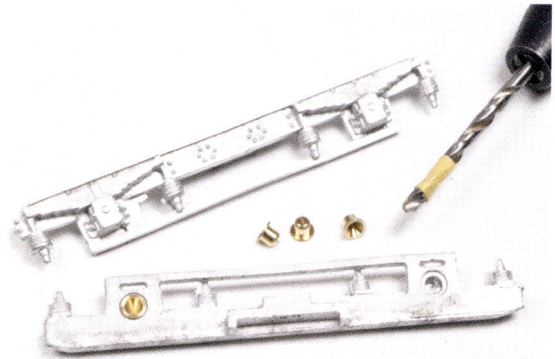

After cleaning up any flash, ensure that the white-metal bogie frames are straight and true. Bearing holes will need opening out with a hand drill, marking the necessary depth on the bit with tape to avoid cutting right through the frames. Glue (epoxy) or solder the bearings in position.

MIDDLE: 'Tin' both joint faces and fit one side to the central frame, using a set square to check for a perfect 90-degree angle and make a quick 'tack' solder bond. Recheck the alignment before making the bond permanent, adding plenty of flux and flooding the joint with 100°C solder. Make sure that the parts don't move before the solder cools completely.

BOTTOM: With the other side held loosely against the stretcher, place the axles into the bearings and, after checking for adequate side-play, free running and alignment, add flux and 'tack'-solder the frame in position. Work with the wheels on a sheet of glass to ensure all is square. Add more flux and flood the joint with solder.

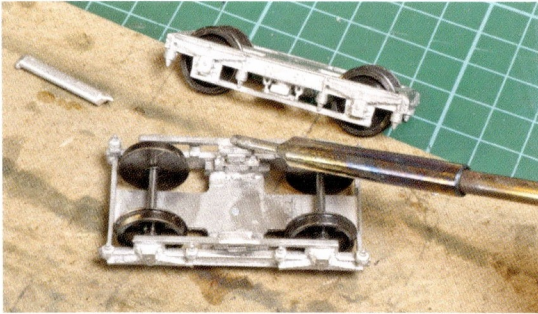

Add smaller detail parts, such as cross-members, suspension and brake gear with either solder or glue. If soldering, take care not to loosen the main structural solder bonds with further heating, employing a 70°C solder – having formed the main frames with 100°C solder – and lowering the temperature of the iron slightly.

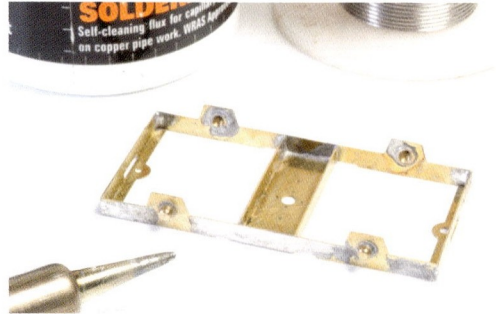

Rigid brass bogie frames are best fitted with bearings before folding up. The holes may need reaming to give the bearings a snug fit. Check that everything is square and true while soldering the inner corners to create a sturdy frame. 'Tin' the outer frames with 145°C solder, ready for the white-metal overlays.

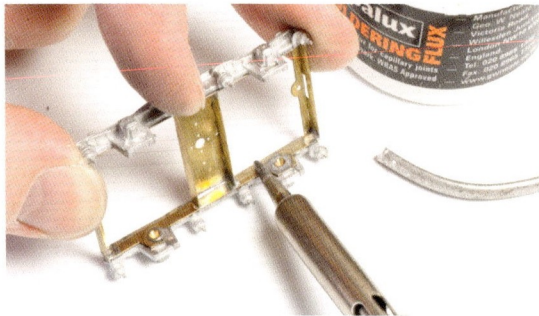

The overlays are also 'tinned', this time with 70°C or 100°C solder. Add more flux, clamp securely and sweat the parts together by applying heat from the inside, with the iron set to around 200–250°C. As soon as the solder between the parts begins to flow around the joint, remove the iron and allow the parts to cool undisturbed.

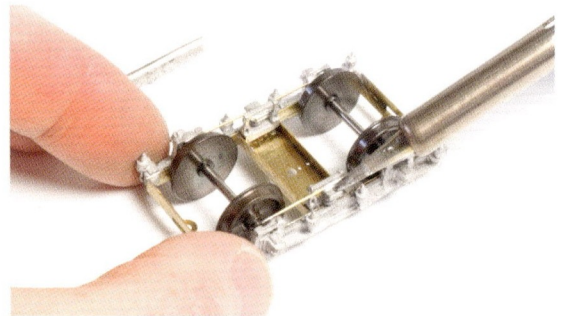

Gently pop the axles into the bearings and check for smooth running on a sheet of glass and a length of track. Fine details can be installed, such as suspension and brake gear, ensuring that nothing comes into contact with the wheels and flanges. A mix of white-metal and brass parts calls for lots of 'tinning' of each surface before the soldered bonds are made.

As demonstrated in the previous chapter, soldering white-metal to itself and other materials requires a temperature-controlled iron and a little extra effort, but is otherwise straightforward. The 'tinning' of all parts, and particularly unlike metals such as brass and nickel silver, with the appropriate solder formulas, is fundamental to success. Furthermore, cleaning away all traces of flux is of paramount importance, ensuring structural integrity for years to come. Pay special attention to the bearings, as flux residues often linger in the recesses and will prove corrosive to the pinpoint axles.

BOLSTERS

Most kits, be they complete carriages, underframes or bogies, will provide some form of bogie bolster arrangement. Designs vary, with some being glued, bolted or soldered to the underframe, with or without the need for separate shims, while the

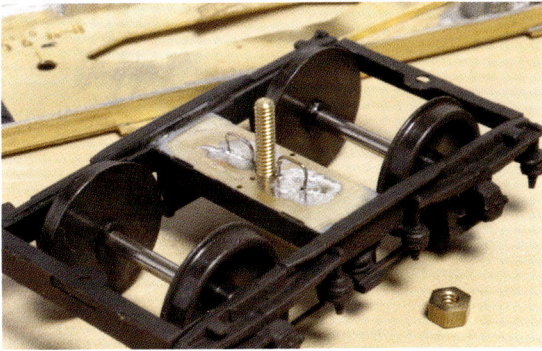

These No Nonsense Kits bogies feature a novel bolster arrangement, with a pair of wire hoop spacers soldered either side of the mounting bolt on one bogie and fore and aft of the bolt on the other, thus evening out any lateral forces (in theory at least). Setting the wire hoops at a uniform height is important and, frankly, can be a right pain.

The bolsters supplied with most cast metal bogies are simple to install to the underframe, either via drilled mounting holes, glue or solder. Test-fit the bogies and check the ride height, adding plastic shims if necessary (I've used 60 thou' plastic card here).

matching bearing plates may be formed integrally to the main bogie frames, or added from separate components. I've come across some weird and wonderful takes on a seemingly simple principle, involving folded-up, half moon-shaped brass bearers, metal washers and even wire hoops. Whatever is provided in your kit, there's usually the facility for some fine-tuning, as gaining the correct ride height is of the greatest import.

Another vital factor is a degree of free vertical movement around the pivot bolster, as well as rotational freedom, with sufficient clearance for the wheel flanges beneath the underframe. The need for model carriages to cope with un-prototypically sharp track curvature often leads to slightly underscale wheels being installed as a compromise. The kit's instructions should advise on the subject of recommended wheel sizes.

When the time comes for final assembly, the bogies can be fastened just enough to keep them in position without impairing the rotational or lateral swing. Add a couple of drops of Loctite onto the bolts to prevent them wearing loose in service.

RIGHT: **Plastic kit-built or RTR bogies are an option worth considering, not least as a weight-saving measure. These Ian Kirk bogies boast an impressive level of surface relief and, once extra brake gear has been installed, will look the part. Note the round Southern Pride bolsters and brass fastening bolts, as well as the Keen Systems close-coupling unit.**

COMPENSATION

There's no doubting that a well-built compensated chassis or bogie offers a far superior ride than rigid bogies or axles. Compensated carriages fairly glide along the rails, taking any humps and bumps in their stride. In theory, they should be less prone to derailments and couplings tend to function more reliably (especially finer options such as the Spratt & Winkle and Alex Jackson types). The track needs to be equally well built, however; working suspensions should not be expected to compensate for poorly laid permanent way.

If you're prepared to put in a little extra time and effort, there's no reason why adding compensation should be too onerous a task. Repetition certainly speeds up the process and good design on the part of the kit maker definitely helps. There are plenty of fiddly and frustrating options out there, especially in 2mm, 3mm and 4mm scales, but there are also some simple yet highly effective products too.

I've been fitting MJT Carriage Compensation Units (CCUs) to most of my kit-built and scratch-built coaches for the past decade and been very happy with the results. Formed of two separate sections, plus an independent central bolster, the CCUs offer a gentle amount of flex, allowing each axle to pitch up and down and absorb any irregulari-ties in the track. Other than threading a length of brass wire through each section, there is nothing remotely fiddly about them. After making a few mistakes on the first unit, the rest proved plain sailing and I can knock the things out in about half an hour these days – about the same time as it takes to build a rigid metal bogie kit, in fact.

In contrast, compensated bogies from the likes of Bill Bedford or Model Railway Developments feature individually sprung pinpoint bearings that slide up and down the axleguards, just like the real thing. Some brands also feature secondary suspension, with springs mounted over the central bolster too. Such products inevitably demand more time and patience from the builder and the painting and weathering stages must not clog up the working surfaces, lest the moving parts be impaired. That said, the extra effort is rewarded with greatly enhanced performance, especially for those working in the finer scales, with hand-built trackwork.

Some form of compensation is particularly recommended for fixed-axle stock, especially long-wheelbase and six-wheel vehicles, whose reliability will be greatly improved. The Bill Bedford components showcased here offer a satisfying assembly project, with the reward of the model operating in a similar fashion to the real thing. As always, by following the supplied instructions carefully there is very little to worry about, save for preventing ingress of paint into the moving parts while the model is being finished.

Compensation systems are available in bogie and fixed-axle format and vary in their design and operation. MJT, Model Railway Developments, Comet and Bill Bedford are just some of the many suppliers who offer effective solutions.

MJT's Coach Compensation Units (CCUs) are perhaps the most straightforward of compensated bogie kits. Erected in two halves per bogie, the various bearing and wire suspension holes require reaming out before shaping and assembly.

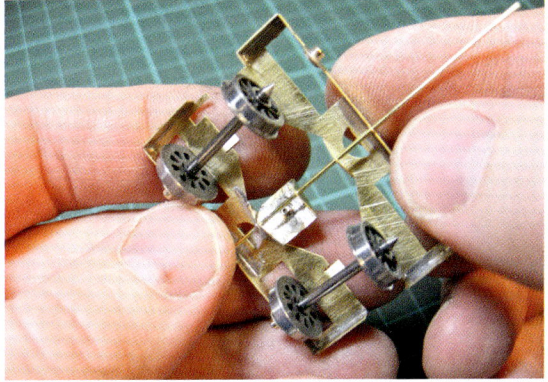

Standard brass wire is inserted into one half of the bogie and secured to the mounting brackets. The female element of a press-stud is then soldered to the central bolster unit, which is also threaded onto the wire, followed by the other bogie frame and axles.

RIGHT: **Working on a flat surface, check that the axles are aligned and, with a fractional amount of slack between the three frame elements, solder the wire to the other bogie frame. The male press-stud is secured to a bolster bracket, which is fixed to the underframe. Once everything is satisfactory, the excess wire can be snipped away and the bogie sides prepared for the overlays.**

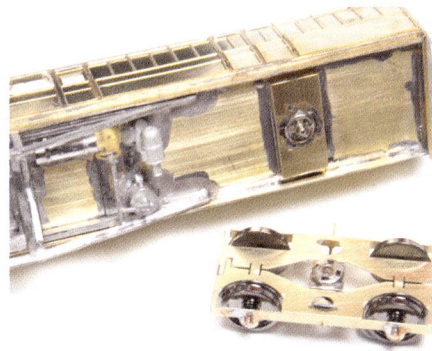

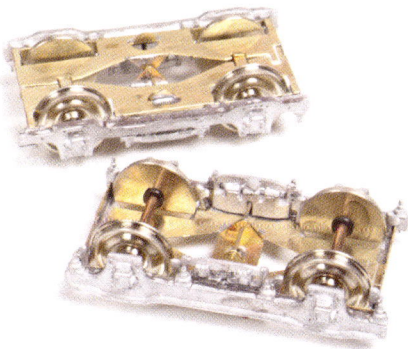

I prefer to fix the bogie overlays to CCUs with epoxy rather than solder, lest the pivoting wire be disturbed. Open out the inner faces to clear the bearings. Note that no cross-member overlays are installed, as the halves of the CCU must be allowed to flex freely.

Suspension systems for fixed axles come in a variety of forms. This is a MARC Models version, with each axleguard unit pivoting on a central bracket, with a length of brass wire acting as a retaining pin and soldered to the protruding prongs from the lower bracket. Smear a little Vaseline onto the axleguard to avoid excess solder impairing the free movement of the parts.

While the axle is allowed to pivot vertically, the fixed solebars and axleboxes must be milled out to give clearance to the pinpoint bearings.

This alternative, and more prototypical, compensation system is from the Bill Bedford range and involves the bearings being fitted to brackets that slide within the axleguards. Springing is provided by fine steel wire (guitar strings).

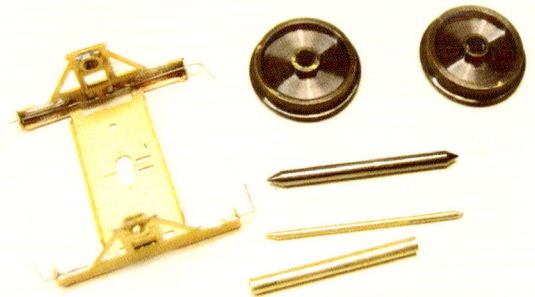

Care is needed during painting to avoid clogging the axleguard slots with excess paint. The bearings are designed to move freely in the slots, aided by a little light grease. The vehicle demands a certain amount of ballast for the suspension system to operate successfully but, once set up correctly, the ride quality is superb.

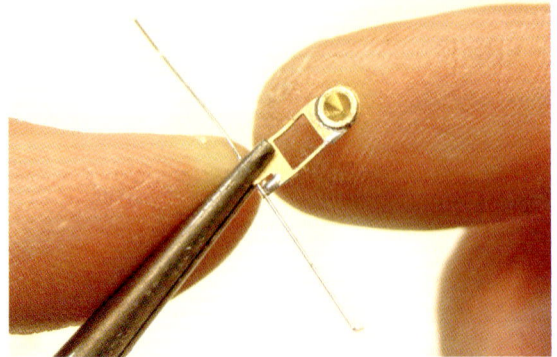

For six-wheel stock, it helps for the central axle to possess a degree of extra side-play, allowing the vehicle to cope with tight curves. Creating a hollow axle from brass tube, with a loose inner axle, is a simple but highly effective solution. For this 'OO' coach, the outer axle is formed from 2mm brass tube, with the inner axle formed from 1mm brass rod.

LEFT: Form the pinpoint ends of the inner axle by mounting the rod in a mini-drill and turn it against a file and successive grades of abrasive until a smooth, sharp point is created. Take care to ensure that the overall length of the axle matches the other two wheelsets (typically 26mm in 'OO').

Push the wheels onto the hollow axle, setting the back-to-back measurement and ensuring that they sit concentrically to the axle. Also, check that the insulation washer is not compromised or short circuits will occur. Add a drop of light oil onto the inner axle and slide it into the tube. If brake gear is to be installed, sufficient space will be required to allow for the sideways movement of the wheels.

RIGHT: *A more resilient, and refined, option is to drill holes in the bogie frames and solebars and add brass wire to the boards to act as mounting brackets. Some kits provide footboards with integral mounting brackets that simply require folding up and soldering to the solebars.*

Footsteps are typically formed from hefty timber boards on the real thing and plastic strip can be ideal for replicating these features.

LOOKING AHEAD

The fact that I've devoted the best part of three chapters of this book to the tenets of soldering and working with different metals is a clue to their significance in carriage kit building. Taking the time to assimilate this information and, more importantly, to consolidate these fundamental practical techniques will pay dividends; the best way of doing this is through practice, practice and yet more practice.

Honing your skills on scrap materials or spare parts avoids the stress of working on an expensive kit. Asking around your local club or browsing swap-meets will likely turn up one or two unwanted or incomplete metal kits. Forget about whether it's in your scale or your area of interest – just try building it anyway.

With the rough handling out of the way, smaller parts can be safely installed at this point, such as buffers and brake gear. Once all soldering tasks are completed, the model must be cleansed thoroughly of all flux residues and debris before any remaining details are installed with cyano or epoxy adhesive.

CHAPTER THIRTEEN

DOING IT YOURSELF

Scratch-building refers to the process of creating something out of nothing, usually by crafting most or all of the separate components ourselves. Going to such extreme lengths may be the only route to achieving an accurate replica of a particular carriage in a specific scale. Scratch-building may not entail constructing the entire vehicle. Indeed, it may be a means to creating part of a bodyshell, underframe or even just an individual component.

Building complete carriages from scratch is not something to undertake lightly, especially if multiple vehicles are envisaged. It's not impossible, though, and I've been lucky enough to come across some truly wonderful scratch-built coaches over the years. Most notably, when I was a conservator at the National Railway Museum, an 'EM' gauge recreation of Queen Victoria's train found its way onto my workbench. Damaged after returning from loan, the models needed a little tender loving care and it was an honour to work on such exquisitely crafted models.

Built by the late Cliff Newell, the bodyshells were surprisingly rendered in plastic, being lami-nated from various thicknesses of Plastikard. Some years later, I found a series of articles by Cliff in *Model Railway Constructor* describing his building process in detail: I'd recommend any interested readers to track down the relevant back issues (*see* Bibliography). Not surprisingly, it apparently took a decade to produce the whole train, although he created a number of jigs and formers to aid the process and ensure consistency.

The plastic bodyshells were carefully designed with an in-built resistance to warping. Sensibly, the underframes and bogies were constructed from brass and nickel silver, with many common parts being reproduced as castings, such as the side over-lays for the bogies. The masters for these were scratch-built from metal and the castings made with Plastic Padding, a car-body filling compound.

The interiors were fully furnished, which, being a replica of a royal train, was no small feat. Interior lighting was also installed, taking power from the compensated axles; in my youthful ignorance, I hadn't expected such things in models built in the 1970s.

This exquisite rendition of Queen Victoria's Royal Train in 'EM' gauge was entirely scratch-built, including the locomotive, by Cliff Newell. I was lucky enough to be tasked with repairing a number of the vehicles during my time at the National Railway Museum and they offered plenty of inspiration for my own scratch-building efforts. PHOTO COURTESY OF MODEL RAIL MAGAZINE

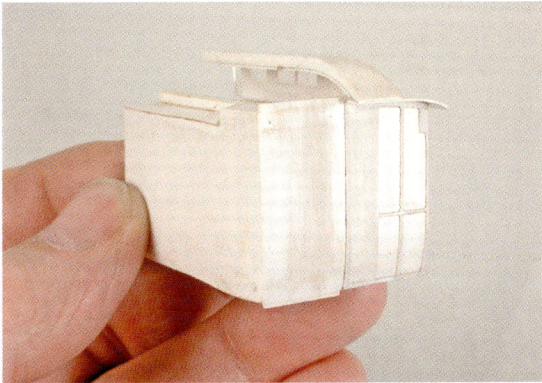

The carriages were constructed from laminated plastic card, with a punch system devised for creating the panelled overlays, as this mock-up section illustrates. Careful design meant that the bodyshells were incredibly strong and resistant to warping. PHOTO COURTESY OF MODEL RAIL MAGAZINE

The effect of the layered construction evoked the appearance of the real things perfectly, even before one considers the exquisite livery application and lining. Working interior lights also allowed the handcrafted interiors to be appreciated. PHOTO COURTESY OF MODEL RAIL MAGAZINE

TO SCRATCH-BUILD?

That is, indeed, a good question. This is a potentially massive subject, but the following pages will showcase a range of techniques, materials and tools that can help you tackle subjects that may prove difficult by any other means.

The issue of building your own chassis is a subject that I'm often asked about. It can be an enjoyable and rewarding exercise, whether starting from scratch or making use of the many 'universal' etched underframe kits that are available for most scales. Many of these 'kits' can be adapted to suit particular vehicles and avoid the hassle of cutting sheet metal to a particular size and length.

Economy is an important factor to consider, both in terms of time and financial outlay. Making your own castings can offer savings in both, although the need to craft a master and moulds, as well as obtaining the necessary casting materials, will require a significant initial investment. Various materials can be employed for certain tasks, including plastic, wood and metal. If more than one vehicle is to be built, creating a series of jigs and building aids will make life much easier and the results more consistent.

Coach sides in particular can be a tricky prospect, with countless apertures to form and door seams to scribe. Commissioning brass or nickel silver etches, or perhaps laser-cut wood or plastic components, is worth considering. As has already been described, 3D printing is proving popular for such situations. The cost of designing and production work is much lower these days, thanks to modern technology, and you can always try to sell

Metals and plastics are available in a vast range of sheets, sections, strips, rods and tubes. Albion Alloys, K&S Metals, Evergreen and Slater's Plastikard products are available from most good model shops.

any surplus stock to fellow enthusiasts as a way of covering your costs.

Whichever way you decide to progress, careful planning and research is essential. Take the time to draw up a list of the necessary parts, with all scale dimensions worked out and with an idea of how the parts will fit together. It will be worth mocking up a few prototypes in order to trial your design for strength and reliability, as well as prototype accuracy.

Plastic is a great material to work with, but it does have its drawbacks. I was thrilled with a fleet of Warflat wagons that I built from plastic sheet and strip over a decade ago but, after storage in various sheds and attics, some of them have now taken on a warped appearance. If the upper side of the wagon's floor could have been braced in a similar way to the underneath, things wouldn't have been so bad.

START WITH THE FOUNDATIONS

Building a chassis from scratch may appear daunting, but it's actually a less complicated prospect than tackling a bodyshell. DIY underframes may be required to upgrade a RTR model, to enhance a fairly rudimentary offering contained within a plastic kit, or to form the basis of a completely hand-built vehicle.

The importance of rigidity is a common factor to consider, whatever the intended use for an underframe. Unless the frames and floor are concentric then the running characteristics will be less than reliable. Bogie vehicles demand a high degree of square-ness in the chassis, or the carriage is likely to lean or wobble awkwardly while in transit. Articulated bogies may cope with any slight unevenness, but they can't compensate for an inferior chassis.

Although the aforementioned Mr Newell had well-founded doubts about hand-built plastic underframes, it's not impossible to use this material, as long as a few precautions are taken. Styrene is a material sensitive to fluctuations in temperature or humidity, with shrinkage and warping a real possibility, especially with long-wheelbase vehicles. In the past, I've built a number of vehicles from styrene sheet and section that have looked great for a year

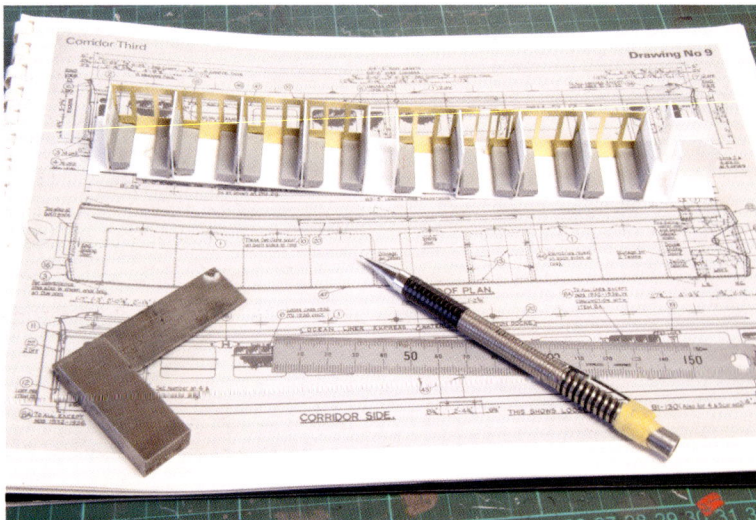

Although the seats and corridor partitions are from the trade, the rest of this interior has been built from scratch, using plastic card. Interiors offer the perfect subject for a first foray into scratch-building.

or two but, after longer periods stored in the attic, some of them have warped badly.

A well-built plastic bodyshell can counteract contraction and expansion in a plastic chassis. Indeed, I can vouch for the use of plastic for the underframes of four- and six-wheel vans and carriages, but I've yet to employ the same methods with total success on longer bogie stock.

Employing thick plastic for the main chassis structure is preferred, especially where the chunky profile of such parts can be disguised. It is for a good reason that RTR and kit manufacturers mould their underframes in generous thicknesses, save for the more decorative features, and we ought to follow suit if possible. Finer profile material can then be installed for more visible areas, such as the solebars and trussing, with less expectation of them providing the resilience and stability to the chassis that their real-life counterparts do. Incidentally, if your prototype vehicle featured timber frames, then plastic strip can be subtly distressed with a steel brush and abrasives to give a textured surface (as was shown in Chapter 6).

For steel-framed carriages, shallow 'C' channel section, as offered by Evergreen, is ideal for solebars, although it may need some discreet strengthening in certain areas, depending on the facets of your particular model. Small right-angle plastic section is an ideal reinforcing medium that will back up the inner faces of the headstocks in particular. This will be essential if fitting heavy cast-metal buffers and, particularly, if employing scale couplings that will put significant pressure on the bufferbeams.

If a bodyshell is not to be glued permanently to the plastic underframe, the chassis will benefit from the addition of longitudinal ribs on the upper surface of the floor to counteract the twisting forces on the underside. Further integrity can be added by fixing the interior floor, seating, corridors and bulkheads to the underframe.

As for plastic bogie frames, they'll also need to be thick enough to remain rigid and free from distortion, with cross-members helping to keep them straight and true and a sturdy bolster to take the weight of the carriage above it. A decent amount of mass is desired to help keep the wheels on the rails, especially as they encounter curves and points.

There's certainly plenty of choice amongst off-the-shelf bogie kits in plastic, brass and white-metal, as well as RTR units offered as cheap spares from the likes of Bachmann. These may not meet your criteria in terms of high levels of detail, but they can be readily modified and upgraded. As we've already mentioned, kit and RTR manufacturers employ a tougher grade of plastic for their bogies, suggesting that the commonly available styrene scratch-building materials may not be entirely suitable for the purpose.

Fixed axle carriages and vans also have their demands, as the interface of the metal axles and bearings with the plastic is of vital importance. Again, the use of tough plastic like ABS and butyrate by commercial manufacturers reveals the need for a level of resilience that styrene can't match, so substituting another material for the axleguards is recommended. White-metal and brass axleguards are freely available, so it makes sense to employ this type of component within your plastic underframe. Besides, the extra weight of metal parts will mean that less additional ballast will have to be squeezed into the interior to get the vehicle up to the necessary mass.

PLASTIC SHELLS

As the bodyshell is probably the most prominent part of any model carriage, getting it to look right is crucial. Arguably, it's the most challenging aspect of a scratch-building project, equalled only by the bogies. Getting the sides, ends and roof shaped correctly and consistently, then joining them squarely is no mean feat. Moreover, cutting out the various windows and the rendering of any planked or panelled bodywork will require hours of marking, cutting and fettling.

Laminating the sides from several layers of styrene provides greater strength and is particularly suited to panelled stock. This approach also offers the opportunity for fitting near-flush glazing. By cutting the apertures on the lowermost layer slightly oversize, handy recesses are created in which to secure the glazing material. The 'glass' will then appear set back from the outer surface just enough to appear realistic.

Another benefit of a multi-layered approach is to refine the window apertures by means of individual frame overlays. Either hand cut or commissioned as fine etched metal or laser-cut components, they'll ensure a consistent appearance across the carriage. There are plenty of sources of bespoke etching and laser cutting services, who will be able to offer quotations based on your specifications (see Useful Addresses).

As with a kit, having each of the main components fully formed 'in the flat' will make them easier to handle and work on. Creating the sides and ends, with all profile shaping complete and apertures and door seams created, allows them to be married up in a simple jig. Once the shell is assembled, perhaps with the roof fitted now (and the chassis bolted on later), it should be strong enough to withstand careful handling while the smaller details are installed and the painting is carried out.

WORKING WITH PLASTIC

Styrene sheet and section is certainly a rewarding material to work with. Cutting, shaping and bonding is easy and very few tools or expensive workshop aids are required. As well as cutting or filing parts to shape, it can also be manipulated with hot water.

Forming roof panels or body sides to the necessary profile can be achieved by immersing sheet styrene in a bath of hot water for a few minutes and then lashing it around a suitably prepared former that is close to the desired curvature. Once cooled, the parts ought to be assembled as soon as possible.

The roof will need to be formed from material of a decent thickness, say at least 40thou' for 4mm scale models. It will also demand plenty of internal support, in terms of contact area with the sides and ends for the adhesive to work on, and also along its length, to maintain an even contour and resist any twisting or warping forces over time. Incorporating internal bulkheads and partitions as part of the main

fabric of the bodyshell, rather than as a separate, removable interior, is an effective option.

Marking out the components on flat sheet material demands a high degree of accuracy, as is common to all materials. Rendering visible markings is not so easy, however, without recourse to a fine permanent-ink pen. More preferable is a sharp scriber tool that will also be effective for locating centre lines, datums and hole positions, being far more accurate than pens or pencils. Always check that your reference edge is square and straight, as

Marking out sheet plastic demands precision. A sharp scriber is preferred to pencils and a dark enamel wash will highlight the lines clearly. With underframes, mark out the centre lines and wheelbase at an early stage to help with positioning subsequent components.

A profile cutter is less prone to wandering away from the straight edge and will form squarer edges, demanding less fettling later. Make several passes with the tool before the plastic is snapped apart.

To help file the edges to their exact dimensions, while keeping the edges square, create a simple 'shooting board' from a scrap of plywood or MDF. A strip wood fence will keep the parts at 90 degrees to the edge.

For smaller parts, such as lengths of plastic strip or section, a craft guillotine is a handy tool, especially one with the ability to cut at a variety of angles. This device was obtained from Expo Tools.

To keep the plastic chassis flat during assembly, screw it to a strip of MDF or plywood. Fix the solebars and headstocks, using a set square to ensure that they are straight and true. Evergreen $\frac{1}{8}$in-wide 'C' channel is the perfect size for carriage and van solebars in 'OO'. I like to reinforce my headstocks with strips of right-angle section on the inside.

With the basic frame complete and the parts cured, key mechanical parts can be installed. These white-metal axleguard and suspension units have been fitted with brass bearings and fixed to the chassis (use epoxy or thick cyano), taking great care with their alignment. As the assembly jig is small and lightweight, the entire thing can be tipped over and the chassis tested on a sheet of glass, as demonstrated in earlier chapters.

sheets of plastic card are seldom cut with the edges true.

Cutting the material also demands a careful approach and a profile cutter is preferred to a regular scalpel or knife. With a hooked blade, profile cutters are drawn towards the user and the blade will follow the edge of a steel ruler more reliably than a knife. After several passes, a trough begins to form. Cutting should cease just before the blade pierces the underside of the plastic. There will be a small burr on the

TOP: *Once free of the assembly jig, the upper side of the chassis has been reinforced with similar sizes of plastic strip. This should avoid any issues of warping in the future, with the bodyshell also offering extra rigidity once it has been fitted. A flat steel bar provides the necessary ballast, fixed with epoxy.*

LEFT: *The various underframe fittings can now be installed. Note that the battery boxes and fusebox have been salvaged from a scrap RTR chassis, while everything else has been assembled from proprietary detailing parts or stock materials.*

Prior to the Invicta/Bachmann release of a RTR Mk1 CCT, modellers wanting a high-fidelity rendition had to set about scratch-building a new chassis for the rather primitive Lima model.

edge that can be dressed flush with a broad, flat file and some blocks of wood mounted in a vice can help to achieve a square edge.

Cutting rod, tube, strip and section is best undertaken with a mini-mitre box and a sharp razor saw, to help get the cuts at the correct angle and to minimize the amount of fettling required before assembly. A craft guillotine, as offered by Expo Tools, is also of great assistance, especially when many parts have to be fabricated, with varying angles to be cut cleanly and accurately.

Drilling out holes can be aided by working over a block of hardwood or thick plywood to absorb the pressure of the drill bit and prevent distortion. Punching the centre of each hole keeps the drill bit from wandering off course and cutting each hole before assembly begins is often more convenient, certainly in terms of clamping the parts safely.

One final piece of advice regarding the use of plastics: always store scratch-built plastic vehicles in a stable environment, free of fluctuating temperatures and humidity levels, just to be on the safe side.

Taking inspiration from those wonderful Cliff Newell carriages, my plastic bodyshells are built up over several layers, starting with a base formed from 30 thou' sheet. The apertures are marked out with a scribing template (as seen in Chapter 8) to ensure consistency. Holes are drilled near each corner and the bulk of the waste cut away.

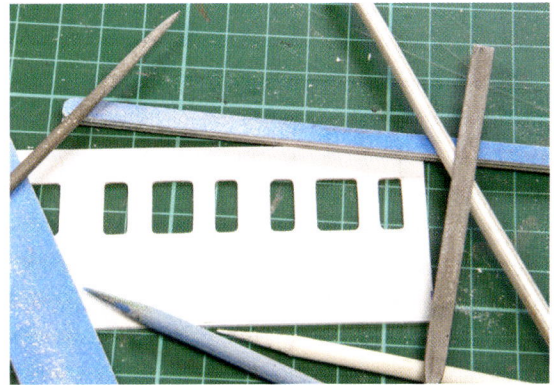

The openings are then formed to the correct dimensions with files and Albion Alloys' sanding needles and sticks.

The base layer is then backed up with thicker material, such as 40 or 60 thou' sheet, leaving clearance around the banks of windows for the glazing to be inserted later. Clamping the sides to an MDF jig will ensure that everything stays straight and true.

When the cement has cured, the side can be flipped over and any necessary profiling attended to with sanding pads. Cut a profile template from wood, card or plastic to act as a guide, ensuring a consistent profile along the whole length of each side.

For the outer layer of beading, I drew up some plans and sent them off to York Modelmaking for laser cutting in 10 thou'-thick Mylar (including recessed door seams). The overlays can then be carefully aligned and secured with liquid poly cement, clamping with masking tape, especially along the curved lower edges.

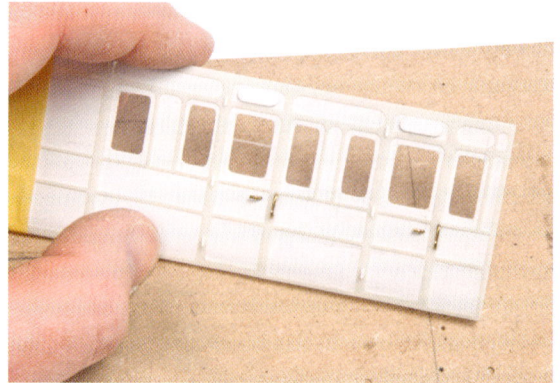

Once extra details have been added, such as door vent panels, hinges, handrails and door handles, the carriage sides soon come to life. The ends are treated in exactly the same way.

For flush-sided carriages, the process is simpler, with single layers of 40 or 60 thou' sheet pierced for the window apertures and profiled as necessary. Custom-etched metal window frames are then installed for a touch of finesse.

METAL

Brass and nickel silver offer a more reliable foundation for a model, although the benefits come at a price in terms of cost and difficulty. Freely available in sheet form, rod and various 'C', 'H' and 'L' sections, once soldered together, a strong, rigid vehicle can be produced.

The need for accurate marking out is important and metal will demand more in the way of scribing and punching. Creating clear lines to work to is essential and the use of sharp tools and a weathering wash (or engineers' blue) to aid identification will make the task less onerous. Cutting sheet metal can be effected with heavy-duty shears or a fret saw, with the edges dressed squarely with a flat file.

In common with plastic underframes, the need for the chassis to be absolutely true is paramount and sturdy plywood assembly jigs are essential. With all the 'gubbins' being fitted to the underside, there's a risk of the floor section being distorted unless it is kept flat against the work surface. Therefore, fixing the floor to the jig with a couple of round-headed screws helps enormously. Plan ahead and site these mounting holes so they can be reused to fix the body or bogies later.

Furthermore, marking and drilling all necessary holes before assembly begins is heartily recommended, both in terms of convenience and accuracy. A fine centre punch, tapped lightly with a pin hammer, will guide the drill. It is important to work with the sheet metal over a tough timber background to avoid distortion. If the metal does kink or twist, hammer it flat again on a small anvil

Brass underframes benefit from erection on a plywood or MDF assembly jig. Drill fixing holes strategically so that they can be reused for mounting the body or bogies later. For this 'OO' underframe, 10 thou' sheet brass is being employed and, just like the plastic chassis, $\frac{1}{8}$in 'C' channel forms the solebars, tack soldered to begin with while alignment checks are made, before the joints are made permanent.

block. Beware, though, that this may cause the edges of the metal to spread out, so be prepared to dress them square again before assembly.

A small bench drill press is preferable for this work, greatly increasing accuracy and reducing the risk of deformation. Apertures are most likely to be needed for the buffers, drawhooks, bogie mounts and certain underframe fittings such as a dynamo, depending on the detail parts to be installed.

Once a metal underframe has been assembled, with solebars, bufferbeams and the relevant trussing arrangement, an incredibly strong and rigid construction will be produced. Accurately cut and jointed components are vital as although solder provides a resilient bond, it has little in the way of mechanical strength. Ideally the parts must all be carefully fettled for a close fit.

In common with forming body sides, fabricating bogie frames from sheet metal takes time and a high degree of accuracy. Ensuring that the axles will be mounted squarely is of paramount importance, so the marking out, drilling and cutting stages are vital. The frames need only be basic in nature, as the prototype realism will be added with the side overlays. However, we need to make sure that most of the side frames will be hidden once these overlays have been installed, so some forethought at the design stage is necessary.

A razor saw and mitre box combine to form accurate components from stock materials.

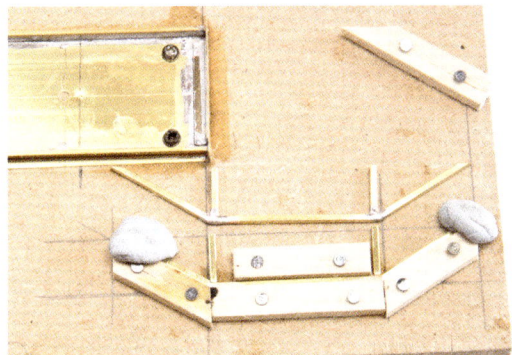

Headstocks are formed from thin strip, reinforced with brass angle, while the trussing is made up from $\frac{1}{16}$in square tubing. A simple assembly guide ensures that the parts are held still during soldering and that the trusses match exactly.

Another simple aid ensures that the truss components are shaped correctly, allowing the file to work at the desired angle.

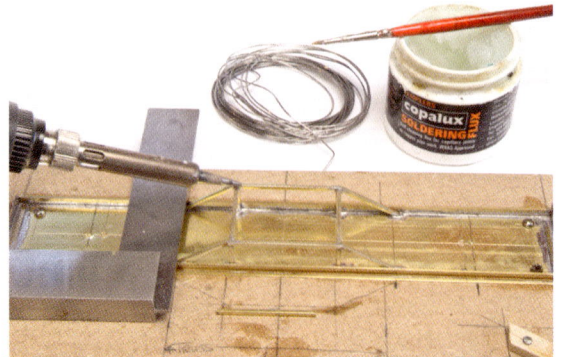

Once the pair of trusses has been installed, cross-members can be cut and fitted. Although the underframe began with a flimsy sheet of 10 thou' brass, it will now be surprisingly strong.

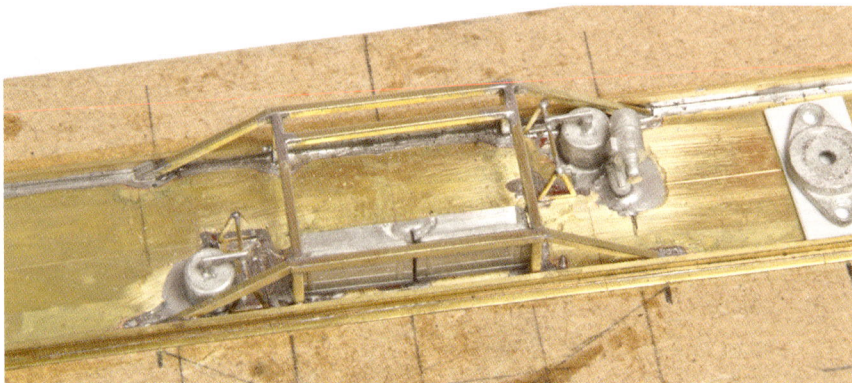

With the main fabric complete, the smaller details can be installed, using parts fabricated or from the trade.

As already mentioned, there are so many excellent bogie kits available from the trade to make this part of a project far more achievable, with less stress and hassle. At times, though, I do like to make my own overlays, especially when building something rather obscure. After all, I often only need to build one to act as a master, with the rest cast in resin.

Bolsters for the bogies to rotate on are simple affairs. They provide clearance and a bearing surface, with a mounting hole drilled in the centre for the bogie to be retained via a nut and bolt. Again, off-the-shelf parts are freely available in a range of materials, but a square, round or rectangular pad of metal or plastic will suffice, suitably shaped to allow whatever bogie you're employing to move freely in terms of rotation as well as a little vertical play. Even

a couple of steel or brass washers can be effective.

The necessary ride height of the chassis over the bogies will have to be ascertained before the height of the bolsters can be finalized. Leave adequate clearance for the wheel flanges while checking the height above the rail to see that the vehicle stands at the correct scale height and the buffers and gangway align with other stock.

Metal bodyshells are easy enough to fabricate, in terms of the sides, ends and roof, even if the prototype incorporates a curved profile. What isn't straightforward is the forming of the various apertures and door seams. That's what etching was invented for! If you are still keen on forming your own body, the windows will have to be cut with extreme care to avoid distorting the sides. Thicker material will be more appropriate in this case. Indeed, a tougher material all round, such as nickel silver, would be better suited and drilling and cutting with a fretsaw is likely to take many, many hours. It's best to undertake this before the sides have been cut from the sheet, thus offering even more support for the metal while it's in the vice.

Some other points to bear in mind include the fact that the sides, if rendered in thin metal or plastic, are liable to distortion unless reinforced. This may take the form of interior bulkheads fitted direct to the body or as a set of longitudinal members, at the top and bottom edges, that can act as locating aids for the roof and floor. As carriages are likely to be picked up and handled in the centre of the body, resistance to compression forces is essential.

The availability of extruded aluminium roofs, from the likes of MJT, to suit a variety of prototype profiles, takes away much of the hard work without compromising the scratch-built nature of a model. If the right shape, scale or size is not available, some recourse to shaping sheet brass will be required.

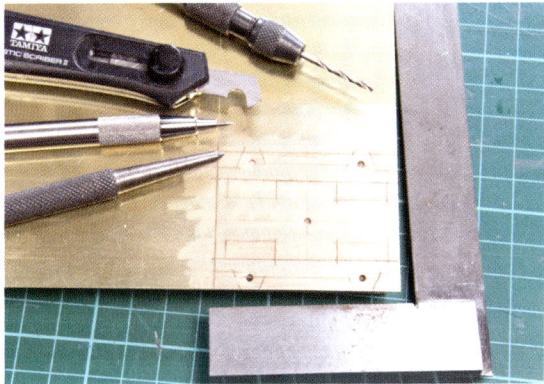

As with sheet plastic, the brass was marked out with a scriber and weathering wash. It's best to drill any holes before the parts are cut from the sheet, using a centre punch to mark the locations precisely.

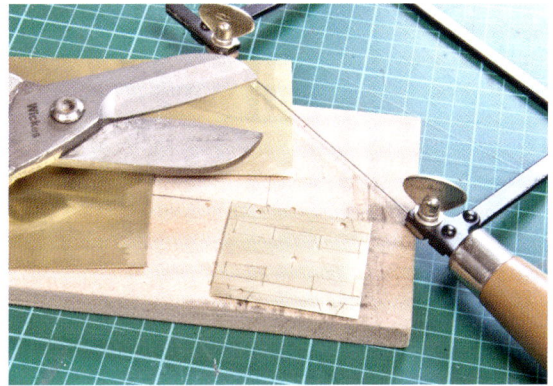

A set of good-quality, heavy-duty metal shears will make easy work of thin brass and the long jaws allow straight lines to be formed. Just watch that the material doesn't curl, by applying minimal pressure.

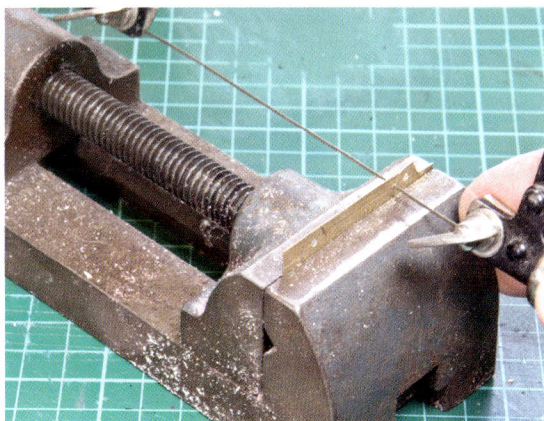

For intricate shapes and for reaching into awkward spaces, a fret saw is the answer. It'll be hard to keep exactly to a straight line with such a fine blade, however.

Use files to take the material back to the final dimensions and ensure straight, square edges. For captive areas, such as the flangeways on this bogie frame, drill a couple of access holes and pass the fretsaw blade through to cut away most of the waste, finishing the job with files.

To create effective fold lines, use a profile cutter to scribe wide troughs on the inside face of the fold.

Mount the frame securely in a vice or Hold 'n' Fold and form the fold gently with a straight edge used as a lever.

LEFT: **Push in a set of axle bearings and add the wheels. A wheelbase gauge ensures correct spacing and alignment. When you are happy that all is well, solder the bearings into place from the outside.**

BELOW: **Bolsters for the bogies are not too difficult to make, but I had these white-metal castings knocking around, shimmed with plastic card in order to give the correct ride height and fixed with epoxy.**

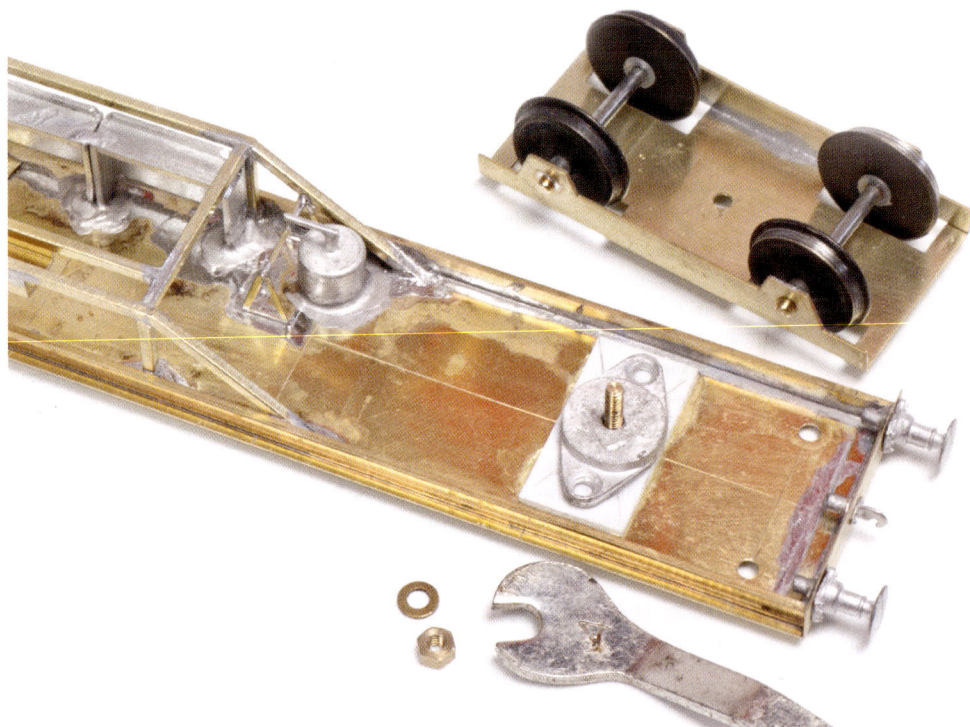

After an enjoyable afternoon's work, the sturdy underframe is ready to receive its bodywork. There's something extremely rewarding about this sort of modelling and, despite the initial outlay on stock materials and tools, it can also be economical.

While there's plenty of choice among off-the-shelf bogie side overlays, it is possible to make your own, especially if you are modelling an obscure prototype. Plastic section and a variety of materials have been employed, including wound guitar strings to simulate springs. Think about making a single overlay and casting copies from polyurethane resin, as described in Chapter 6.

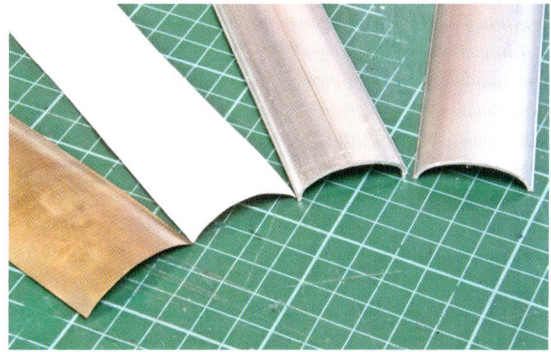

Prefabricated roofs are available in most scales, to suit the most popular profiles. But you can form your own by rolling sheet metal. Plastic and thin plywood are also viable options, soaking the material in hot water before clamping over a suitable former.

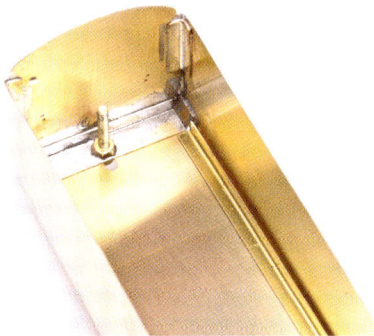

Sheet-brass bodyshells can be assembled in the same manner as brass kits, although it may be necessary to reinforce the corner joints with angle strip. An improvised bottom bracket, with captive nut mounting arrangement, has also been installed. Note too the angle strip that is about to be secured along the edges of the floor, offering greater strength to the sides.

OTHER MATERIAL OPTIONS

The pros and cons of wood in carriage building have been discussed elsewhere, along with the material's sensitivities to external environmental conditions. The material, though, does have many potential uses to the scratch-builder, especially in miniature plywood, MDF and veneer form.

Birch-faced plywood is available in various thicknesses, generally down to about 4mm (⅛in) thick. The rigidity of plywood and MDF makes it a viable alternative to metal or plastic sheet for the construction of the main underframe floor unit as well as bulkheads, interior and even the body itself in some instances. Plywood, after soaking and heating, can be formed into curved shapes relatively easily, so gentle tumblehomes and other side or end profiles are manageable, certainly in 4mm scale and upwards.

What is not so easy, as with all scratch-built coaches, is the creation of multiple window apertures. Careful use of a fretsaw, after the drilling of pilot holes, is the best way forward unless you have access to powerful die-cutting or sophisticated laser-cutting equipment (again, commissioning a laser-cutting specialist may be worth considering if your budget allows). The saw must be sharp and using a fine, single-sided marking knife is recommended to help avoid splitting the grain.

Resin ought not to be discounted either. Creating masters and casting multiple copies saves hours of work and plenty of cash. As was demonstrated in Chapter 6, the material takes a bit of getting used to, but parts required in multiple, such as seats and underframe detail, are perfect fodder for replication. With a bit of experience and bravery, you can start thinking of progressing to casting carriage ends and maybe entire bodyshells.

A carriage does not have to be built from one type of material only and opting for plastic, metal or wood to suit a specific task is highly recommended. As we've seen with many of the kits featured so far, employing a material in a context that suits its inherent properties can certainly prove the most convenient option. Weight remains a factor, however, and employing plastic for most of the vehicle's structure is likely to demand the addition of extra ballast.

A RIVETTING SUBJECT

Employing flat sheet material or plain lengths of metal or plastic may provide the basic three-dimensional outline of the model but, when it comes to adding surface relief, we'll have to score recess and seam lines, add door hinges and bump stops, handrails and all other raised or recessed details. Much depends on the prototype, of course, but there is likely to be a demand for rivet or bolt heads, or maybe rows of countersunk screw heads.

Where raised rivet or bolt detail is required, it can be punched out from the rear of the material. However, whereas etched metal kits will have the rivet locations marked by half-etched depressions, there's no such luxury with scratch-built models. Accordingly, I find that it can be far more injurious to the materials, especially thicker sheet metal, as the punch has to push more of the metal outwards, leading to greater risk of distortion.

Thinner metal (10 thou' and less) is easier to work with, while thin plastics can also be embossed with a punch. Whatever the material, rivet punching should be effected before assembly, while the parts can be freely accessed. If you make a mistake, simply file down the outer surface until it is flush and try again, perhaps filling the inner face with a little solder (on metal) or putty (on plastic) to repair the depression.

Alternatively, a less fraught option is to add raised rivet and bolt detail with a Nutter punching tool, which can also form hexagonal nuts and bolt heads in a range of sizes. The desired forming tip is fitted to the punch and a sheet of thin, flexible metal foil is held within the Nutter. After punching out the individual embellishments, they can be fixed to the model with clear varnish.

Rivets are also available in sheets of textured waterslide transfers (from DCC Supplies – see Useful Addresses), offered in a variety of sizes and spacing, so it's not always necessary to apply them individually. Both methods may prove laborious or therapeutic, depending on your prevailing mood, but there's no doubt that each offers a more accurate and less risky option than wielding a hammer and punch at your delicate, handcrafted components.

Recessed rivets are not seen too often on railway subjects, but a wooden-bodied carriage may have boasted rows of countersunk screws. These can be punched from the outside in a similar way, again watching out for potential distortion. If working in plastic and being faced with long rows of recessed rivets or screws, a special riveting wheel tool can be employed. Designed mainly for model aircraft, the wheels boast fine prongs set a certain distance apart and the tool is simply trundled against a straight

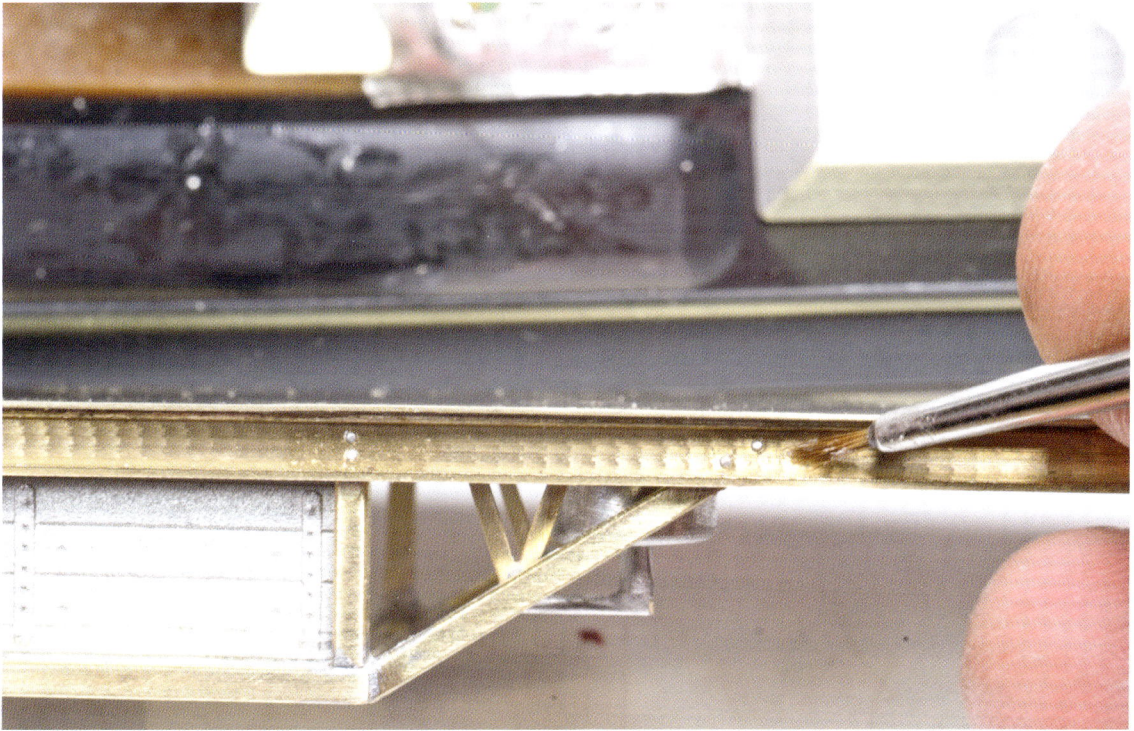

Add finesse with individual rivet or bolt head relief. These rivets were formed with a Nutter punch tool and metal foil, fixed with Johnson Klear.

edge to form a row of perfectly spaced depressions. If anything goes wrong, apply filler, sand smooth and try again.

It is to be hoped this chapter has provided a flavour of what is possible through making your own components, underframes and bodyshells. There's very little to match the satisfaction of seeing your own handiwork running on a layout and creating castings is an equally rewarding experience. Scratch-building need not be the preserve of the skilled miniature engineer with a shed full of tools and equipment. Indeed, most of the projects featured in this chapter have been crafted on a modest budget, with simple materials and processes.

Rows of recessed rivets or countersunk screws can be created with a wheel punch. This Trumpeter tool comes with a choice of wheels, for a variety of rivet sizes and spacings.

CHAPTER FOURTEEN

PAINTING

The painting stage is a 'make or break' moment. Scrimping on preparation or tardy application of topcoats will render the many hours of assembly and detailing wasted. Indeed, the best model in the world can still be ruined by a lumpy paint job.

Taking the time to get the model's surface as close to perfect as possible will reap great rewards. Moreover, time invested at the preparation stage will likely avoid hours of remedial action later. We talked about the use of primers as a proving medium back in Chapter 6 and it is worth reiterating the importance of these initial coats. Here, we'll look at priming in more detail, along with other subjects such as the application of topcoats by hand and airbrush, as well as paint formulas and compatibility.

The cost of good-quality airbrushes and equipment is only a fraction of what it was a decade ago, with some excellent budget tools released in the past few years. Indeed, a decent set-up can now cost about the same as a new DCC-fitted 'OO' gauge locomotive. A brief guide to airbrushing is provided here, but readers are directed to my previous Crowood title, *Airbrushing for Railway Modellers*, for a more detailed discussion.

If you've been upgrading RTR stock, then perhaps a full repaint isn't required. In such cases, knowledge of how best to touch in small areas of a finish, blending as seamlessly as possible, is advantageous. Accordingly, some tips are contained herein.

ORDER OF SERVICE

The point at which a model carriage enters the paint shop depends on personal preference and the nature of the model. Frustratingly, a kit's instructions will seldom talk you through the whole painting stage, although they may offer a snippet of general advice. Some modellers swear by painting and lining the carriage sides before the bodyshell has even been assembled, while others will treat the body in isolation from the roof and underframe or paint the whole thing as a single, fully finished object.

Like most facets of modelling, I prefer a flexible approach, tailoring the sequence to suit a particular project or my prevailing mood. Illustrated here are a number of different finishing methods aimed at specific 'types' of kit or RTR projects. What is common throughout each endeavour is that the painting stage was considered from the very outset, taking into account the peculiarities of the components and the livery scheme. After all, it's in our own interests to make the finishing process as straightforward as possible.

On a number of occasions I've finished a model fully on the inside, glazing and all, before the outside was painted. This is rarely ideal, but at the time it may seem like the only way forward. In other instances, the body has been painted and lined prior to the roof and chassis being installed. Choosing the right adhesive is vital in such instances, lest it interfere with the painted sides or glazing.

Plan the finishing stages from the outset. There is likely to be a need for rubbing down between coats and masking jobs, so leaving the fitting of handrails, door furniture and other fiddly bits until later will make life much easier.

Some parts will have to wait until the painting is complete, especially self-coloured window frame overlays and the like. The use of Johnson Klear as an adhesive medium means that such parts can be installed as part of the clear-coating phase, offering a neat and invisible bond.

Where there is likely to be much in the way of masking to separate multiple colours, or if lining is to be applied, then it makes sense to keep the sides as flat as possible until after the colours and lining are in place. Indeed, I can confirm that there is nothing more frustrating than having to work around and over lots of raised detail, prolonging what can be a tedious job at the best of times. The amount of handling that a model receives during the finishing process inevitably puts delicate components at risk of breakage.

With the most simple of paint schemes, such as plain British Rail blue or crimson, there's little point in holding up construction for the painting stage, as only the roof and underframe (and maybe the ends) will need masking, which can be achieved readily enough. This also saves the need for touching in any details afterwards and – heaven forbid – having to cure any resulting gaps or imperfections. However, this depends on how readily accessible the interior will be once the model is assembled.

As described in Chapter 3, laser-cut glazing is usually designed for installation from the outside, which can be a godsend in most instances. The added fact that the glazing can be fixed with varnish makes it naturally suited to fitting at the clear-coating stage. Indeed, employing an acrylic varnish, such

as Johnson Klear, not only provides the ideal base for waterslide decals on the carriage body, but also improves the transparency of the glazing while also adding a durable, protective coating.

Treating demountable fittings separately often makes good sense, such as the bogies and gangways. It helps if the wheels can be easily removed, although the axle bearings should be masked to keep the working surfaces clean. Other moving parts, such as close-coupling units, must also be installed after painting or covered to avoid clogging up the workings.

But we're getting ahead of ourselves a little here; we must first take a look at preparing the bare surfaces, ready to accept the primer coats.

STRIPPING YARNS

When building kits, we're inevitably dealing with bare materials that are ripe for priming and painting without the need for much prior preparation, save for cleaning (we'll come to that shortly). However, upgraded or modified RTR models – or those simply earmarked for a different livery – will require some extra intervention. Existing factory finishes can be employed as primers/undercoats, without the need for complete removal, as long as the paintwork is smooth and thoroughly clean.

If the finish has been abraded away in certain areas, however, or if lining, logos or multiple livery elements are rendered, then these various layers will show through any subsequent coats of paint. To avoid such issues, a complete rub-down with abrasives will be necessary, followed by cleaning and, preferably, priming in order to provide a perfect base for the new livery. But, with delicate detail and awkward shapes to cope with, this may be no easy task. Instead, resorting to paint stripper will be necessary in order to start again with a clean slate.

Various model paint strippers exist, with most being suitable for use on plastic components,

although only a handful of formulas will prove effective on factory-applied finishes. My personal recommendation is Superstrip, a liquid formula from Phoenix Paints. This can be decanted into a long container and the carriage body left to 'pickle' for a few hours before lightly scrubbing the surface with an old toothbrush.

To avoid irreparable damage to the clear plastic, all glazing must be removed before the stripping formula is applied. The same applies to small detail components, as the glue bonds are likely to break down and parts can get lost in the 'soup' of stripped paint. I find it helpful to dismantle a model as much as possible before dipping into a bath of Superstrip: Bachmann's Mk1 stock is especially

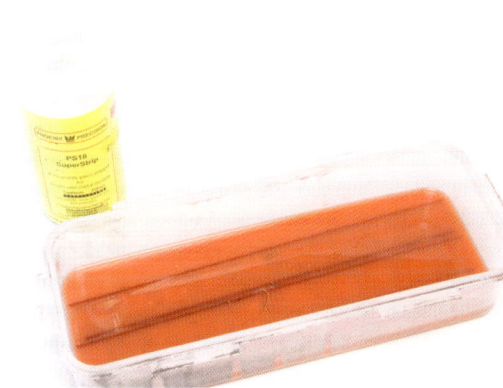

Phoenix Paints Superstrip is my favoured paint-stripping medium. Decanted into a solvent-proof container, the coach body can be soaked overnight to remove all traces of paint, even factory-applied finishes.

Deluxe Materials' Strip Magic is a less toxic option. Brush on the fluid and leave for a few minutes. The paint will soon blister and more Strip Magic can be worked into the surface until the bare material is exposed. Clean with methylated spirit or isopropyl alcohol to deactivate the stripper before rinsing in water.

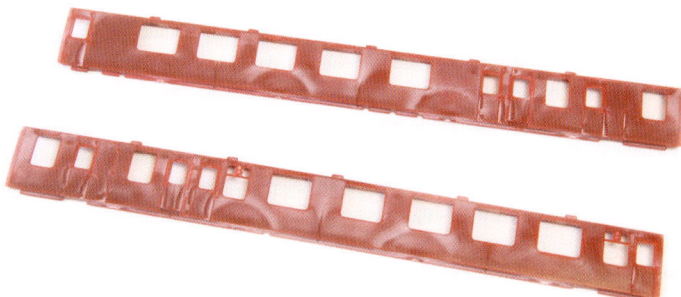

Scrub with an old toothbrush to shift any stubborn deposits and wash the parts thoroughly in clean water and mild detergent. The Superstrip fluid can be reused almost indefinitely.

It is vital that surfaces are spotlessly clean before applying paint. After washing with a mild detergent, allow the model to dry before employing a plastic-friendly alcohol-based cleaner, as offered by Finescale Model World and Phoenix Paints.

convenient in this respect as the sides can be treated individually.

After a few hours of soaking, the layers of paint will begin peeling away. A light scrubbing with an old toothbrush will help shift paint from recesses (always wear gloves and eye protection) and, once the bare material is revealed, parts can be washed thoroughly with a mild detergent before rinsing in clean water and setting aside to dry. The Superstrip can then be filtered and returned to its container, ready for reuse. Indeed, the stripper can be reused indefinitely, making it extremely economical, albeit not the cheapest option in the short term.

Another stripping fluid that I can recommend is Strip Magic from Deluxe Materials. Containing much less in the way of noxious chemicals, Strip Magic can be applied by brush and immediately deactivated with methylated spirit or isopropyl alcohol. Effective on all types of paints, even factory finishes, Strip Magic is also great for working on smaller areas, without the need for complete dismantling.

PERFECT FOUNDATIONS

As well as being clean of loose debris, a surface must also be devoid of any traces of oil and grease. As previously mentioned, plastic and resin components are likely to be contaminated with mould-releasing chemicals that ought to have been cleaned before assembly. Etched and cast metal parts are liable to be covered in traces of chemicals linked with their manufacture, which must also be removed. Flux, solvent residues and oil deposits from our hands will also react unfavourably with paint unless cleaned away completely.

A thorough wash and gentle scrub with a mild detergent is recommended, followed by a day or two of storage in a warm, dry location. By way of a 'belt and braces' approach, I also like to employ an alcohol-based cleaner to ensure any stubborn residues have been removed. Mild formulas of isopropyl alcohol (IPA) are available from hardware stores, often branded as electrical switch cleaners.

Beware, though, that some formulas of IPA can be rather potent and may damage softer plastics (especially styrene) or loosen previously applied paint and primers. Gentler, alcohol-based cleaners designed specifically for use on models can be obtained from Phoenix Paints or Finescale Model World (see Useful Addresses), which are safe to use on virtually any surface.

Alcohol-based cleaners evaporate rapidly, leaving the model ready to paint again within an hour or two. To maintain cleanliness from this point onwards, it is best to handle the model only with gloved hands.

A CRASH COURSE IN AIRBRUSHING

Airbrushes were developed as a means of applying regulated, thin layers of a liquid medium with a high degree of accuracy. Amusingly, the genesis of the concept came from two contemporaneous sources: a doctor desiring a better means of applying medicine within his patients' throats and watercolour artists wishing to overlay different colours without the previous layer being disturbed.

Although the principle of the airbrush can be traced back to the late 1800s, there have been many refinements in their design since then, opening up their use to all manner of art, craft and modelling applications. Having said that, those early tools do not look too dissimilar to many of the airbrushes we see today. Indeed, the basic process of using compressed air to blow liquid paint onto a surface remains unchanged.

There are two main types of airbrush, defined by where on the tool the air and paint are combined: internal and external mix. Taking the latter type first, these airbrushes are often to be found in budget 'spraygun' packages aimed at first-time users. They are fairly crude in some respects, but they can offer acceptable results, albeit in a narrow field of operation. As the paint does not enter the tool itself, being drawn into the airflow by means of suction from a glass jar, there are fewer parts to clean and maintain. The main drawback, however, is that the paint flow is difficult to adjust and the paint particles are not mixed with the air (atomized) sufficiently to produce a high-grade finish.

Internal mix airbrushes employ gravity or suction to draw the paint into the tool, where it is mixed

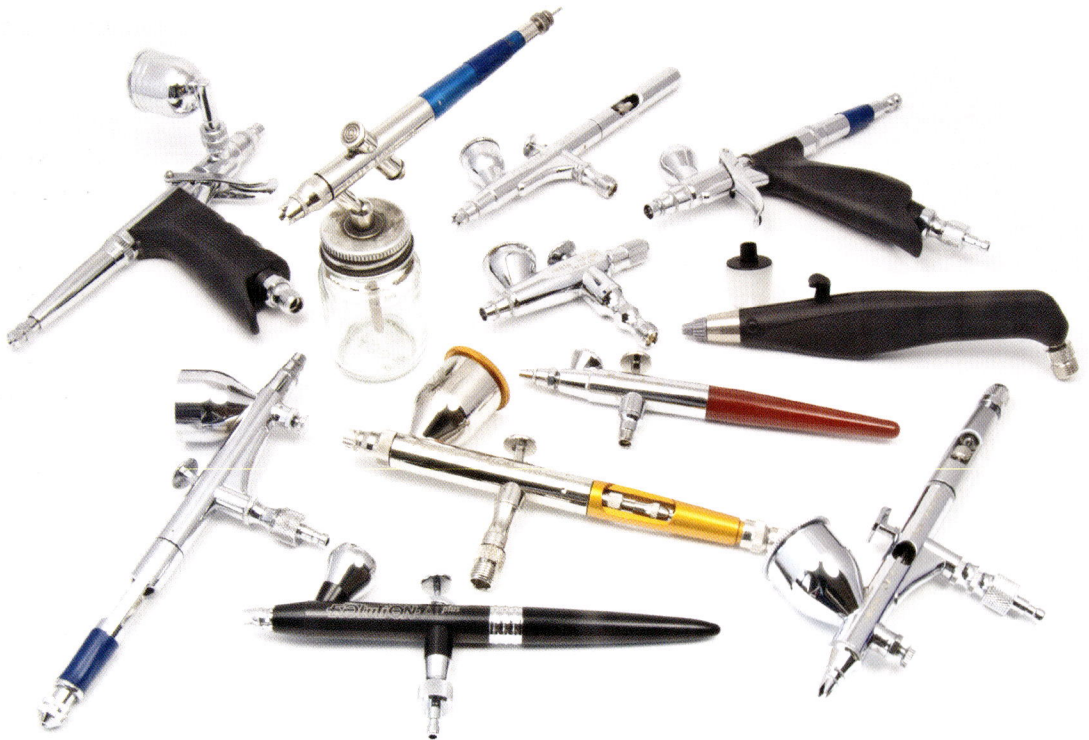

Airbrushes offer the potential for a vastly superior paint finish and there is plenty of choice in terms of price, specification and type. Invest wisely and choose a well-known brand such as Iwata, Harder & Steenbeck, Aztec or Badger.

Single-action airbrushes are relatively simple to use, with the main trigger controlling the air flow and the paint governed by turning a wheel at the rear of the tool.

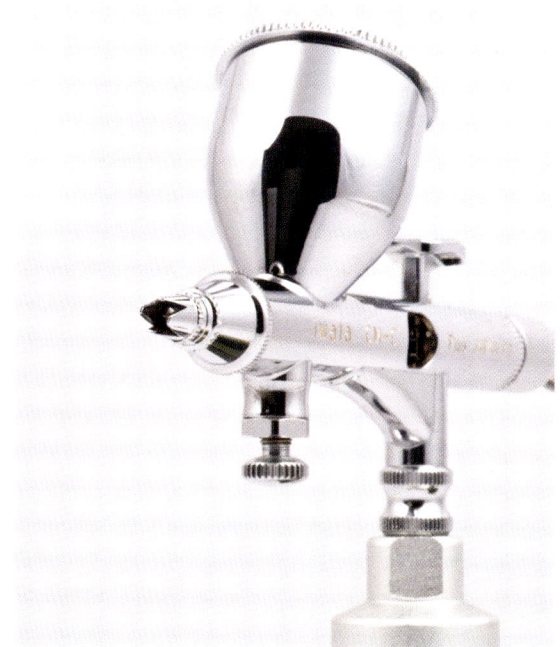

Double- or dual-action airbrushes offer greater control of both the paint and the air, using a single button or trigger.

with the air inside the nozzle. The cone-shaped nozzle creates a Venturi effect whereby the force of the air is multiplied (despite the air pressure remaining constant), thus creating a very fine mist of paint that can be controlled more readily. A needle fits within the nozzle and, by drawing it backwards, the opening is enlarged and more paint can flow from the tool. There is more effort involved in keeping these airbrushes clean, but the enhanced quality of the output more than makes up for any inconvenience.

We can separate internal mix airbrushes into two further camps: single- and double-action. Single-action tools see the trigger controlling the flow of air only (on or off), with the amount of paint emitted governed by turning a small knob at the rear of the tool. These airbrushes are generally cheaper than double-action tools (though not always) and are somewhat less versatile and user-friendly.

Double-action tools feature a trigger that is depressed to release the air and a back and forth sliding action also moves the needle within the nozzle, thus governing the paint flow. They may be a little harder to master, but the increased level of control lends these tools to very intricate work, such as painting small areas without masking, or applying weathering effects.

For those who dislike the feel of the traditional 'top button' trigger style, various pistol-grip devices have appeared in the past decade. These are much more comfortable to use, especially when working for long periods, although they tend to be on the bulky side.

Prices range from budget-priced tools in the sub-£50 category, up to several hundred pounds for those rendered in high-grade materials with fine needle/nozzle sizes aimed at the specialist user. For general modelling use, in 4mm and 7mm scales, an airbrush with a 0.4–0.5mm nozzle will suffice. For those intending to work in 'N' gauge, or who envisage plenty of fine weathering work, a tool with a 0.3mm nozzle will be useful. Large-scale modellers may want to consider a 0.7mm nozzle; anything larger is straying into spray-gun territory with a need for a more powerful air supply. It's worth noting that some airbrushes are available with interchangeable needle/nozzle combinations, essentially offering two tools in one package.

One thing to note with nozzle sizes is that, generally speaking, the smaller the aperture, the more likely it is to clog with paint unless it is thinned

Nozzle sizes lend certain airbrushes to specific jobs, such as general spraying or intricate weathering work. A close look at the needle and nozzle will reveal the importance of thinning the paint properly, so that it can pass through the minuscule aperture cleanly and efficiently.

correctly. Acrylics are particularly prone to blocking nozzles, and the airbrush must be flushed thoroughly with a cleaning agent at regular intervals during painting.

AIR SUPPLIES

Any airbrush, no matter how much it may cost, is only as good as its air supply. We need a reliable, steady and controllable flow of compressed air, generally between 10 and 18psi. Aerosol-based propellants are convenient and cheaper than a mains-powered compressor, at least in the short term. The cans will prove expensive in the long run, however, with the precious air also required for cleaning out the airbrush at regular intervals. Aerosols also tend to freeze up after prolonged use and there is no way of accurately regulating the pressure.

Compressors may not be cheap, but they will repay their cost instantly with superior, reliable results. In fact, over many years of teaching airbrushing techniques, I still recommend that my students invest more in a compressor than in an airbrush: there are more good-quality, low-price airbrushes to be had than decent, cheap compressors!

As well as a controllable supply of air, some form of moisture filtration is also essential. The act

of creating compressed air is a hot business and, as the air makes its way through the hose to the airbrush, it naturally cools down. Condensation thus forms and, if the droplets of moisture mix with the paint, the results can be messy. Some compressors come supplied with a filter as standard. If not, small in-line filters are relatively cheap and fit between the hose and the airbrush as a last line of defence against errant water droplets. I employ a filter on the compressor as well as an in-line unit at the airbrush.

Anyone likely to be spray-painting by airbrush or aerosol is encouraged to invest in a fume extraction booth. Airbrushing creates a very fine mist of paint and solvent, neither of which ought to be inhaled. At the very least, a good-quality facemask, with the correct filters to suit paint vapours, should be worn at all times. Other safety precautions to observe include wearing gloves when employing solvent airbrush cleaning fluids, some of which can be very aggressive.

As will be appreciated by looking at the tiny aperture on a decent airbrush nozzle, the paint and air have to make their way through a very small opening. Thick, gloopy paint, therefore, doesn't stand a chance of being atomized finely, so we need to ensure that any paint is thoroughly mixed beforehand and thinned to the correct viscosity. There is often talk of paint/thinner ratios, but I never concern myself with these, not least as ratios differ widely from brand to brand and even jar to jar. So many factors are at play, including how long a jar has been opened or even what colour it is (darker paints have more pigment, so are likely to need thinning more than lighter shades).

Instead, I aim to judge the viscosity of the paint on an individual basis. This has proved to be a far more helpful approach, especially for beginners. Decant the paint into a mixing jar before adding a few drops of thinners, stirring gently and adding more thinners until the mixture takes on the consistency of skimmed milk. Additionally, watching how the paint drops from a spatula is another foolproof test. The paint should drop in self-contained blobs: stringy globules show that the mix is too thick while the

The air supply is just as important as the airbrush. Investing in a good quality compressor will be worth every penny.

Other essential gear includes a pressure regulator, moisture filter, good quality hoses, airbrush holder and cleaning pot.

paint running off in a torrent means that it's too thin. It is really that simple.

MAKING A START

Getting the paint mixed correctly and setting up a constant supply of air at a low pressure are the two fundamentals of airbrushing that are non-negotiable. With the compressor set to around 12–15psi,

load the airbrush with paint and try spraying onto a scrap of card or plastic. The paint should flow easily with the mist evenly dispersed. For optimum performance, we need to work with the airbrush's nozzle about 3 inches (75mm) from the surface of the subject.

We can play about with the air pressure and distance, adjusting each factor until everything is working correctly. However, if the paint is still not flowing evenly above 18psi, you need to add more thinners to the paint. If it's flowing too freely, ease off the pressure until you feel in complete control. It's always easier to deal with paint that is too thin rather than too thick as we can work right down to just a few psi if necessary, although this may not always prove ideal.

Taking the time to get the paint, air and distance right will set you up nicely for trouble-free airbrushing. Fail to master these basics, though, and you'll be flailing around wondering why the tool isn't doing what it's meant to do. Exercising on sheets of card or scrap models is highly recommended, as it is with any method of painting, rather than jumping straight in at the deep end.

To make the most of the airbrush's potential, it's important to build up layers of colour as thinly as possible. This will avoid the risk of clogging up fine surface relief as well as guarding against runs and pooling of excess paint. 'Little and often' is a mantra worth repeating, building up livery elements over several coats. It's a myth that airbrushing offers a rapid solution to the painting stage but, with practice, it's a tool that can produce superb results efficiently.

The paint must be thinned to the consistency of skimmed milk. Regardless of the paint type, brand or formula, this simple system is a far more reliable gauge than worrying about paint–thinner ratios.

If the paint spatters out of the airbrush, the paint is too thick, the air pressure too low or the nozzle may be blocked.

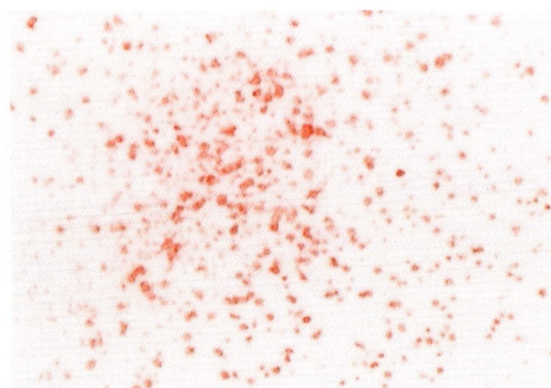

If the paint runs, puddles and feels out of control, then it may be too thin. Try reducing the air pressure. The airbrush must be kept moving while paint is being emitted and only small amounts of paint should be sprayed at a time.

Begin by laying a thin mist of paint into recesses and around raised details. With the paint thinned correctly, and pressure set to around 12–15psi, the airbrush should be kept at a distance of 2–3in (50–75mm) from the surface.

Overall horizontal strokes can follow, again spraying a fine mist. As soon as the paint looks damp on the surface, allow it to dry off for 10–20 seconds before continuing. A very patient approach will be rewarded with a better finish.

Once the paint appears opaque, it will start to appear 'wetter'. This is a good sign, showing that the paint is building up to an even finish. But don't overdo it, as adding too much paint will cause puddles and runs. Leave the model to dry for a few hours before assessing whether it needs further coats.

A rough, orange-peel effect is produced if the paint is sprayed from too far away. Try to keep the airbrush at a consistent distance from the surface (2–3in/50–75mm) or the paint will be drying in mid-air. This effect can also be a result of working with the air pressure set too high (above 20psi).

Don't expect your airbrush to produce good results unless you keep to a rigorous cleaning and maintenance routine. This need not be too onerous. Indeed, regular quick flushes will avoid the need for lengthy strip-downs at the end of each job. There are plenty of cleaning fluids available, along with brushes and lubricants. A decent airbrush will include instructions for cleaning and maintenance – make sure you follow them.

A handy tip, once most of the paint has been flushed through the airbrush, is to fill the cup with cleaning fluid and place your finger over the nozzle. Press the trigger and the air will cause the fluid to bubble away, forcing any solid matter or residual paint back into the paint cup, which can be wiped out. Repeat the process until the fluid remains clear, but watch your eyes.

otherwise the primer is likely to cause the underlying finish to blister and peel away. In nearly all cases, such aerosol primers can be used atop RTR factory finishes with no such problems.

As with all aerosols, thorough shaking of the can beforehand and application in a warm, yet well-ventilated space is essential. Aerosols will always be limited in terms of spray pattern and pressure. As a result, smaller models or those with intricate shapes may see the paint struggling to reach into all of the nooks and crannies. Indeed, trying to aim the paint into awkward spots can easily result in messy puddles.

With this in mind, cellulose primers designed for airbrush application are a particular favourite

PRIMERS

As modellers, we're spoilt for choice in terms of high-quality primers, available in a variety of formulas. Most leading hobby paint brands include primers in their ranges, with Phoenix and RailMatch's enamel formulas and AK Interactive's acrylic primers being particularly good. To get the best from a primer, however, it really needs to be sprayed. The enamel primers mentioned above are great when thinned and applied by airbrush, while there are also a number of aerosol-based primers that offer superb results.

Automotive primers, such as those retailed by Halfords, are usually cellulose or synthetic acrylic formulas, resulting in super-fast drying times and incredibly hard-wearing finishes. They also contain self-levelling, micro-filling compounds to help cure any minor surface blemishes and promote a smooth overall coating. They're ideal for use on plastic, resin or metal models, provided they have been stripped of any previously applied enamel or acrylic paints,

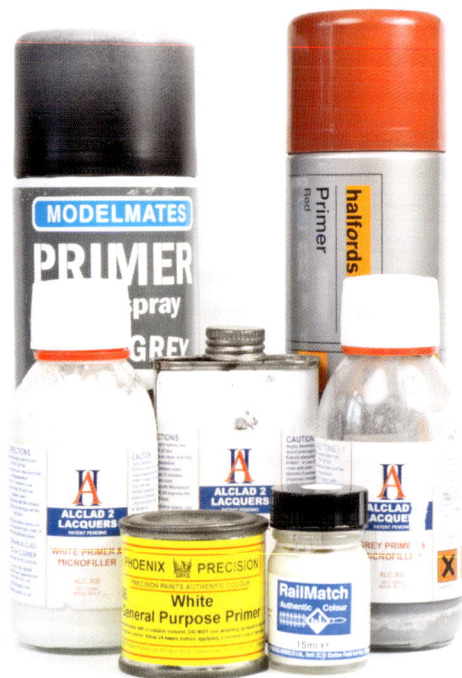

Primers come in a variety of formulas and formats. Aerosol primers offer convenience and generally high-quality results, but the aggressive spray can obliterate delicate detail on smaller models. Airbrushing primers offers greater control and finesse and Alclad2's lacquer-based primers are optimized for spraying.

Grey primers are ideal for creating a base coat, showing up any surface blemishes more effectively. Paint handles and turntables are strongly recommended, allowing the model to be rotated while keeping both hands free. This unit is from Tamiya.

Some primers can be hand-brushed effectively, especially enamel or acrylic formulas. However, it is difficult to achieve a smooth finish without recourse to abrasives in between coats, which is not always appropriate where fine surface detail is involved.

of mine. Alclad2 primers come pre-thinned for convenience and produce excellent results when airbrushed, although they take a little getting used to. They can be buffed to a super-smooth finish and are dry within about thirty minutes. Being lacquer based, they must be treated with respect and the fumes avoided at all costs, so some form of fume extraction is vital, or a high performance facemask must be worn at the very least.

While regular primers offer increased levels of adhesion on any surface, so long as it has been correctly prepared, there are others containing chemical additives that literally 'etch' their way onto the model's surface. Offered in single- or twin-pack form, some are more powerful than others, while certain formulas are tailored for use on either metal or plastic surfaces.

As may be supposed, such etching primers contain some rather nasty ingredients and I tend to steer clear of them. I've tried a number of them over the years and they certainly work. However, the cheaper, safer, non-etching formulas can also be highly effective, thus making the extra hazards of etching primers seem pointless, insofar as my needs are concerned. Indeed, any product that carries carcinogenic warnings has no place in my workshop.

UNDERCOATING

The colour of the primer can have a significant impact on the appearance of subsequent colour coats. It will also dictate how many coats are required before the livery colour reaches full opacity. In general, white is the preferred undercoat shade as it is less likely to influence the perception of subsequent layers of paint, especially with lighter colours such as cream, crimson or yellow. Furthermore, paint manufacturers tend to colour-match all livery shades on a white backing, so we ought to follow suit in order to maintain authenticity. Unfortunately, a greater amount of paint is required before the topcoat colour is rendered to its full effect.

Darker livery elements, such as maroon, plum, deep green or a faux wood finish, will generally perform satisfactorily over a mid-grey shade of primer. Colours that are darker still, such as greys, browns and black will be fine over a darker, more general shade of grey primer. Earlier chapters have already mentioned how useful grey primer can be as a proving tool, showing up imperfections in a surface far more effectively than other shades. With this in mind, my usual approach is to employ a grey primer initially as a matter of course and, once any

Lighter, vibrant livery colours demand a white undercoat.

It may take time to build up a livery colour to an even coating, without traces of the white undercoat showing through.

blemishes have been made good, another grey coat follows. If necessary, a white undercoat can then be applied, either using a white primer (as long as it's compatible with the preceding primer formula) or a matt white paint.

The necessity for very light primer coats cannot be stressed enough, as excessive layers of paint have the potential to obliterate fine surface relief. The ability to apply the minimum amount of paint, while producing a quality finish, is where an air-brush excels. Aerosols are great for many tasks but are difficult to control over intricate and small-scale surfaces, leading to the risk of 'over-cooking' the job. But we'll return to application methods shortly: the paints themselves are our immediate concern.

PAINTS

Any reader in the UK over the age of thirty is likely to have been weaned on Humbrol enamel paints during their formative modelling years. Like many others, I stuck with Humbrol for decades, excusing some erratic changes to the formula and, I have to say, they're still user-friendly and great value. Their wide availability is also a welcome factor.

Enamels, as also offered by Revell, Railmatch, Phoenix and a host of others, have the potential to produce very high standards of finish. Easy to work with and hard-wearing, drying times may be long (around 6–12 hours), but this can prove beneficial when working by hand or airbrushing. The fumes can be harmful, however, and some specialist brands still add lead chromate to certain colours, making safe working practices essential.

Enamels are easy to thin, with white spirit if brushing, or with proprietary thinners if spraying. They're also easy to wipe away if a mistake is made, with plenty of working time available before they start to 'go off'.

Acrylics are less toxic than the aforementioned paints, being formulated from water- or alcohol-based ingredients. Indeed, the term 'acrylic' is rather a vague term, encompassing products that differ radically in performance. On the 'water' side are the likes of Vallejo and Lifecolor, along with the acrylic variants from Revell and Humbrol. Tamiya acrylics, in particular, have a much higher alcohol content that renders them easier to spray, albeit with a more noxious haze. As a result of these differences, I always recommend employing the same brand of thinner and paint.

The other main variety of paint is cellulose, or 'lacquer'-based formulas, which are now regarded as specialist paints and are therefore not so freely available. The Alclad2 range of primers is classed as lacquers, although these modern paints are more sophisticated than the cellulose paints of old. For livery colours, the only source I'm aware of is the Chris Wesson range, along with a handful of automotive paint finishes that are close matches to certain railway company schemes.

Only suitable for spraying, cellulose is not an easy paint to use, as ultra-rapid drying times can be both a blessing and a curse. The need for high-quality thinners adds further to the costs involved. Its hazardous nature means that cellulose is a substance to use only with the greatest respect – and the correct safety equipment.

All paints are composed of a mixture of solid pigments and a liquid medium that allows the colour (or clear varnish compound) to flow easily over a surface. The liquid eventually evaporates, leaving the hardened pigment behind. It is often this liquid medium – the thinners – that causes compatibility problems. By necessity, thinners need to be of a volatile nature, so that they can evaporate readily and offer drying times within set parameters. However, the higher the volatility of a thinning agent, the more likely it is to damage soft plastics or underlying paint finishes.

Therefore always follow the instructions supplied with paints, most notably in terms of drying and recoating times. Although a surface may be touch-dry relatively quickly, there's likely to be traces of the thinners that have yet to evaporate. Applying more of the same paint too soon will reactivate the residual thinners and loosen the pigment, resulting in a gloopy mess. Similarly, introducing a different type of paint, before the previous layer has hardened completely, can also produce a negative reaction.

On the subject of compatibility, cellulose can have an adverse effect on previously applied enamels or acrylics, while the latter two formulas will happily sit beneath or atop each other. Enamels and acrylics can be applied safely over a cellulose background. Confusingly, some modern cellulose-type paints, especially Alclad2 products, are formulated for use over almost any type of surface. Indeed, there are exceptions to many of these 'rules', and two fundamental factors to observe, when applying different types of paint, are to apply the minimum amount at a time and to ensure that any previous layers are completely dry before recoating. If there's any doubt about compatibility, test the paints on a scrap surface beforehand, leaving for a week or two to be sure that no adverse reaction takes place.

Sticking to one type of paint throughout the finishing process is more likely to bring reliable results: acrylic paints, in particular, tend to benefit from application over previous acrylic layers. But I can't profess to follow this edict myself: I nearly always choose a lacquer-based primer, usually as offered by Alclad2 or – for sheer convenience – an aero-

There is a massive amount of choice amongst paints for the modeller these days, although specific railway-themed colours are limited to a smaller range of brands.

sol-based automotive primer. Livery colours tend to be the preserve of enamels (either Railmatch or Phoenix), although I'm happy using acrylics, in particular from Lifecolor, Tamiya or Vallejo, when I can find a suitable colour match. Clear coats tend to be enamel-based whenever a hard-wearing finish is desired. I also regularly employ Alclad2 clear lacquers, while acrylic clear coats have also found favour in recent years.

*MIDDLE: **Spraying livery colours with aerosols offers quick results, albeit without the finesse of airbrushing. Shake the can well and always work in a warm, well-ventilated area. Wear a facemask and keep the can moving all the time.***

*BOTTOM: **Thinning paints is often necessary before applying by hand. Good-quality white spirit is compatible with most hobby enamels and offers a slower drying time than proprietary thinners, which is ideal when working with a brush. Always take the time to shake and/or stir paints thoroughly before and during use.***

APPLICATION FACTORS

As with the priming stage, the surface must be as clean and smooth as possible before any paint is applied. If hand brushing – and occasionally when airbrushing – you must be prepared to rub down each individual layer before applying the next, which can be a labour-intensive business.

At least the use of an airbrush allows the paint to be layered more evenly and, with some paint formulas, the coats may be built up in a much shorter time span. That's not to say that it's a rapid finishing method. A high-quality paint finish demands time, regardless of how it's applied, and overnight rests between colour coats and especially before applying any masking are essential, even when using fast-drying acrylics.

Drying times depend not only on the type of liquid medium, but also the ambient temperature and humidity level, so working in a warm, dry environment is always recommended. Conversely, painting in overly hot conditions can cause problems with paints drying too quickly. Temperature has a major role to play in paint performance. I refuse to apply paint in ambient temperatures below 10°C as results can be unpredictable and, besides, it's too cold for me to be hanging around in the shed anyway.

Applying the main livery colour via an airbrush offers more chance of a smooth, even finish, although the other elements, such as the roof, underframe and end detail can be added by hand if desired.

Although we don't get many days of blistering sunshine where I live, 30°C is my nominal maximum as, again, paint may behave erratically above this threshold. As you can imagine, installing a thermometer near to your painting station is a handy means of gauging when is or is not a good time to be painting, especially with an airbrush or aerosol.

PAINTBRUSHES

Choosing the best brushes you can afford will be rewarded with superior results, as long as great care is taken to keep them in perfect condition. Readers may be forgiven for assuming that solvent- and oil-based paints are the most damaging to a brush's lifespan. However, in my experience, it is fast-drying acrylics that tend to be more destructive. Slower-drying paints allow more time for cleaning after each job and, provided any traces of cleaning solvents are also removed before the brush is left to dry out, good-quality brushes will give many years of service.

Sable-haired brushes offer unparalleled performance and can be used with acrylics and enamels, especially for overall livery applications. Flat and long-bristled brushes are recommended for covering larger areas, such as carriage bodyshells, while round brushes are suited to picking out details or covering small areas where a higher degree of accuracy is required. Synthetic bristles are acceptable for many general tasks, especially for painting underframes or applying weathering. The act of working paint into the nooks and crannies of chassis frames and bogies is likely to ruin the bristles of a good-quality brush. Accordingly, holding a range of brush sizes and bristle types in stock will prove useful, saving the best tools for the showcase jobs and the cheaper or older brushes for the 'dirty' work.

Over the years I've developed a preference for certain brands, such as Kolinsky and Lifecolor, neither of which are particularly cheap, but they have the potential to give years of sterling service. Your local model shop may stock a selection of Humbrol (or similar brand) brushes that are fine for general work. Indeed, Humbrol has greatly expanded its range of brushes recently, with various bristle types

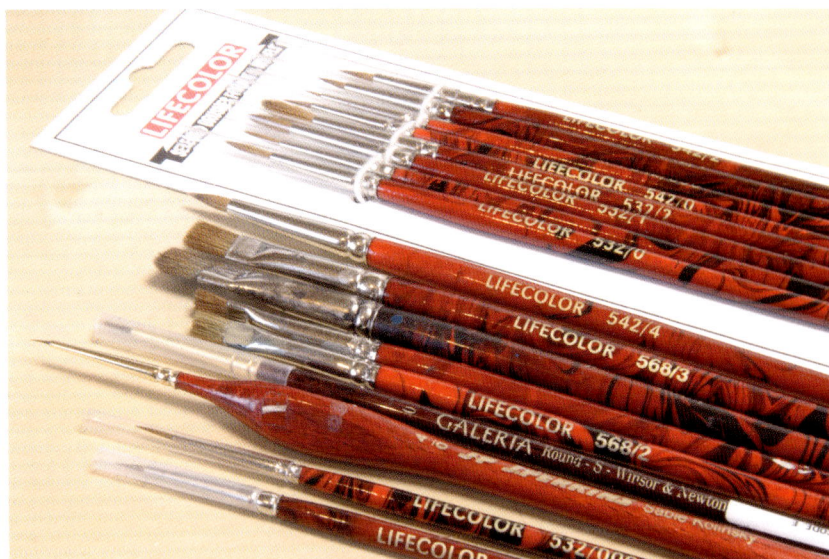

Choose the best paintbrushes that you can afford, with Lifecolor's range being among my favourites. They're not cheap but, as long as you pamper them, they will last for years.

and patterns to choose from. Tamiya brushes are also excellent and widely available, with the very fine pattern tools being especially useful, not least as they feature ergonomically shaped handles. Art and craft stores will offer a wider variety of brush types and brands, so it may be worth shopping around.

PAINTING BY HAND

A good paint finish relies on two main factors: preparation and application. Ensuring a clean, smooth surface and mixing the paint thoroughly count towards the preparation stage. Choosing the best paintbrushes, keeping them in tip-top condition and building the layers of paint gradually are essential, thinning the paint if necessary to maintain a smooth, workable flow. Perfecting both of these facets takes a little practice, but the effort is ultimately worthwhile.

Moreover, getting the first few coats applied to a good standard from the offing allows subsequent layers to be built up successfully and avoids the need for repeated remedial work after every individual layer. Apply light coats, paying attention to the direction of the brushstrokes, and allow the paint to cure fully before gently abrading with fine abrasives, used wet to avoid clogging.

Much depends on the paint formula and brand, but thinning is usually necessary to some degree. Acrylics can be thinned where necessary with specific acrylic thinners, although some brands are compatible with water (read the label), thus offering a little extra in the way of drying time and so workability. Some acrylics can be a joy to apply by hand, particularly Lifecolor's range, but the rapid

When painting by hand, do not overload the brush and apply light coats at a time. Thin the paint, if necessary, to ensure that it flows readily and can be spread easily. Flat brushes are recommended for larger areas. Slower-drying oil-based paints make life easier, although Lifecolor acrylics are a joy to brush, as long as you don't hang around.

Allow each coat to dry thoroughly, preferably overnight (even with acrylics) before de-nibbing with fine abrasives (10,000–12,000 grit) to remove any brushstrokes or lumps. Clean the surface and repeat the process. It is not uncommon for a deep colour to demand up to six individual coats.

Cleaning brushes at regular intervals and especially at the end of every session is vital. Shampoo is a great cleaning agent, especially for acrylic paints, leaving sable bristles as good as new. If paint deposits linger, or the brush dries up, try dipping in Brush Magic. The cleaner will restore even the crustiest brush.

drying can be unforgiving with other brands, such as Tamiya.

Enamels, on the other hand, can be thinned with white spirit and the long curing time of most brands allows for plenty of manipulation on the surface, reducing the appearance of brushstrokes markedly. Annoyingly, some brands will insist on adding fancy new ingredients to speed up the drying time, but this can often be counterproductive to a hand finisher. Railmatch enamels, in particular, are a pleasure to apply by hand, being generally thin and easy to spread, although the weaker formulation does demand several coats before full opacity is achieved. They also tend to dry more quickly than some other enamels, so there must be no shilly-shallying with the brush.

CLEANING UP

My usual cleaning routine, when brushing enamels, is to give the brush a few swills in white spirit, wiping gently on a tissue between each 'dip'. Don't be tempted to scrunch the brush against the bottom or sides of the solvent container, especially if there are deposits of old paint suspended in the fluid. Rather, submerge the bristles only and agitate vigorously

to dislodge the paint, using the tissue to collect the bulk. Also, avoid any rough handling of the bristles with the tissue – just let the solvent do its work over several minutes and many immersions.

As soon as the last of the paint traces are revealed on the tissue, wash the bristles in warm soapy water. Shampoo is rather good in this respect, especially on sable-haired brushes. Rinse thoroughly, shake away the excess moisture and, while still damp, manipulate the bristles back into their intended shape and set aside to dry naturally, preferably stood in a jar or old mug. When working with acrylics, the process is basically the same, but omitting the use of white spirit and heading straight for the water and shampoo.

TOUCHING UP

Where carriages have been modified with new parts, they can often be touched-up without the need for a full repaint. The new paint can then perhaps be blended into the surrounding finish without any obvious transitions. If this isn't possible, the act of weathering will come to the rescue, effectively hiding any discrepancies in the overall finish.

Take your time to get all of the detail parts installed neatly and, once the glue has cured completely, treat the carriage to a thorough clean to remove any debris or greasy deposits. Bare metal parts will benefit from a light coating of primer to ensure that the finish adheres reliably, applied with a fine brush or sprayed, having carefully masked up the surrounding areas. An enamel-based primer is preferred for hand brushing, ensuring that the paint has been shaken and stirred thoroughly beforehand. Primers contain very heavy pigments that are prone to settling in the jar at the earliest opportunity, so a good stir every few moments is necessary. Only a small amount of primer is needed, just enough to give the final colour coat a suitable surface on which to stick.

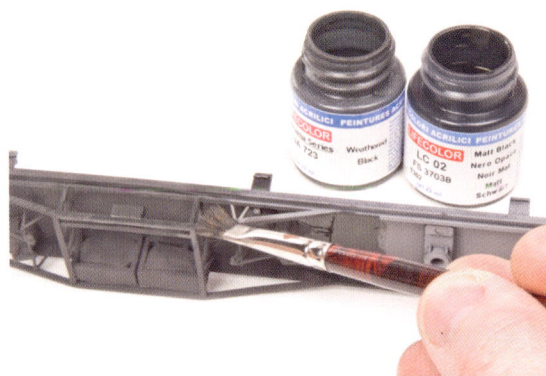

Spraying underframes can be tedious, with the airbrush or aerosol having to be directed in and around all of the various components. Painting by hand may be quicker, especially if using acrylics and the added texture from brushing can actually be beneficial. Two coats of Lifecolor Weathered Black are my usual treatment for chassis that will subsequently be weathered with an airbrush.

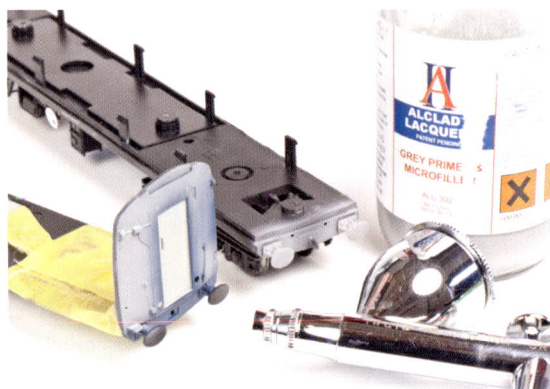

Where only small areas are being touched up, such as the ends and chassis of this Mk1, the coaches are masked up where necessary (or dismantled if possible) and a light misting of primer applied over the new parts and modified areas.

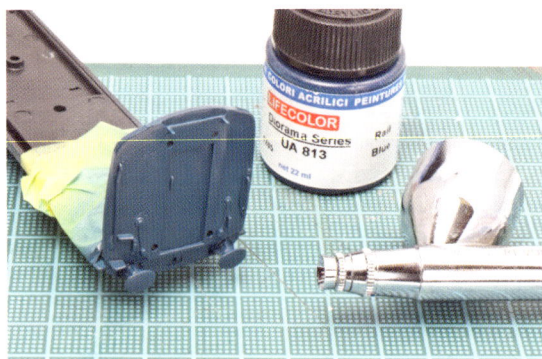

The livery colour is then applied over several light coats until full opacity is achieved. Different paint brands offer slightly different takes on railway livery shades, some of which are closer to those colours employed by the likes of Hornby and Bachmann.

The same process can be followed if hand-brushing the primer and topcoats, although more care is needed to avoid drowning the surface relief with excess paint or damaging it with abrasives in between coats.

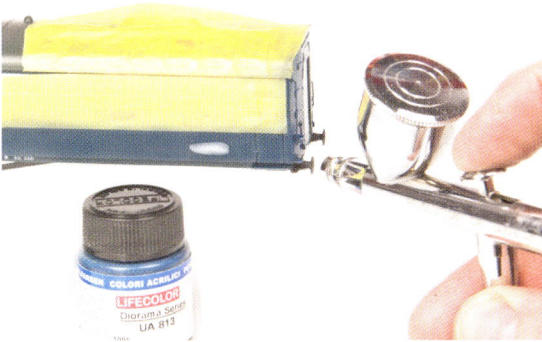

If the new paint doesn't match the existing finish exactly, either disguise the inconsistency beneath a weathered finish or 'feather' the paint over the factory finish with an airbrush. Mask up other livery elements carefully, including any numbers and logos.

To cure an area of damaged paintwork and disguise an ill-fitting roof, this Southern Pride Pullman kit has been masked carefully and the umber shade sprayed in light layers to avoid building up a pronounced ridge of paint against the edge of the mask.

Making use of natural boundaries against which to mask, such as the cream band and roof of this Pullman car, makes the job of blending in new paintwork easier.

Once the primer is completely dry, brush on the livery colour, building it up over several light coats if necessary until the finish is opaque. While touching-up small areas can be easy, larger expanses can offer more of a challenge. Good results are possible, though, rubbing down each coat with ultra-fine abrasives and following with an overall layer of varnish to create a more harmonious appearance. Working with an airbrush offers the best results, as the new colours can be 'feathered' over the factory paintwork to create a seamless finish.

Now that we've covered the core skills of painting, the following chapter will delve deeper into the subject, looking at masking, lining, varnishing, woodgrain effects and decals.

Touch in smaller details, such as handrails or water pipes in situ. Bare metal always benefits from a coat of primer, avoiding the risk of paint flaking off during handling.

CHAPTER FIFTEEN

FURTHER FINISHING

Finishing a model carriage involves much more than applying paint and this chapter delves into the swirling tide of masking, lining, varnishing and the use of transfers or decals, as I prefer to call them.

Unless you're intending to paint the entire carriage in a single colour, you'll need to plan ahead vis-à-vis the order in which the colours are applied. Life will be simpler if working with the lightest colours first, adding progressively darker shades in separate stages. Working in the reverse order requires extra white or grey undercoat layers, posing the risk of obliterating subtle surface detail.

Carriage modelling is seldom straightforward and it may be unavoidable that the colour progression cannot follow these rules. However, contained in the following pages are a number of hints and tips to help you navigate these tricky waters.

MASKING

Separating different colours cleanly and effectively will demand the use of some form of masking medium. Masking allows different livery elements to be applied as well as protecting delicate features, such as glazing or axle bearings, from unwanted paint ingress. Available in the form of tape, film and fluid, there is a masking medium to suit almost any situation.

What is important is that the masking offers a secure bond to the model, preferably with the ability to cope with shaped or undulating surfaces, while not being so sticky as to remove the underlying paint. Tapes are the most common, with Tamiya and Tristar producing some excellent waxed cloth-backed tapes in a variety of widths. Possessing just the right amount of 'tack', the tapes can be manipulated over and around a variety of shapes while still providing a robust barrier to any paint. Where even more flexibility is needed, for example over a panelled carriage side, thin vinyl tape is recommended, such as offered by Phoenix Paints.

Masking film is a helpful alternative to tape, although even the supplest versions tend to lack the necessary flexibility to cope with intricate surface relief. Film does have many uses, though. Ultra Film, from Artool, is a translucent medium that is easy to

Masking media comes in a number of forms: tapes, films and fluids. Vinyl tapes from Phoenix Paints offer flexibility, while Tamiya and Tri-Star wax-backed tapes are great for general use.

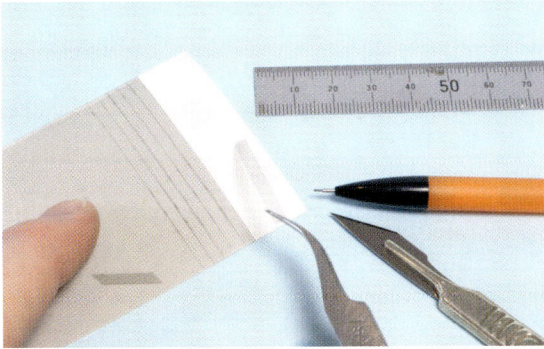

Masking tapes and, especially, films can be cut to form simple or complex shapes. I particularly enjoy using Artool's Ultra Mask film as the masks can be used many times, although it's only suitable for flat surfaces.

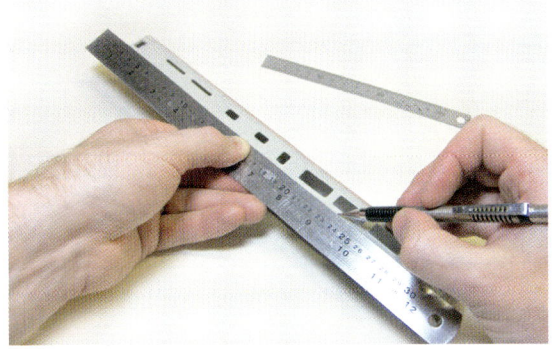

Planning the order in which colours are applied is important. For this BR Mk3, the light grey element has been applied first, over a white undercoat. Accurate marking-out is required to help mask the panel before the blue is applied.

Align the edge of the tape against the feint pencil lines, checking with a straight edge to ensure they're lined up correctly. It's possible to trim the ends of the tape in situ, but be careful not to damage the underlying surface – always use a fresh, sharp scalpel blade. Clean the masked edges with a cotton bud dipped in a tiny amount of white spirit to remove the pencil lines and any stray adhesive.

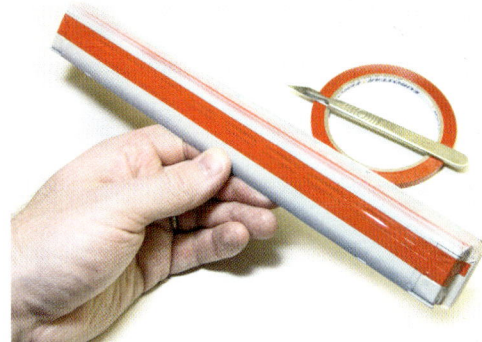

Where strips of tape have overlapped, apply masking fluid with a brush or cocktail stick and allow it to dry fully before painting.

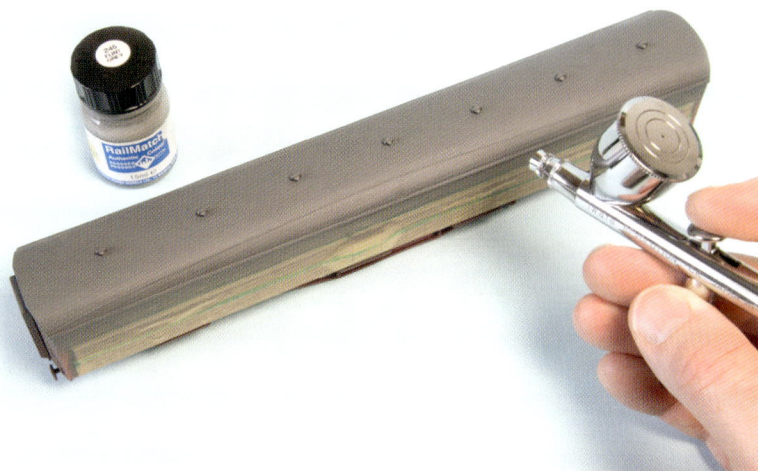

Try not to work the paint directly against the edge of the masking, either when brushing or spraying, otherwise the masking may be disturbed or ridges will be created.

I nearly always treat the sides first, with whatever separate elements are required, before masking and treating the roof, ends and underframe. Roofs and ends can be tricky to mask, but this is where fluids come to the rescue.

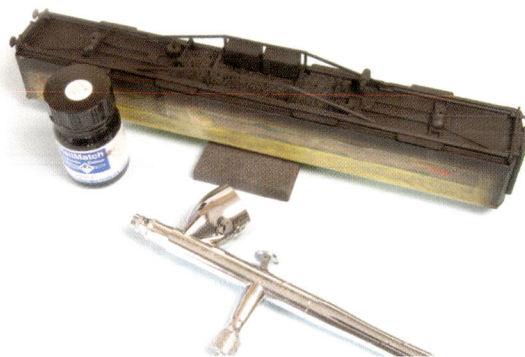

Before painting underframes and chassis, don't forget to mask up the axle bearings and any other working parts beforehand.

Allow the paint to cure before removing the masking. Pull it away gently, avoiding the use of sharp tools. Clean away any residual marks with a cotton bud and a little white spirit.

position accurately and marking out and cutting into intricate shapes is simple; just the thing for many modern liveries applied to contemporary smooth-sided vehicles. In fact, Ultra Film can even be fed into a desktop printer and computer-generated masks created.

Latex- or resin-based masking fluids, such as Humbrol's Maskol, dry to a flexible, low tack film. Resistant to all paint formulas, it is simply peeled away when necessary and leaves behind no residue. This is ideal for coping with very awkward surfaces where tape would struggle to adhere, or for sealing different layers of masking to prevent any paint from creeping through the gaps.

Careful planning of the painting stage is essential. Masking can be a tiresome activity, so plotting ways of speeding up the process is heartily recommended.

VARNISHING

There are plenty of varnishes about that are suitable for use on models, with enamel and acrylic formulas easy to obtain from the likes of Humbrol, Phoenix and Railmatch. And then there's DIY polyurethane varnishes aimed at finishing wooden furniture and joinery, which some modellers endorse (but I don't). The point of using the latter is lost on me, with many superior hobby grades available at a fraction of the price.

Clear coats are probably a more appropriate umbrella term to adopt, encompassing a broader range of translucent finishes, some of which may be optimized for spraying or brushing. There is also much choice in the final sheen of the clear coat, ranging from shiny gloss to dull matt in a staggering number of increments, especially in the Alclad2 range.

Applying a clear coat serves many purposes. First, it's a useful device for unifying a finish that is made up of numerous separate colours, each of which may have dried to a slightly different level of sheen. Second, a high-gloss clear coat provides the optimum surface for applying decals and lining. Third, clear coats work to seal these embellishments, rendering

any carrier film invisible and protecting the model's finish against everyday handling. As seen in previous chapters, there are many other uses for high-quality clear coats, such as improving and repairing plastic glazing or as an adhesive for fine etched components.

Enamel varnishes offer tough, high-lustre finishes that will last for years, although some brands are prone towards yellowing with age. Drying times are long, especially for gloss finishes where the coating will take around a week to harden completely. Most acrylic formulas will not stand the same kind of handling as enamels, and so are not recommended for stock liable to constant handling, for use outdoors or haulage by live steam traction. They do dry much more quickly, though, as well as offering less in the way of harmful fumes.

Modern acrylic formulas are improving constantly, in terms of performance and ease of application. Humbrol's recent 'Clear' formula is a good case in point, as it aims to replicate the fabled Johnson Klear floor polish that turned out to be a fantastic clear varnish ideally suited to finishing plastic models. Although the formula has been tinkered with over the years, Klear (or Future as it is branded outside the UK) has many uses, can be airbrushed without thinning and is a joy to apply by hand. Naturally enough, being a floor polish, the liquid dries to a very hard-wearing finish. In practice, it does have some limitations, not least that it adheres best to matt acrylic paints and it is not wholly solvent-proof, even when dry.

Clear cellulose-type lacquers are the *pièce de résistance*, with the potential for super-fine finishes, although they demand a higher level of painting expertise. Lacquers can only be sprayed, either from an aerosol or airbrush, although, once fully cured, the finish is durable and lustrous. As mentioned in the previous chapter, most lacquers will react against underlying paints of acrylic or enamel formulas – and are highly toxic – so they must be used with care. Curiously, Alclad clear lacquers are fine when airbrushed over acrylics and enamels, provided that the paint finish is absolutely dry and the clear coats are built up in light layers. If in doubt,

Clear coats are essential as a means of unifying a number of separate livery elements, as well as providing the necessary base for decals and lining.

Johnson Klear and Hornby's Gloss Clear are acrylic-based finishes that are optimized for both hand and airbrush application.

read the label before use and try out on a scrap surface to be sure.

APPLYING CLEAR COATS

The same vital factors that govern a successful paint application – spotless, grease-free surface and patient build-up of very light coats – apply equally to clear coats. Moreover, a very gentle rubdown with some ultra-fine abrasives (grades 12,000 and upwards), lubricated with warm water, will serve to flatten the painted surfaces and remove any raised ridges where different colours merge. Allow the model to dry naturally before wiping with mild isopropyl alcohol and, once this has also dried completely, begin brushing or spraying your chosen clear coat. Apply light layers and allow each to dry before continuing.

Creating a high-quality deep gloss finish takes time. Rubbing down each hardened coat to ensure no imperfections are trapped between the layers can be laborious but ultimately worth the effort. I'm often asked about the use of gloss livery paints, as a quicker route to achieving a final gloss finish and my answer remains the same: they're not worth the effort. As the assembly of a multicolour livery demands the overlaying of certain elements, getting fresh paint to cling to a gloss backing is not easy, unless it is first rubbed down to a semi-matt sheen, thus rendering the hassle of slow-drying gloss paints pointless. Similarly, the paint will need to be rubbed down again, prior to the final clear coat. As with gloss varnishes, gloss paints take much longer to build up no matter how they're applied, so it's far better to employ matt or satin paints and worry about getting the desired final sheen at the varnishing stage.

Once decals and lining have been applied to the gloss surface, I prefer to add another gloss clear

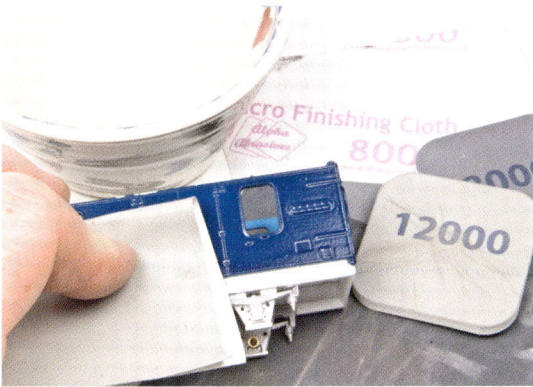

High-grade gloss finishes take time to achieve. Build up several layers, rubbing each coat down gently (when completely dry) with fine abrasives, such as Micro Mesh, lubricated with water. With patience, a glass-like finish can be achieved.

coat in order to render any decal carrier film completely invisible. Once this has cured, the final finish can be tailored to your own preferences.

Matt and satin varnishes are far less demanding in their application. Matt, or 'flat', clear coats contain heavier pigments and thus require fewer coats (in general). They can also act to change our perception of the underlying colours. Indeed, some varnishes, such as Humbrol's Matt Cote, have the nasty habit of adding a greyish hue to the livery. This is not such a bad thing with carriage roofs, but is undesirable on the bodywork. Testing various brands is worthwhile to gain an appreciation of how each behaves and to choose whatever suits your needs most accurately. One brand's satin is another brand's matt and vice versa, so taking what's on the label with a pinch of salt is also to be recommended.

DECALS

As discussed briefly in Chapter 2, decals, or transfers, come in a variety of different types and they offer a quick and effective way of adding numbers, logos and other markings. Lining is also available in decal form for those of us who don't fancy using a ruling pen and paints or, indeed, for occasions when ruling the lines by hand will be impractical. There's

certainly no shame in adopting transfers for these tasks, as the quality of certain brands is superb.

You may have noticed the qualifying remark in the previous paragraph: when I say 'certain' brands I mean that transfers are not of a universally high quality, so it helps to look in the right places. Brands such as Fox Transfers offer a massive range of decals, across all scales, covering a vast selection of prototypes, so they're usually my first port of call. The fact that the range is searchable online also helps. Other brands I can happily recommend include Precision Labels, Railtec and the various packs from the Historical Model Railway Society (HMRS). Replica Railways also offer a number of packs suitable for BR-era carriages, as do Modelmasters. Nairnshire Modelling Supplies commissioned a few sets of TOPS-era coaching stock transfers from US firm Microscale, who have an enviable reputation for producing high-quality decals. Lastly, Cambridge Custom Transfers offer various transfer packs for BR steam-era coaching stock in virtually any scale (*see* Useful Addresses for details of all transfer sources).

Most of the aforementioned ranges are supplied in waterslide format, save for Replica (dry-transfer) and HMRS (Pressfix and Methfix). Waterslide is the commonest application method for good reason: it's very simple. A high-gloss surface is paramount for maximum adhesion and to ensure that the clear carrier film, on which the individual characters are printed, remains invisible. A further sealing coat of gloss varnish is recommended before the final sheen is applied to suit your own tastes. These extra varnishing stages can be tiresome in some instances, but the results are more than worth the extra effort. Take shortcuts here at your peril, as the 'silvered' carrier film will potentially ruin the model.

Waterslide transfers may need a little help to adhere to undulating surfaces, or where a recessed panel or line of rivets lie beneath. Most brands produce waterslide decals that can take a degree of manipulation but, if you fiddle with them for too long they're bound to break apart. Accordingly, there are liquid decal setting and softening solutions to make the carrier film more flexible and to help the transfers adhere to the surface. They also

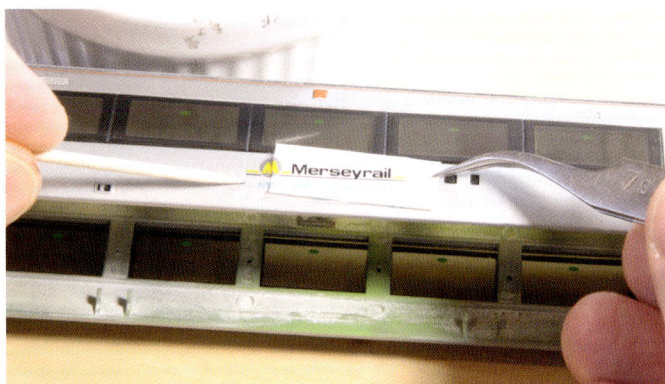

Waterslide decals offer the convenience of easy application and, if used correctly, can offer great results.

Decal softening fluids help waterslide transfers to settle over uneven surfaces. Apply the fluid before and after the transfer has been positioned, leaving a few minutes for it to work its magic.

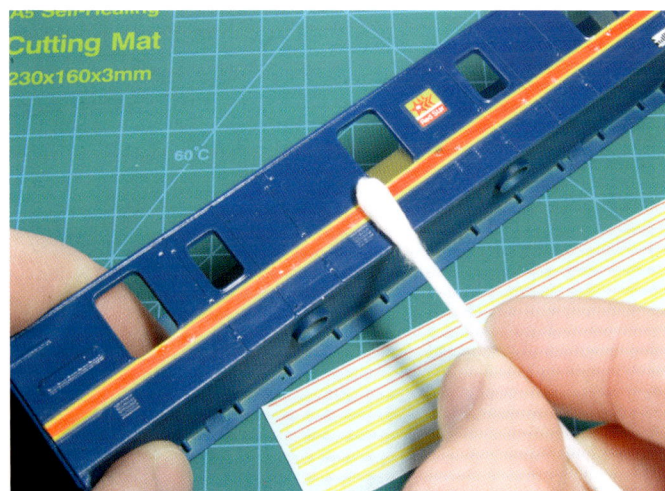

help disperse any air bubbles trapped beneath the film that can cause the 'silvering' effect that we so desperately need to avoid.

Dry transfers do not necessarily demand a gloss backing but the printing process limits the number of colours that can be replicated. Unlike waterslide decals, there is no room for adjustments. Once the character has transferred to the model it cannot move, so it's vital to get things perfect first time. Ideal for renumbering RTR models or adding extra small printed detail here and there, their wider use is, however, rather limited.

Pressfix and Methfix offer good results (especially Methfix), but application can be a long-winded process. The various characters are printed in reverse with a sticky covering applied to the lower face. After cutting and peeling from the backing sheet, the transfer is pressed into position. This is not as straightforward as it seems, as the opaque paper does not make for precise adjustment. Once the character is aligned, the paper is dampened with water (Pressfix) or a mix of diluted methylated spirit (Methfix). After a few minutes, the backing paper can be peeled away. While Pressfix decals can be a little on the bulky side, Methfix decals offer an almost 'painted on' appearance that is hard to beat. The dilute meths takes much longer to soak the backing away, however, so you can't be in any sort of hurry.

LEFT: **With a little gentle manipulation with a blunt cocktail stick or damp cotton swab, the softened transfer will meld itself around the detail. This is essential when applying large livery elements, bodyside stripes or lining.**

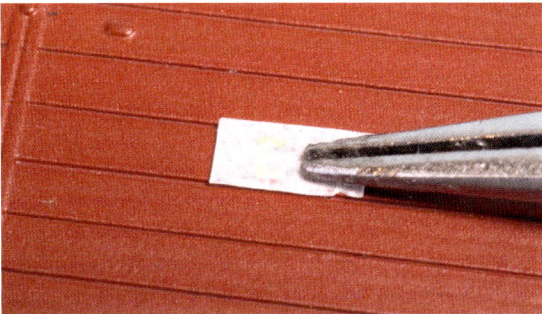

Pressfix and Methfix decals are a little more challenging, with accurate positioning not helped by the opaque paper backing.

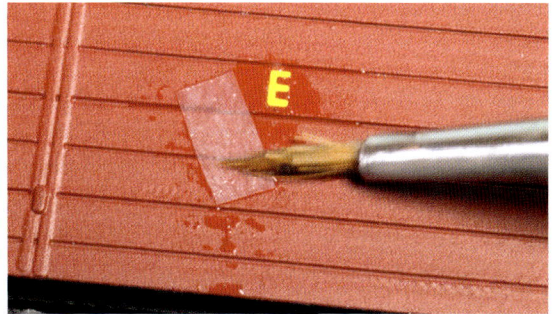

Once aligned and pressed onto the surface, the backing paper is soaked away, leaving behind no carrier film. Use water or Micro Sol for Pressfix and a mix of methylated spirit and water for Methfix.

Choosing decals is a matter of personal choice and we all have our own preferred mediums and brands. Convenience also plays a role as it may be possible to obtain all the necessary livery elements and markings in a single package, perhaps with enough to cover a number of similar vehicles with the one pack. Other times, we may have to spread our custom around in order to track down all the necessary bits and pieces. This can be frustrating and not a little expensive, so it may be worth contacting the likes of Railtec, Precision Labels or Cambridge Custom Transfers who each offers a more flexible service. Indeed, they can all produce hitherto unavailable transfers to suit your particular project, especially if you can help them out with the necessary prototype information.

An increasingly viable alternative is to make your own decals, using sheets of waterslide transfer paper that can be fed into a home desktop inkjet or laser printer. It means doing all the research and artwork yourself, which can be either a chore or a pleasure – depending on your predilections – and the printed sheets will need sealing with a clear varnish before application. It's not an expensive option, however, provided you have a decent printer and some form of design software on your computer.

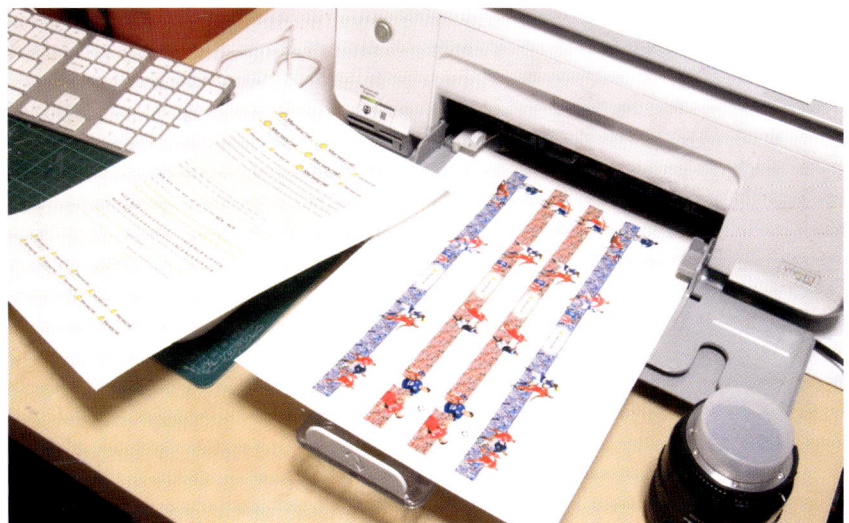

You can even make your own water-slide decals on a home computer, printed via an inkjet or laser printer. The sheets will need sealing with a few coats of varnish before application.

WOOD EFFECTS

Creating realistic wood grain effects is an enjoyable challenge, injecting a little bit of artistic endeavour into our carriage modelling. The pre-British Railways era saw a variety of coaching stock boasting a varnished wood finish, with some of the most famous being employed by the LNER. So keen was the 'North Eastern' on this livery, that even Thompson's later steel-sided stock was painted in an 'ersatz teak' scheme to match vehicles from earlier periods.

Plenty of natural wood finishes were to be found elsewhere, including on the Metropolitan Railway. As these coaches were invariably built in the panelled style, attention to the direction of the grain on the prototype is important (something Hornby overlooked on some of its early Gresley teak stock).

There are a number of ways to recreate this type of finish in miniature, with my preferred strategies outlined here. However, I've seen other modellers employ some vastly different materials and techniques to amazing effect, so I'm not stating any claim for superiority. They're simply the methods that I've found effective and reasonably quick – once you've had a bit of practice, of course.

Study of the prototype will reveal plenty of tonal variation across a natural wood finish. The grain figure itself is seldom a single shade, while the rest of the timber will also exhibit fluctuations in tone, even without the consideration of weathering effects. A combination of paints can be harnessed to create a suitable background colour, aiming for subtle variations to mirror those of the prototype, especially

Creating authentic wood-grain effects can be great fun, but careful study of the prototype is essential. Note how the grain direction varies across this carriage.

around the edges (darker) and central areas (lighter) of each panel. I prefer to undertake these preliminary applications with an airbrush, tinkering with the paint shade regularly to avoid an overly uniform finish. Although not impossible, I find it much more difficult to achieve similar effects by hand, especially on smaller scale subjects, without the risk of smothering the fine surface detail under excessive layers of paint.

However, the use of special 'filter' paints offers the modeller much more scope for working by hand. These are diluted paints that leave a translucent finish over a base colour, helping to create high- or low-lights across a specific tonal range without depositing high quantities of heavy pigments onto refined surface relief. Employed extensively by military and aviation modellers, a choice of oil-based, wood-themed filter washes is available from AK Interactive and they can also be sprayed directly through an airbrush with no need for thinning.

I prefer to build up a variety of acrylic base shades. Darker shades are concentrated around the edges of each panel and in recessed areas, with lighter tones aimed towards the centre of each panel.

With the base layers rendered, the grain figure can be applied with careful dry-brushing, with only traces of paint left on the brush's bristles. A good-quality flat brush is essential for this task and, again, varying the shades slightly will create more lifelike results. Allowing each application of paint to dry completely in between is paramount. Indeed, following acrylic basecoats with enamel washes and filters will only work if the previous layer has hardened entirely. Rushing will only soften the underlying paint and spoil all your hard work.

A viable alternative, seldom mentioned in model railway circles, is the use of wood grain decals. Available in many different shades and grain patterns, they're aimed at modellers of early aviation subjects. Although marketed to suit specific

When the first stage is complete and the paint dry, an enamel dark wash is brushed over the body. The excess is wiped away with a swab, leaving the dark pigment in the various recesses.

Enamel-based filters are then employed to fine-tune the base shades (enamels are used so that the Tamiya acrylics won't be disturbed). AK Interactive offers a range of washes and filters aimed at creating lifelike wood finishes. Brush or spray the filters as desired, wiping away any excess.

The grain figuring is created by dry-brushing with a flat brush. Nearly all of the paint is removed from the bristles on a tissue before lightly dragging it over the model, working in the direction of the grain. The shades are varied slightly from panel to panel, with several repeat passes made where necessary. I like Vallejo acrylics for this task, as they come in a perfect consistency: not too thick and not too thin.

aircraft modelling scales, a quick browse will reveal colours and grain patterns suited to a variety of carriage prototypes across virtually any scale. There will often be a need to apply a suitable buff under-coat shade, as I've found some wood grain decals to be ever so slightly translucent, plus the essential high-gloss clear coats on which the transfers can adhere correctly.

Cutting the decals to size and applying to many individual panels can prove time-consuming and the raised areas of beading pose their own problems (I paint these separately before the decals are applied). Recourse to decal softening solutions will be essential to get the film sitting evenly across any undulating features.

The grain effect can be toned down slightly by more applications of filters, either sprayed or brushed. It is vital that the model is left to dry overnight between each of the various stages.

Elements of lining, according to the prototype's scheme, can help blend everything together, as will a sealing clear finish and some degree of weathering – again, using images of the real thing as inspiration.

Brushing or spraying 'filters' over the sealed decals is also worth mentioning, as these dilute media can help to tailor the finished colours more precisely, as well as creating a more unified overall effect.

Whether employing the dry-brushing method or decals, it's important to study the grain patterns of the prototype, as the direction of grain was oriented in specific directions across certain areas. Wood grain effects are also well worth applying to coach interiors, especially in larger-scale models where bulkheads and partitions are readily visible through the windows or when interior lighting is installed.

A viable alternative to painted renditions of wood grain is to employ waterslide decals. There are numerous packs available, such as these sheets from the Uschi van der Rosten range, distributed by Albion Alloys (see Useful Addresses).

LINING

Not solely confined to the steam age, lining is still to be found on the twenty-first-century railway, albeit in a more simplified form than in days gone by. In modern terms, the obvious example is the obligatory orange warning line at cantrail level, while certain post-privatization liveries have included some form of bands, stripes or lined accents. Even the seemingly drab BR corporate image livery had a delicate white lining separating the blue and grey elements.

Move further back in time and carriage lining becomes more complex, attractive and vital. Indeed, it's unthinkable to not include the lining on panelled stock, especially on pre-1940s vehicles where the railway companies really went to town on their carriages. Even if we're talking about etched carriage kits, there's a strong chance that the painting and lining stages will take longer than the actual construction. Therefore, mastering lining application methods will provide a valuable asset for the budding carriage builder.

A choice may have to be made whether to simplify a prototype's lining scheme, if it's deemed too difficult or impractical for a small-scale rendition. Scaling down lining elements, in the same way as you'd scale down the size of a window aperture or wheel, may not always be possible, especially without recourse to some highly sophisticated printing equipment. Lining by hand or with decals comes with certain limitations regarding the size of coloured line that can be formed on a three-dimensional surface (or what may actually be visible) so, in some cases, be prepared to make some degree of compromise.

The use of an artist's bow pen (or ruling pen as they're also called) is not an easy skill to attain, not so much due to the tool being difficult to use, but because good-quality bow pens are difficult to find these days. Specialist art shops are a potential source and choosing the best you can afford is important. Rather like a plasterer's trowel that has been worn-in over many years, so that it has a feather-light working edge, so a bow pen also benefits from age and use. Mine have seen regular employment over the past twenty years and they're better now than they've ever been, although they have been carefully maintained and pampered. More recently my wife bought me a beautiful set from an antiques dealer and this century-old tool has proved even more effective. You can try to grind

The tools of the lining trade: bow pens, draughtsman's pens and inks, compasses, templates and straight edges.

the edges of a new pen on an oilstone, but it's a very tricky business – far more difficult than the lining itself.

Choosing and mixing the paint is just as crucial as honing the bow pen, with the pigment needing to flow freely across the model, yet with the ability to remain between the jaws of the pen until needed. Slower drying paints, such as enamels, are recommended although this means that only a small number of lines can be ruled at a time before the model has to be left overnight to dry, lest the straight edge

Stir the paint thoroughly, adding a drop of thinners if necessary. Gloss enamels are the easiest to line with, as they dry very slowly and remain workable for longer. Load the bow pen and wipe the outer faces of the jaws clean.

Perfect your technique on scraps of plastic card, adjusting the bow pen until the desired width of line is created. If the paint struggles to flow, clean the tool completely, stir the paint again and add a little more thinners.

disturb the wet paint. I've used acrylics on many occasions when I've had deadlines looming and their faster drying does permit far more rapid progress. However, the paint is only useable in the bow pen for a minute or so before it clogs up and demands a thorough clean. Being forced to rush is never conducive to fine modelling, so I'd recommend taking your time and sticking with enamels.

As well as a traditional bow pen, the Bob Moore Master Lining Pen is also, apparently, an effective device, although I've never tried one personally. Furthermore, it was designed to offer a more user-friendly option than a bow pen, with interchangeable tips to create lines of a consistent width (from 0.2mm). It's certainly not a cheap option (hence why I've yet to invest in one), but it may well prove a worthy asset if lots of lining-out jobs are envisaged.

My old Rotring ink pens, intended for technical drawing, also see plenty of use for lining tasks. I've had these pens since my art college days and the various nib sizes allow a range of fine lines to be rendered accurately and cleanly. The surface must be clean, dry and, preferably, glossy and the ink demands a few hours to dry properly before the risk of smudging has passed (following with a spray coat of varnish is also essential).

A very limited palette of colours is possible, however, with Rotring only offering black, white and red inks. Available in a variety of tip sizes, from 0.1mm up to 1.0mm, they may not be cheap but they will last a long time if cleaned and maintained regularly. Incidentally, if using white ink in a Rotring pen, be sure to empty the reservoir and clean out the tip as soon as you've finished the job. The heavy, chalky pigment has a nasty habit of drying up after a couple of days and is murder to clean out.

Lining is a technique worthy of trialling on scrap models first, rather than taking the plunge directly onto a freshly assembled kit. Improvising a suitable cradle for the model will help keep both hands free and your wrists should ideally have plenty to rest themselves on. A simple wooden contraption is easy enough to knock-up from offcuts of baseboard timber to make yourself as comfortable

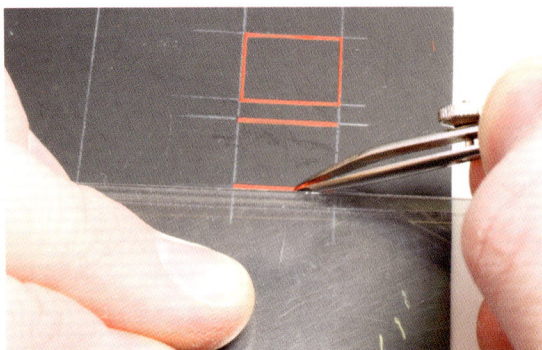

Mark out the location of the lining elements with a finely sharpened tailor's pencil, following with the bow pen as closely as possible. Be careful not to smudge the paint as you remove the straight edge. Working onto a high gloss surface allows any mistakes to be wiped away with a white spirit-soaked swab.

To introduce curved elements, stop short with each straight line and either touch-in the missing areas with a brush by hand, employing a curved template, or use a compass-type bow pen.

Previous applications must be completely dry before layering subsequent colours.

Provided that the model, straight edge and your wrist are well supported, there's no reason why the skills you've honed on flat plastic can't be transferred to a three-dimensional object. A single thin stripe, such as an orange cantrail warning line, is an ideal subject to start with. Clamping the straight edge to the body with pegs or spring clamps can be helpful.

Thicker lines or stripes, such as the white separating line, can be achieved with one broad stroke, but it is unlikely that the bow pen will hold enough paint to cover more than a few inches. Instead, build up several adjacent thin lines that will merge into one another. It is very difficult to join lines seamlessly end-to-end if you run out of paint mid-stroke.

With lining consisting of multiple colours, such as the straw/black of this maroon BR coach, apply the lighter colour first.

as possible, which will help you to keep a much steadier hand.

As already mentioned, lining is possible by means of transfers, either in waterslide, Pressfix or Methfix formats. It's not uncommon for professional model-lers, including myself, to adopt a mixture of both decals and hand-applied lining, depending on the model in question. Sometimes a bow pen simply won't reach a certain area, especially on smaller-scale models, so unless you can fill in the gaps with a fine paintbrush, resorting to decals is a natural solu-tion. Colour matching may be an issue, however, so it's never a quick fix solution. If the carriage is

When the first layer is dry, the black element is then overlapped slightly to render the straw to its scale thickness to create a neater join between the two.

Alternatively, try a Rotring pen to add fine lines in black, white or red ink. Various tip sizes are available and they work best on a glossy surface.

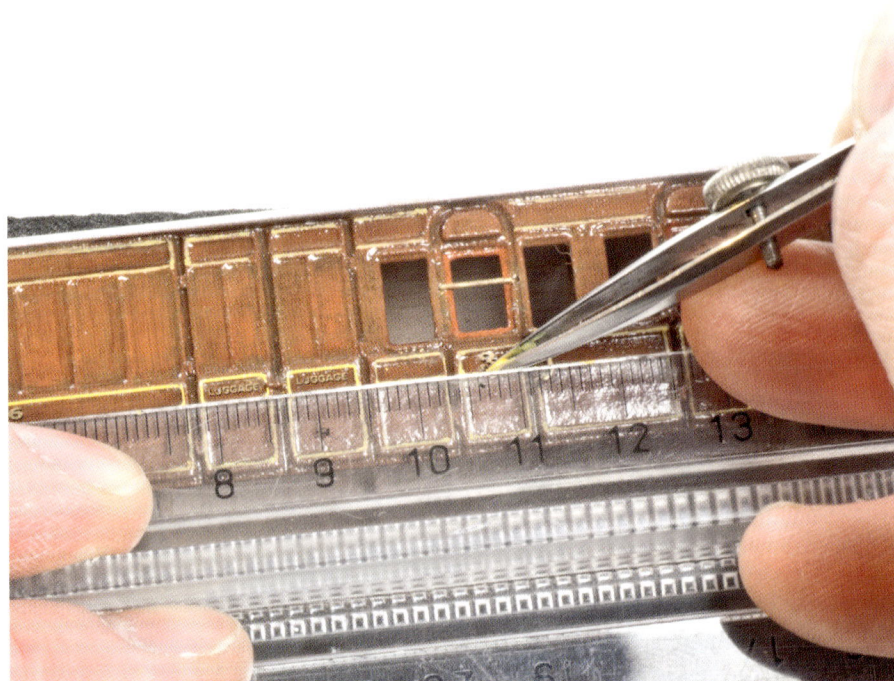

Lining the edges of panels and raised beading takes plenty of time. It is all too easy to smudge the lines by being impatient. Work in short bursts, over several days, to stop yourself going mad!

Lining by hand can be complemented – or replaced – by the use of decals. Both the yellow First Class banding and the fine white lining separating the blue and grey were applied with waterslide decals, ensuring that they sat cleanly around any raised or recessed surface detail.

to receive a mildly weathered finish, then any small inconsistency can always be disguised.

Lining decals come in straight lengths and a variety of corners and curves. It's then a question of cutting and pasting the various elements together. Depending on the scheme, it may be necessary to layer a variety of colours on top of each other. If so, the previous layers must be fully dry or subsequent wetting will simply loosen all surrounding decals. Far better to apply one layer, leave to dry out and spray a light coat of varnish and then continue. Once again, there's the prospect of waiting around between tasks, but remember that the finishing stage should never be rushed.

FINISH THE FINISH

In order to unify all of the various livery elements, transfers, lining and any small details that have been picked out by hand, an overall sealing coat of varnish is always recommended. The final sheen is down to personal preference, but bear in mind that the entire carriage does not have to carry the same sheen all over. Treating the sides to a semi-gloss, while the roof and underframe receive more of a matt finish can have a pleasing visual effect. Use of an airbrush at this stage offers particular benefits as the different clear coats can be applied with no need for masking, the lines between each being 'blurred' for maximum effect.

Another tip is to add a drop or two of black paint to the varnish in order to give the surface a slightly lived-in feel and to temper any bright livery elements or logos. The paint must be of the same brand and type as the varnish to ensure compatibility, and practising on a scrap model to perfect your mix ratio beforehand is recommended. This is probably a subtle form of weathering, but we'll look into that subject in detail in the following chapter.

Don't forget other small details, whether they are added from decals or with the paintbrush, including data panels, warning stickers, jumper cable sockets, axlebox covers, springs and piping.

Pick out polished metal door furniture and handrails with metallic paints, such as AK Interactive's True Metal range. Once dry, these paints can be burnished to a realistic finish. If such fittings had previously been omitted, now is the time to install them.

With all but the glazing installed, treat the body to an overall sealing coat of varnish. This helps blend all the different elements together as well as protecting the finish below. For greater realism, tailor the sheen of the clear coats over different areas: matt for the roof, underframe and ends, with a gentle gloss on the sides.

CHAPTER SIXTEEN

WEATHERING

You may think that the weathering of carriages is a fairly condensed topic, but such is the wealth of potential techniques and variety of available materials that it's actually a rather complex subject. Not everybody appreciates 'dirty' carriages, however, and I'm not one to argue against a fellow modeller's preferences. Therefore, what this chapter aims to do is to give an overview of how I aim to make my model carriages more lifelike. That may involve a faded livery, patches of rust or peeling paint and a general air of decrepitude. At the other extreme, it may simply consist of a little dust and soot here and there, with some patches of grease on the buffers and the odd scuff on the footsteps.

Indeed, the term 'weathering' is often misconstrued. I'm not sure what the official definition is in terms of model railways, but I've always interpreted it as making a model as realistic as possible rather than simply daubing it with filth. As the following demonstrations illustrate, there are many simple techniques as well as a few complex methods that can each have a dramatic influence on the appearance of a finished model.

Having come this far with a kit build or RTR upgrade, it may be a daunting prospect to then try and take things even further. Once again, though, trying out some of these techniques on older or less prized models beforehand is heartily recommended.

No matter how well built a carriage is, it will always look like a model unless some effort is made to help it blend into a scenic layout.

The same carriage looks considerably more lifelike with the aid of some simple weathering. In this case, enamel paints have been applied via an airbrush for quick but effective results. However, there are plenty of other methods and materials to employ.

Even RTR carriages can be brought to life with a little effort. The finish of the plastic sides has been given a deeper lustre with the use of T-Cut automotive finish restorer, while the contrast with the dusty roof, ends and underframe is an accurate depiction of the real thing.

I'd also suggest looking at as many prototype images as possible, preferably in colour. Different vehicles tended to attract dirt in specific manners, whether as a result of their peculiar operating areas, the nature of their outline or the common traction types employed in their haulage.

Other relevant factors include the importance of the vehicles. Were they employed on top-link expresses, suburban commuter services or work-man's trains? How often would they be cleaned and by what methods? Was it just the sides and windows that were treated? The period in which your layout is based is also important. For instance, the imme-diate post-war and early nationalization era saw a shortage of cleaning staff and a rundown of certain pre-war carriage types, as the new 'standard' stock was being designed and introduced. You don't need to be an expert in railway history in order to answer all of these questions, as the clues will be there in contemporary images.

WEATHERING MATERIALS

PAINTS AND DYES

Most hobby paint ranges offer either dedicated weathering shades for railway subjects or a wealth of similar colours under different branding. I tend to go through phases of using one or two brands, more out of habit than anything else. Most recently, Tamiya's acrylics have been in vogue in the Dent workshops, mostly due to their ease of use when airbrushing and ultra-rapid drying times. Other paints that I happily employ include Lifecolor and Vallejo acrylics, plus RailMatch enamels.

Going more from the shade of the paint rather than what's written on the label, it's usually a case of finding a handful of browns, greys and dirty blacks, with a couple of rusty reds thrown in. With Tamiya and Vallejo, that may mean paints as exotic sounding as Linoleum Deck Brown or German Camouflage Black. Whatever they're called, a collection of a dozen or so shades usually suffices, with intermix-ing common to achieve the exact shades that I'm after. It can be surprising just how much tonal variety can be achieved with such a narrow palette

of paints, although it's very much a question of personal interpretation, helped by reference to prototype images.

As for dyes, the ModelMates range of water-based dyes is a useful medium, being a halfway house between a dilute wash and a regular paint. They can be airbrushed without need for thinning or can be readily applied by brush, sponge or swab. Rather like dry pigments, they demand a matt surface on which to adhere, while offering the unique ability to be manipulated with water for an indefinite period. Anything from a finely misted smoke stain to heavy streaking is possible and, once the intended result is obtained, a coat of clear varnish seals the dye in place.

POWDERS

Dry weathering powders and pigments, if applied carefully, can create a wide variety of visual effects. Lightly misted areas of dusty deposits provide similar results to an airbrush, yet with the added dry texture that paints can never truly replicate. They can also be mixed with enamel or acrylic paints in order to create a textured finish. Indeed, adding a greater proportion of powders turns the paint into a thick paste that also has its uses. Alternatively, some pigments can be mixed with pure turpentine to create similar effects.

Powders struggle to adhere to gloss finishes, so a prior coating of matt varnish is important. Much depends on the quality of the powders, but they'll often stay put once applied with a soft flat brush. Removing any excess should be done with another soft, clean brush or dry air from an airbrush. Try to resist the temptation to blow the dust away with your breath, as any moisture will cause staining on the model. If necessary, the powders can be sealed with a liquid fixative. Most weathering powder ranges offer a fixing solution and this can be applied in various ways. I prefer misting the fluid through an airbrush with the air set at the lowest possible pressure. The liquid does have a tendency to 'clean up' the weathered areas slightly, which may or may not be desired. More pigment can then be applied if necessary and the process repeated.

WASHES

As glimpsed in the previous chapter, weathering washes are essentially heavily diluted paints. MIG and AK Interactive produce some superb enamel-based formulas, while the Lifecolor acrylic Tensocrom range has its own merits. Designed for creating streaking effects (leaking water, oil or grease) as well as rust and other grubby deposits, they can be applied with fine brushes, sponges or cotton swabs. They're also ideal for overall washes, especially on surfaces with plenty of relief, such as planked or panelled bodyshells. The pigments find their way into recesses and around raised details while the carrier liquid tends to dry to an almost translucent finish.

With a bit of practice, some very realistic effects can be created with relative ease. The benefit of enamel-based formulas in particular is that they remain workable for up to an hour and can be manipulated or removed altogether with a little white spirit. The better formulas of washes contain pigments that dry to a flat matt sheen, except for those intended for replicating greasy deposits. Any previously applied finishes must be completely dry before applying washes, especially enamel- or oil-based formulas, or they'll damage the paint or varnish.

Other types of wash are available, including artists' oil paints, suitably thinned with turpentine, or water-based formulas containing finely ground clay pigments. You can also create your own washes by diluting suitable shades of enamel or acrylic paints, although getting them to the optimum consistency is a matter of trial and error. Ready-made washes offer greater convenience and, as long as they're thoroughly shaken beforehand, they frequently produce superior results.

OTHER MATERIALS AND TECHNIQUES

Recreating specific effects, such as peeling paint or rust patches, is possible using a variety of materials and techniques. There's also the matter of introducing wider tonal variety within a livery shade, adding highlights and shading as well as replicating the distinctive faded appearance common on many vehicle types. Employing less obvious weathering devices, such as coloured pencils and T-Cut automotive finish restorer, can also be highly rewarding.

T-Cut can be employed on factory finishes, applied sparingly with a cotton bud. Don't worry about protecting the plastic glazing, as the compound won't damage it. Work on one side at a time.

Burnish the T-Cut before it dries out, using clean cotton buds or a soft-haired polishing mop in a mini-drill (set to a low speed) and using minimal pressure to avoid damaging the plastic. Follow with an old but clean toothbrush to ensure that all traces of the T-Cut are removed before treating the other side. Leave the coach overnight to allow any solvent traces to disperse.

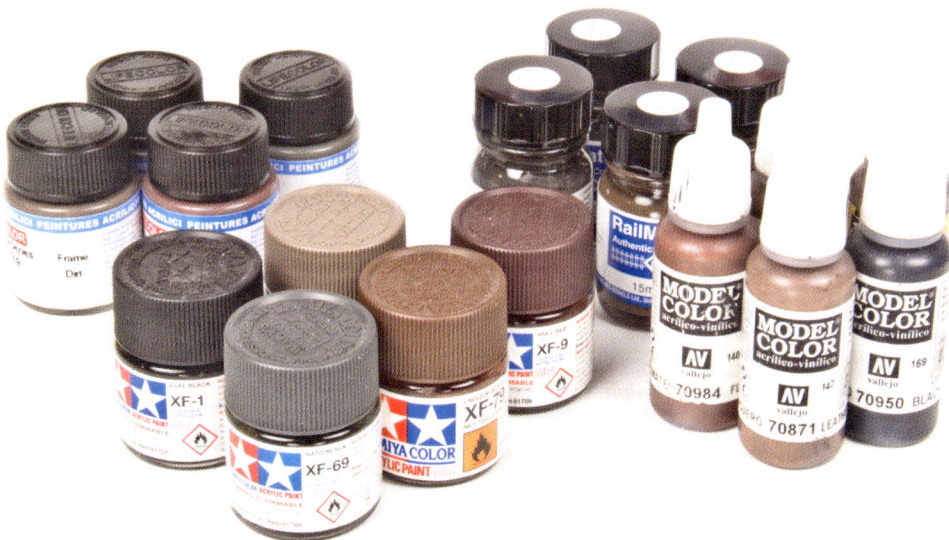

A relatively small palate of paint shades is required for weathering, consisting mainly of various browns, dark greys and black. Matt paints are essential and my personal preferences include RailMatch enamels and Tamiya, Vallejo and Lifecolor acrylics.

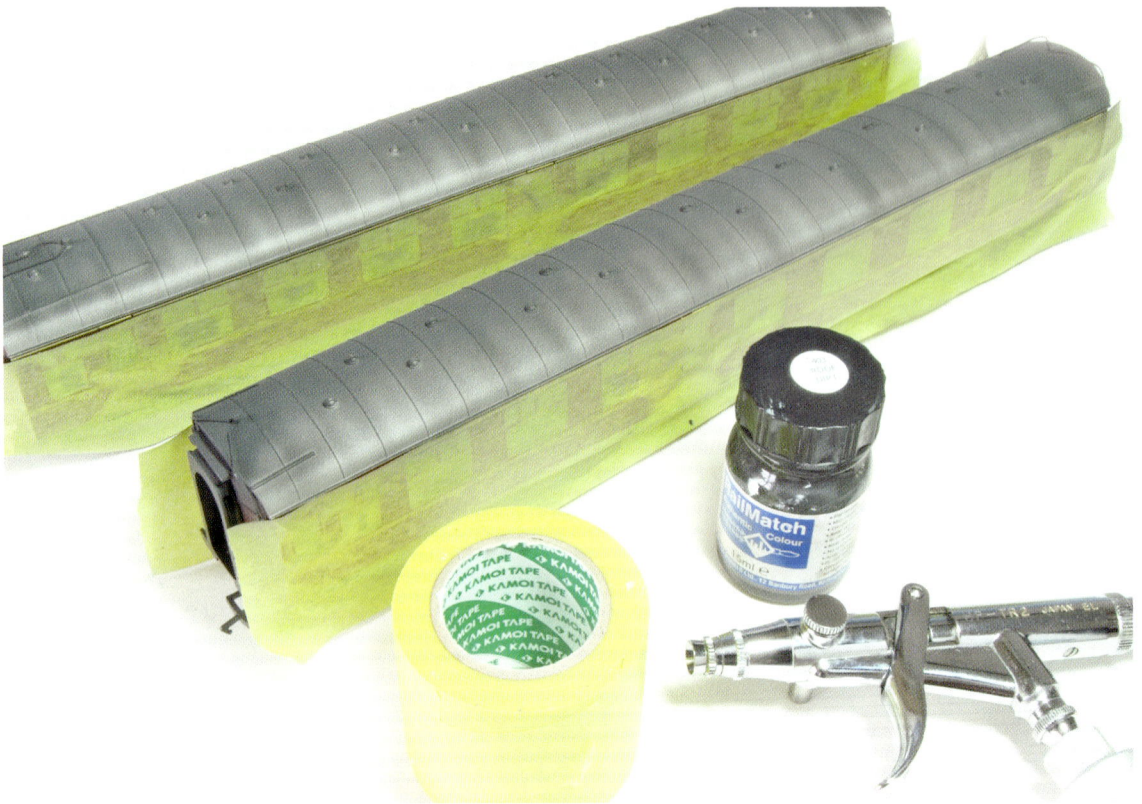

My usual routine for generic airbrush weathering jobs is to begin by masking the sides, while leaving the ends, roof and underframe exposed. A dirty, dark grey, such as RailMatch's Roof Dirt, mixed with a little Weathered Black, can then be sprayed over the roof, concentrating the darker shades towards the ends and working it around any raised vents or ribbing.

The underframe and carriage ends are then treated to a misted spray of various dirty browns. In this case RailMatch Track Dirt is in use, although I'll tweak the mix with a little Dark Rust and a drop or two of the Roof Dirt to introduce some tonal variety.

Once the paint has dried, the masking is then carefully removed from the sides.

When using enamels, you have the ability to loosen and manipulate any of the weathering paint that may creep beneath the masking. A cocktail stick, dipped in white spirit, will do the job, as well as creating streaks by dragging the softened paint.

ABOVE: **Run dark enamel paint into the door seams. Don't worry about getting it perfect yet.**

MIDDLE RIGHT: **Excess paint or wash can be wiped away from around the seam with a cotton swab dampened with white spirit, leaving the dark pigment within the recess.**

BOTTOM RIGHT: **Dry-brushing areas with a slightly lighter shade of the livery colour serves to highlight any raised details. Similarly, metallic paints such as Humbrol's enamel No.53 Gunmetal mimic exposed areas of bare or burnished metal, which is perfect for heavy traffic areas, such as door handles, footsteps, vents and grilles.**

Don't forget the wheels, which are often easier to treat separately, if they can be readily removed. A mix of RailMatch Track Dirt and Humbrol No.27004 Metal Cote Gunmetal provides a convincing finish. Wipe away any stray paint from the wheel treads and flanges with white spirit.

To create a more careworn effect to the sides, brush on an overall coat of a dark, dirty brown shade of enamel (I use a mix of Track Dirt and Roof Dirt), working on a few square inches at a time, having masked or removed the glazing. Immediately, most of the paint is wiped away with a swab, using only vertical strokes in relation to the coach body.

TOP: **Excess weathering paint can be removed from awkward areas with a cocktail stick soaked in white spirit, although the solvent must be kept away from the clear plastic. Traces of the dirty paint will remain in the corners and recesses where the cleaner's brush would not have reached. The effect can be tailored to suit your desired level of soiling. Combined with airbrushed weathering to the rest of the carriage, the results can be impressive, especially with panel-bodied stock.**

MIDDLE: **Carriage underframes, especially in the steam era, could be grimy, crusty places and paint alone struggles to convey this. Try mixing in some talcum powder or, preferably, dry pigments. Lifecolor and MIG powdered pigments are ideal for mixing with acrylic paints and the resulting gloop can be stippled onto and around the bogies and chassis, mixing the shades slightly as you go to avoid too uniform a finish. Add a little thinners if the paint becomes too thick. This technique can also be effective for carriage roofs, tailoring the colours to suit.**

BOTTOM: **The textured underframe may appear a little patchy once the paint dries, but the effect can be refined with a misting of Track Dirt via an airbrush or aerosol. Adding greasy deposits around the axleboxes and brake gear, using washes or gloss paints, can be highly effective.**

The dusty, slightly textured underframe and roof counterpoint nicely the colourful sides, albeit with plenty of dirt remaining in the recesses of the panelling. Careful work with the airbrush to soften the contrast between each of the various weathering stages creates a more harmonious effect.

Weathering powders offer the chance to create subtle dusting effects, akin to what is only otherwise possible with an airbrush. They require a matt surface to work on and are best applied with a soft, dry, flat brush. Wear gloves to avoid leaving fingerprints in the weathering.

Although good-quality powders will adhere well enough, they can be disturbed by regular handling, so it pays to fix them in place, either with a matt varnish or a pigment fixative. Most ranges of powder include fixative fluids and they can be sprayed neat through an airbrush, set at a very low pressure.

Applied with a cosmetic sponge or small brush, Tamiya's dark rust and gunmetal weathering pigments are ideal for accentuating raised details, especially on bogies, brake gear and underframe equipment.

Faded paint effects can be tricky to create, especially when working with an existing finish. A technique I've recently discovered is to brush on a mix of AK Interactive Light Grey Highlighting and Dark Grey Fading oil colours, thinning them slightly with white spirit.

A spirit-soaked swab is then employed to remove most of the paint, in a similar manner to the earlier techniques. The paints leave behind a feint pigment that serves to create a realistic washed-out effect.

Once the remains of the grey oils have dried, reinstate the dark door recesses and any other seams with a dark enamel wash. The ability to work on the sides of Bachmann's 'OO' Mk1 stock in isolation is greatly appreciated during jobs like this.

If any small patches of corrosion are required, there are few better mediums than ModelMates' Rust Effect. Apply in several light layers to create a realistic variety of tones (the more is applied, the darker the shade), with the fluid drying to a grainy finish. A fine brush or cocktail stick, dampened with water, can be used to manipulate the Rust Effect to create streaks, or remove it altogether. As the medium will remain water-soluble, it is necessary to seal it with a few clear coats (sprayed) once the desired effects have been created.

To create the appearance of chipped or worn paintwork, apply a suitable undercoat colour first. This could be a layer of 'rust' or a depiction of whatever would be underlying the outer finish, such as bare metal, timber or previous liveries. Once dry, apply several coats of AK Interactive Worn Effects or Heavy Chipping fluid through an airbrush.

The topcoat shade is then sprayed using a water-based acrylic, such as Lifecolor or Vallejo. As soon as this paint is dry (about thirty minutes), use a stiff brush and a little water to reactivate the AK Interactive chipping fluid, revealing the original, underlying finish. This process takes a little practice, but a vast array of effects can be created. Once happy with the results, allow the model to dry completely before adding any more paints or powders.

Employing a variety of separate materials and effects has the potential to create a disjointed overall appearance, but gently misting a variety of thinned dirty browns and dark greys over the model, especially over the 'joins' between different areas, helps bring everything together into a more coherent whole.

Most of my weathering techniques have been derived from improvisation, sometimes inspired by the appearance of new products or materials. Browsing through magazines from other modelling disciplines, especially aviation and military spheres, has proved especially instructive. Experimentation is one of the most enjoyable facets of this hobby as far as I'm concerned and I'm sure that there are countless, equally effective media and methods that I've yet to come across. As long as the model comes out of the weathering stages intact and looking realistic, then that's basically all that matters.

In a similar manner to the dry-brushing technique, artists' coloured pencils can be harnessed to pick out raised details or mimic scuffmarks. A variety of browns and greys will be required, while metallic pencils are ideal for areas of burnished metal.

It helps to apply a sealing layer of varnish to ensure that the weathering is not disturbed during handling. As mentioned in the previous chapter, employing matt coats to the roof, underframe and ends, with a satin or gloss finish to the sides, can be highly effective.

A combination of fading effects, peeling paint, patches of rust and a textured underframe create a highly realistic appearance. Each technique can be fine-tuned according to your needs, with prototype inspiration proving invaluable.

CHAPTER SEVENTEEN

FINISHING TOUCHES

What final flourishes can we give to a model carriage, now that we've rendered a RTR or kit-built vehicle to the highest standard we possibly can? Having enhanced the exterior and interior with plenty of realistic detail and improved the running qualities, what other options exist for adding extra character?

As we've already discussed, looking at the real thing for inspiration is a guaranteed source of answers to such questions. A good example to start with is the once ubiquitous name and destination boards carried by steam-era coaching stock. This type of detail helps to place the train in a certain time and place, reinforcing the authenticity of our layout and its operations.

NAME THAT TRAIN

From the railways' earliest days it was not uncommon for carriages to be adorned with the destinations and

For prestige steam- and early diesel-era express services, carriage nameboards add a final touch of authenticity. Precision Labels and Pacific Models offer a wide range of printed boards and gangway covers for various scales and regions.

calling points of the routes that they served. Prestige expresses are a prime example, with the stock of the 'Thames-Clyde Express', 'The Caledonian' or 'Brighton Belle' carrying stylish name boards above the windows, either just below or above the roofline, wherever was deemed the optimum position for catching the passenger's eye while standing at a platform.

Indeed, carriages were routinely built with mounting brackets for such boards, including BR Mk1 and early Mk2 stock, well into the 1960s. The gangway cover, on the outer end of the trailing car, was also regularly decorated with the train's name and logo. In BR days the painted boards and gangway covers also took on a regional identity, with the house colours of each region, such as maroon for

the London Midland's 'Merseyside Express'. A few even appeared in the corporate blue of the 'modernized' BR era.

Replica's version of the Mk1 coach featured name-board brackets moulded into the bodyshell, but subsequent 'OO' versions have largely ignored these fittings, save for some of Bachmann's more recent Mk1 variants. Older models of pre-BR carriages have also boasted mounting points to suit the prototype. If your model lacks any brackets – or they're inadequate – they are simple enough to recreate with strips of plastic or brass, spaced accordingly. Check your prototype to see exactly where the brackets were installed and the common board lengths employed, as these differed over the years and between regions.

Many RTR carriages and kits include renditions of nameboard mounting brackets but, if not present, they're easy enough to recreate with fine plastic or metal strip. Precision Labels offers packs of etched brackets to match its range of printed boards.

Choose a fresh, sharp scalpel blade and cut out the nameboards carefully against a steel rule, making the cut in several passes if necessary to avoid snagging the card. Precision Labels' boards are supplied with a self-adhesive backing.

Miniature name boards are available in various scales from Precision Labels, who have exhaustively researched the prototypes (my old boss at the National Railway Museum gets an acknowledgement on the packaging). A range of well-known services is covered, across the various regions, and some packs also include gangway covers for the trailing coach and even a matching locomotive headboard where appropriate. Each board is printed onto high-quality self-adhesive paper.

Pacific Models also offer a broad range of printed coach boards for 'OO' and 'O', with destinations and

If the boards feature a coloured background, touch in the white edges of the card with a marker pen or acrylic paint of a similar shade.

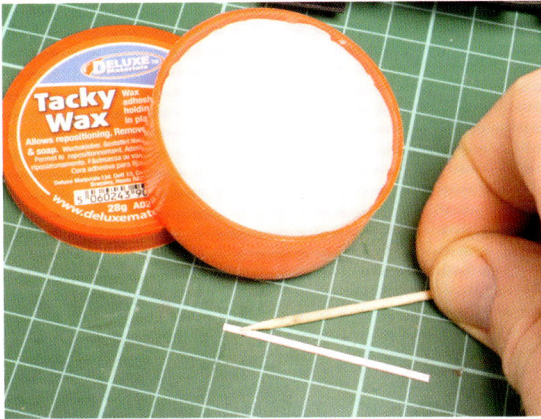

Tacky Wax offers a temporary, yet secure, bond. Apply a small amount of the adhesive with a cocktail stick. Any squeezed-out wax can be removed without damaging the model or the printed boards. For permanent bonds, use clear-setting PVA-type glues, such as Glue 'n' Glaze.

Position the boards carefully, checking prototype images for the correct location. If any adhesive oozes out, remove with a cotton bud or cocktail stick immediately.

With a set of nameboards and gangway covers on the trailing carriage, a top link express is immediately identifiable and will make an eye-catching addition to your layout.

colour schemes tailored to the various BR regions. Moreover, the Western Region packs include renditions of the distinctive three-character locomotive headcodes. Printed onto high-quality paper, each pack offers a number of different regional options. They must be cut from the sheet carefully, using a scalpel and a fresh blade. The white edge of the paper will be revealed, so touch this in with paint or an appropriately coloured marker pen.

Fix the boards temporarily with a small amount of Tacky Wax or, for a permanent bond, add a tiny bead of PVA glue using a pinpoint applicator or a cocktail stick. Keep the adhesive away from the printed face, wiping away any excess immediately with a slightly damp cotton swab.

MODERN IMAGE DESTINATIONS

In the post-steam world, BR perpetuated the use of destination placards, initially with small square boards hung at waist level, outlining the main calling points of express services. Trialled on the experimental XP64 set in the mid-1960s, the boards were initially rendered in matching rail blue with white lettering, but a more eye-catching yellow was soon adopted, with black lettering. The boards measured 22 × 18in (7.5 × 6mm in 'OO'), with 2½in high letters and were formed from painted plywood or coloured fibreglass.

This practice didn't last long, but a trawl through contemporary images from the late 1960s and early

With the modernism of the 1960s came a different type of carriage adornment. These boards were drawn up on a computer and printed onto yellow paper. As with any printed nameboards, it is best to protect the ink from fading by spraying with a coat of varnish.

These 1980s-style paper destination labels were also printed via computer. The destinations are barely legible, but they give a passable impression. Another small but satisfying homemade detail is a complement of coach letters; for 'OO', I employed 5pt Arial bold font. Both labels were fixed to the inside of the glazing with Tacky Wax.

1970s will reveal the use of these small square boards, especially on the sides of Southern and Western Region Mk2 stock. Again, mounting brackets were fitted to the carriage sides, arranged in an inverted triangle pattern, the two upper brackets being set 19in (50cm) apart, 16in (40cm) above the lower fixing point. It took some time for these to be removed, even after the use of the boards had been discontinued.

Replicas of the waist-level destination boards were at one time available in 4mm scale from Signs of the Times. However, despite the range now being run by Ten Commandments, the packs are not currently available, having apparently proved a poor seller first time around. They can be readily recreated on a computer and printed onto yellow paper. Some boards featured a cut-out carrying handle and the lettering was printed as sentence case, using the Rail Alphabet typeface (a close match being bold Helvetica or Arial).

The final version of the BR destination board appeared across the network in the 1980s, in the form of paper banners fixed to the inside of each carriage door window. Even today, this simple system can still be found in use on Mk4 and HST stock operating on the East Coast main line. These are straightforward to create from scratch, printed onto thin paper via a home computer perhaps, or rendered on white waterslide transfer paper for a less bulky option. For true authenticity, though, a few should be missing or half-ripped from the windows, as that's how I recall them. Or, being honest, I remember my bedroom wall being festooned with them. Maybe a group of young trainspotters on the platform could have a few of them hanging out of their holdalls?

OTHER IDEAS

Sticking with the window-mounted theme, reserved stickers were a regular sight in the early BR era, fixed to the inside of the glass over seating bays or compartments, as opposed to the paper tickets or digital readouts that we have on today's network. Part or whole carriages could be reserved for group travel, such as schools, youth groups or works outings.

Seldom seen on layouts, despite being an important part of the railway scene, is the football special. Crammed with supporters and festooned with flags, it would make for a colourful addition to a rolling stock fleet. This could be the famous special from Liverpool Lime Street to 'Rome and back' for the European Cup final in May 1977!

From the late 1960s, 9 × 11in paper labels announced the letter allotted to each coach in a set (arranged alphabetically), pasted to the inside of the carriage windows. These progressed to more professional-looking window stickers, continuing well into the BR Sectorisation and privatized eras. Transfers are freely available for the window sticker format, while anyone with a computer and printer can create the older, paper-style labels.

Football specials are an interesting, yet seldom modelled, subject, despite being a regular weekend fixture in the days before mass car ownership. There is plenty of potential there, with elderly, shabby stock pressed into service and plenty of passengers visible through the windows, clad gaily in the colours of their team. A few flags dangling from open windows and top lights would also be a nice touch. As these services also often saw some rare locomotive haulage, they're an opportunity to add something different to your layout operations.

An increasingly common, if wholly undesirable, facet of the modern railway is graffiti. Mostly confined to buildings and infrastructure, rolling stock and locomotives also succumb to this form of self-expression. Freight vehicles are most at risk, standing as they do in yards over weekends, but I've witnessed coaching stock similarly afflicted on many

It might not be pleasant, but graffiti has unfortunately been a common blight on the railway since the 1980s. Usually confined to buildings and infrastructure, it's becoming more prevalent on rolling stock, especially stuff that sits in sidings for longer periods.

Railtec in particular offers some ultra-realistic modern graffiti decals, ranging from semi-literate 'tags' to recreations of more artistic endeavours, captured from real-life sources. Microscale also provides an option, albeit with more of an American slant.

occasions. Unfortunately it's usually preserved or charter stock that bears the brunt of these attacks, again due to the vehicles being parked up for longer periods in out-of-the-way locations.

Maybe vandalism is not something that you fancy recreating in miniature. But, if a gritty contemporary scene is your goal, then there are a number of high-quality transfers around, catering for the fashionable graffiti styles of the moment. (It was all very basic when I was a kid, so at least some degree of artistic effort can be identified these days.) Railtec and Microscale are two sources that spring immediately to mind.

As described previously, waterslide decals demand a gloss surface, so treating the carriage to several light coats of varnish will provide a suitable base. If the adornments are to cover the windows too, then treat the glazing to the gloss coats as well, ensuring that all surfaces have been cleaned and degreased beforehand – it's all too easy to preserve greasy fingerprints on the glazing otherwise.

Once the transfers have been applied, seal with further coats of clear gloss initially, before a satin or matt sheen is applied. However, before the duller coats are added, mask up the glazing to preserve the high sheen and transparency; matt clear coats in particular are less translucent and will give windows a frosted look.

BAGGAGE MATTERS

While we've looked into adding passengers and enhancing the facilities for our miniature clientele, the luggage and parcel areas of carriages have been overlooked so far. Parcels, newspapers, mailbags, bicycles, luggage, milk churns and even wicker baskets are prime candidates for inclusion, arranged artfully behind the windows and doors to ensure visibility. So typical of mainline and branch line passenger services up to the late 1970s, larger-scale models in particular will benefit from loading up in this way, especially if interior lighting is installed.

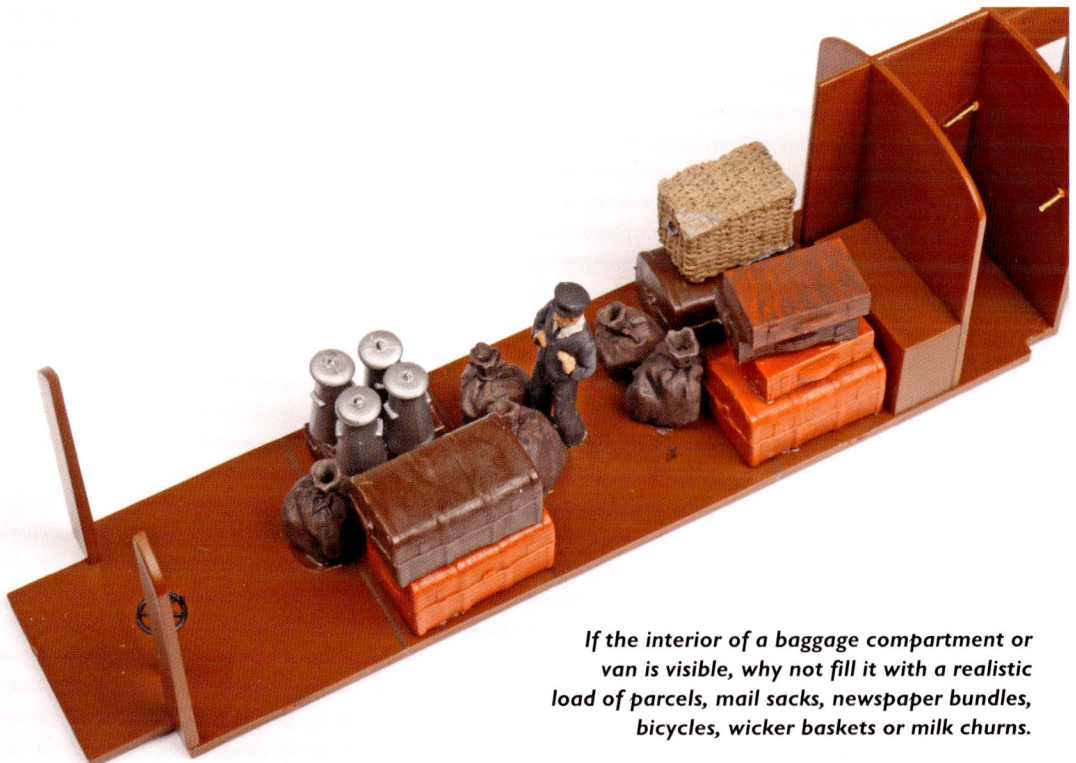

If the interior of a baggage compartment or van is visible, why not fill it with a realistic load of parcels, mail sacks, newspaper bundles, bicycles, wicker baskets or milk churns.

While you are at it, try removing the printed security bars from the baggage compartment windows using a little T-Cut or isopropyl alcohol on a cotton bud. Buff the surface keenly to remove all traces of solvent.

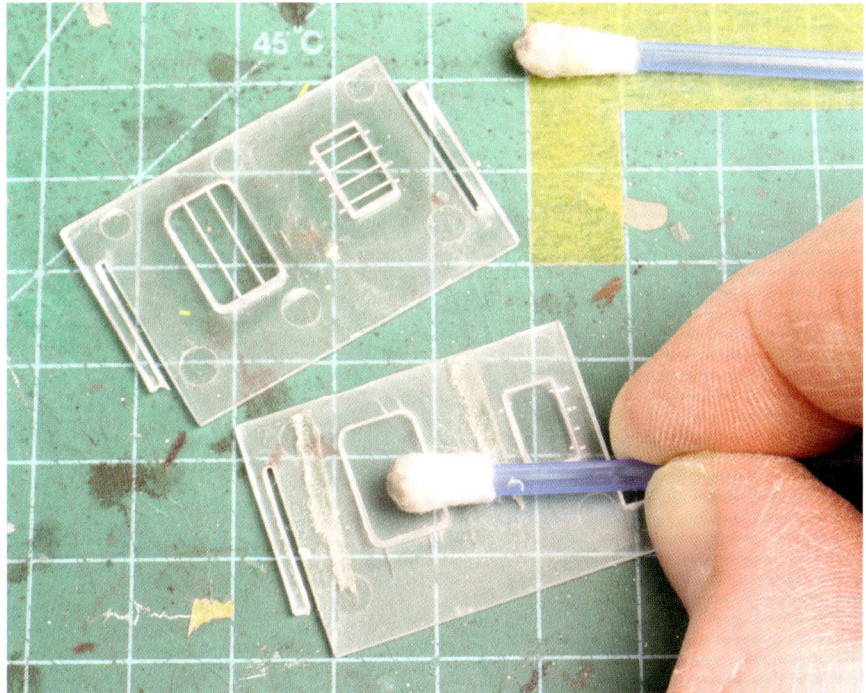

Replacement bars can be cut from nickel jewellery-making wire and fixed to the inside of the glazing with PVA or Glue 'n' Glaze.

The correctly recessed bars add extra depth and the visible luggage, sacks and churns bring the less glamorous end of a passenger train to life.

LIGHT UP YOUR TAIL

As we near the end of this guide to modelling coaching stock, it seems fitting to take a look at adding tail lamps, whether they be illuminated or not. An essential fixture to the last vehicle of any train, only modern services top-and-tailed by locomotives or with a driving trailer car (DVT or DBSO) fitted with working head and tail lights are exempt from this long-standing regulation. BR Mk4 stock was built with integral red tail lights to the end of each car for use in emergencies or unusual circumstances, but even so the humble demountable lamp is still a common feature of the real railway.

Lamps have appeared in various shapes and sizes, according to different practices across the pre-nationalized network. With BR, a standard pattern lamp was issued, rendered in white with an oil-powered red light. This archaic piece of equipment remained in use well into the 1980s before a battery-powered version was introduced, featuring a flashing red aspect.

In miniature form, there are plenty of options. Non-working lamps are available from many sources, such as Springside ('N', 'OO' and 'O' gauges), complete with reflective jewel lenses that are surprisingly effective. Bachmann offers moulded plastic lamps integral to the gangway covers supplied with certain brake carriages, although the lenses are simply picked out with red paint. For those who prefer working lights, there is also plenty of choice, with battery- or rail-powered versions. Similar to the lighting units described in Chapter 9, the lamps can take power from the main interior lighting circuits or be self-contained; DCC users have the option of controlling the lamps via a separate decoder.

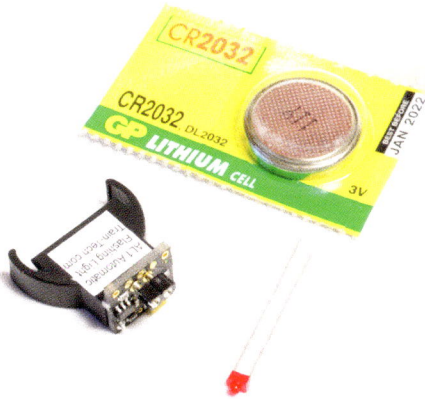

Train-Tech produces a range of illuminated tail lamps for 'OO', featuring motion sensors to power the lights on or off when necessary. Each kit comes complete with self-contained circuit board, LED and long-life 3V power source.

Cut away the upper portion of the carriage's lamp bracket so that the surface is flush. Drill a pair of small holes just wide enough for the lamp tails to pass through.

My favourite 'OO' gauge units, in terms of ease of use, are in the Train-Tech range, featuring a small button cell battery and a motion sensor that switches the lamp on as soon as the model moves. The lamp will stay lit for around four minutes after the model has come to rest, before switching itself off. With no soldering or wiring required, only two small holes for the LED tails are required. A flickering effect enhances the oil-type lamp, while the modern flashing version is equally convincing.

Pass the leads through the holes and secure the circuit board with a blob of Blu-Tack. Make sure that the LED leads don't touch each other, fixing with epoxy or insulted tape if necessary.

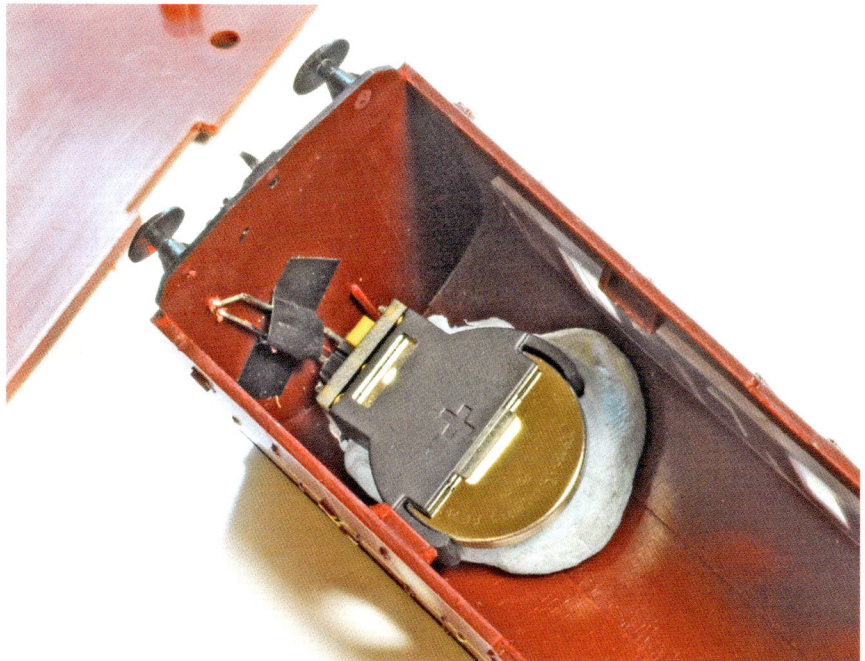

All that's left to do is to paint the outer casing of the LED white or black according to your period. It takes a couple of coats of acrylic to stop the light bleeding through the sides. A wire loop also adds a more authentic appearance.

Although the LED that forms the actual lamp is not especially realistic in shape, it can be modified with paint and a wire loop for a handle to improve matters.

Express Models and DCCconcepts also offer a range of excellent 4mm scale working tail lamps, with an authentic appearance, although more in the way of wiring and assembly is required. For 7mm scale, Modelyard offers a selection of working lamps for the modern and steam eras.

*MIDDLE: **The Train-Tech unit perfectly mimics the paraffin-fuelled lamps of yore, with the flickering effect increasing as the carriage sways. A flashing modern lamp is also available.***

*BOTTOM: **Working lamps from the DCCconcepts range really look the part, even before they're illuminated. Pre-wired with a pair of delicate power leads, they need to be connected to an internal power source.***

Having already installed a lighting unit inside this saloon, the lamp's wires were 'piggy-backed' onto the power terminals from the bogie-mounted pickups.

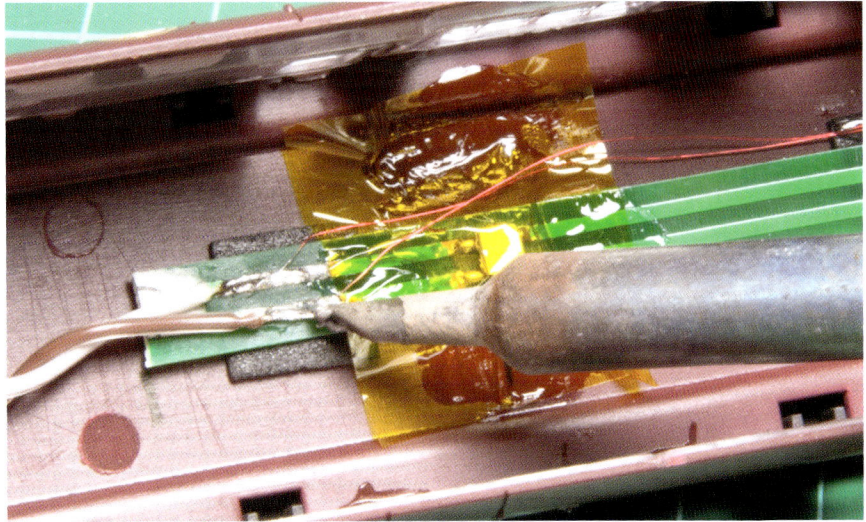

FINAL THOUGHTS

I sincerely hope that this volume has provided plenty of inspiration as well as practical advice on this most engaging of subjects. As we have seen, modelling carriages involves a broad range of materials and techniques, with vast potential in the detailing and enhancement stakes. All depends on how far you want to push the envelope, so to speak. Whether you're happy adding a few extra decorative fittings here and there, or the quest of ultra-prototypical specifications is your motivating factor, either route is equally valid.

Just as there are countless ideas for coach modelling projects, so there are innumerable challenges and opportunities for learning and developing new skills. There is also endless scope for enjoyment and reward, in what is a truly fantastic hobby.

Have fun!

A lamp with a white aspect was installed at this end of the observation saloon so that it can be propelled realistically around my layout.

BIBLIOGRAPHY & SUGGESTED READING

BOOKS

Dent, G., *Airbrushing for Railway Modellers* (The Crowood Press, 2010)

—, *Kit Building for Railway Modellers*, i: *Rolling Stock* (The Crowood Press, 2013)

—, *Kit Building for Railway Modellers*, ii: *Locomotives and Multiple Units* (The Crowood Press, 2013)

Essery, B., *Passenger Train Formation for the Railway Modeller* (Ian Allan, 2005)

Gould, D., *Bulleid's SR Steam Passenger Stock* (Oakwood Press, 1994)

—, *Maunsell's SR Steam Carriage Stock* (Oakwood Press, 1994)

Haresnape, B., *Railway Design since 1830*, i: *1830–1914* (Ian Allan, 1968)

—, *Railway Design since 1830*, ii: *1914–1969* (Ian Allan, 1969)

Harris, M., *British Rail Mark 2 Coaches: The Design that Launched InterCity* (Mallard/Venture, 2007)

—, *LNER Carriages* [1994] (repr. Noodle, 2011)

Jenkinson, D., *British Railway Carriages of the Twentieth Century*, i: *The End of an Era, 1901–1922* (Patrick Stephens, 1988)

—, *British Railway Carriages of the Twentieth Century*, ii: *The Years of Consolidation, 1923–1953* (Patrick Stephens, 1990)

—, *Historic Carriage Drawings*, ii: *LMS and Constituents* (Pendragon, 1998)

—, and B. Essery, *Illustrated History of LMS Standard Coaching Stock*, ii: *General Service Gangwayed Vehicles* (OPC Railprint, 1998)

—, and B. Essery, *Illustrated History of LMS Standard Coaching Stock*, iii: *Non-corridor, Special Purpose and Self-propelled Vehicles* (OPC Railprint, 2000)

Kichenside, G.M., *ABC British Railways Coaches* [1958] (repr. Ian Allan, 1999)

Lacy, R.E., and G. Dow, *Midland Railway Carriages*, i (Wild Swan, 1984)

Longworth, H., *BR Mark 1 & Mark 2 Coaching Stock* (Oxford Publishing Company, 2013)

Mallaband, P., and L.J. Bowles, *The Coaching Stock of British Railways 1976* (Railway Correspondence & Travel Society, 1975)

—, *British Rail Coaching Stock 1981* (Railway Correspondence & Travel Society, 1980)

Parkin, K., *British Railways Mark 1 Coaches* (Historical Model Railway Society/Pendragon, 2006)

Stevens-Stratten, S.W., *Model Railway Constructor Planbook*, i: *Bulleid Coaches in 4mm Scale* (Ian Allan, 1983)

Tatlow, P., *Historic Carriage Drawings*, iii: *Non-Passenger Coaching Stock* (Pendragon, 2000)

Williams, S., *The 4mm Coach, Part One: First Principles and Basic Projects* (Wild Swan, 1994)

ARTICLES

Beattie, I., 'Scale Drawings: BR Mk1 CCT', *Railway Modeller* (July 2002), pp.344–5

Carroll, R., 'Mk1 Pullman Cars', *Model Rail*, 116 (April 2008), pp.56–62

—, and T. Dyer, 'Corporate Image Mail Vans', *Model Rail*, 110 (November 2007), pp.32–5

Dent, G., 'An Irish Recipe', *Model Rail*, 103 (Spring 2007), pp.46–9

—, 'Mallard Mark 4 Stock', *Model Rail*, 78 (April 2005), pp.22–4

—, 'Ultimate Guide to Soldering', *Model Rail* (April 2012), pp.52–7

Hyde, D., 'Victorian Splendour: the GWR 1897 Royal Train in 4mm:1ft Scale', *Model Rail*, 42 (April 2002), pp.52–7

Lavery, J., 'Filling the Seats', *Hornby Magazine* (August 2008), pp.30–33

Leigh, C., 'Carry On Camping', *Model Rail*, 156 (May 2011), pp.44–51

—, 'Pullman Model Luxury', *Model Rail*, 4 (Autumn 1998), pp.38–44

—, 'Waist Level Destination Plates', *Model Rail*, 51 (January 2003), p.42

Moorhouse, C., 'Improve Dapol's Coach Kits', *Model Rail*, 169 (May 2012), pp.88–9

Nevitt, M., 'Stanier Supreme', *Model Railway Journal*, 167 (2006), pp.123–30

Newell, C., 'Fit for a Queen: The GWR Diamond Jubilee Royal Train in EM', *Model Railway Constructor* (April 1983), pp.217–23; (May 1983), pp.284–9

—, 'The GWR Diamond Jubilee Royal Train', *Model Railway Constructor* (April 1981), pp.269–72; (May 1981), pp.332–5; (June 1981), pp.402–3; (August 1981), pp.538–9

Parker, P., 'Fit and Use BK Couplings', *British Railway Modelling* (July 2004), pp.56–7

Smith Wright, J., 'Basic Coach Detailing', *UPDate* (Spring 2002), pp.24–8

Wakefield, M., 'So Near and Yet So Far' [rectifying Hornby Gresley carriages], *Model Railway Journal*, 157 (2005), pp.62–3

Wright, T., 'Done in a Trice' [Hornby Gresley carriage upgrade with brass sides], *British Railway Modelling* (February 2006), pp.50–53

USEFUL ADDRESSES

MODELLING SUPPLIES, KITS & COMPONENTS

Aidan Campbell
22 Queens Road, Hoylake,
Wirral CH47 2AH
Tel: 07801 278044
www.aidan-campbell.co.uk
Figures in various scales

The Airbrush Company Ltd
79 Marlborough Road, Lancing Business Park,
Lancing, West Sussex BN15 8UF
Tel: 01903 767800
www.airbrushes.com
Airbrushes and equipment, paints and tools

Alan Gibson
PO Box 597, Oldham OL1 9FQ
Tel: 0161 678 1607
www.alangibsonworkshop.com
Wheels and detailing components

Albion Alloys
Spacemaker House, 518 Wallisdown Road,
Bournemouth, Dorset BH11 8PT
Tel: 01202 511232
www.albionhobbies.com
Metal rod, sheet and section, modelling tools,
abrasives

Andrew Stadden
41 Cove Road, Rustington, West Sussex
BN16 2QN
Tel: 07526 639890
www.acstadden.co.uk
7mm scale figures

Axminster Power Tool Centre Ltd
Unit 10 Weycroft Avenue, Axminster,
Devon EX13 5PH
Tel: 03332 406406
www.axminster.co.uk
Craft and hobby tools

BH Enterprises
68 Meadow Road, Watford, Hertfordshire
WD25 0JA
Tel: 01923 672809 (7.30–9.30pm)
www.bh-enterprises.co.uk
Coach kits and detailing components in 'N' gauge

C&L Finescale
Aran Lodge, Severn Road, Hallen,
Bristol BS10 7RZ
Tel: 01179 505470
www.finescale.org.uk
Suppliers of Carr's solders, fluxes and blackening
fluids and Exactoscale wheels

Cambridge Custom Transfers
6 Roseland Gardens, Bodmin, Cornwall
PL31 2EY
www.cctrans.org.uk
Transfers for coaching stock in all scales

Comet Models
c/o Wizard Models, PO Box 70,
Barton-upon-Humber, North Lincolnshire
DN18 5XY
Tel: 01652 635885
www.wizardmodels.co.uk
Carriage kits and components

Crafty Computer Paper
Woodhall, Barrasford, Hexham,
Northumberland NE48 4DB
Tel: 01434 689153
www.craftycomputerpaper.co.uk
Materials for DIY waterslide transfers

Dart Castings
17 Hurst Close, Staplehurst, Tonbridge,
Kent TN12 0BX
www.dartcastings.co.uk
Figures in 4mm scale and detailing components

DCCconcepts
Unit E, The Sidings, Settle, North Yorkshire
BD24 9RP
Tel: +61 8 9437 2470
www.dccconcepts.com
Tools, solder, wheels, interior lighting kits

DCC Supplies
Unit 17A Top Barn Business Centre,
Worcester Road, Holt Heath, Worcester
WR6 6NH
Tel: 0845 224 1601
www.dccsupplies.com
Tools and electrical equipment, including Brelec
and Digirails pickups, lighting kits and conductive
couplings, rivet decals

DC Kits
111 Norwood Crescent, Stanningley, Leeds,
West Yorkshire LS28 6NG
Tel: 0113 256 3415
www.dckits-devideos.co.uk
Plastic coach kits and accessories

Eileen's Emporium
Unit 19.12 Highnam Business Centre, Newent
Road, Gloucester GL2 8DN
Tel: 01531 828009
www.eileensemporium.com
Tools, adhesives and materials

Express Models
65 Conway Drive, Shepshed, Loughborough,
Leicestershire LE12 9PP
Tel: 01509 829008
www.expressmodels.co.uk
Lighting units and working tail lamps

Finescale Model World
Tel: 07780 097503
www.finescalemodelworld.co.uk
Specialist cleaning fluids and adhesives for plastic,
resin and metal

Fox Transfers
Unit 5 Prior Business Park,
Wistow Road, Kibworth,
Leicestershire LE8 0RX
Tel: 0116 319 4950
www.fox-transfers.co.uk
Vast range of waterslide transfers and lining in all
scales

Gaugemaster
Gaugemaster House, Ford Road, Arundel,
West Sussex BN18 0BN
Tel: 01903 884488
www.gaugemaster.com
Deluxe Materials adhesives, fillers and applicators,
Preiser and other figures and model kits

Hattons Model Railways
17 Montague Road, Widnes WA8 8FZ
Tel: 0151 733 3655
www.ehattons.com
New and pre-owned RTR stock, 3D printing and
CAD artwork services

Howes Models Ltd
Unit 2C/D Station Field Industrial Estate,
Rowles Way, Kidlington, Oxfordshire
OX5 1LA
Tel: 01865 848000
www.howesmodels.co.uk
Kits, components, Railmatch paints and transfers

Hurst Models
PO Box 158, Newton-le-Willows,
Merseyside WA12 0WW
www.hurstmodels.com
Coach kits, conversion and parts in various
scales

IP Engineering
Carousell, Spilsby Road, New Leake, Boston,
Lincolnshire PE22 8JT
Tel: 01205 270010
www.ipengineering.co.uk
Carriage kits for garden scales

Just Like the Real Thing
26 Whittle Place, South Newmoor Industrial
Estate, Irvine, Ayrshire KA11 4HR
Tel: 01294 222988
www.justliketherealthing.co.uk
High quality 7mm scale rolling stock kits, plus
paints and accessories

LHP Products
Printed, self-adhesive carriage interior kits
http://stores.ebay.co.uk/TRAIN-BOAT-DEPOT

Markits
PO Box 40, Watford, Hertfordshire
WD24 6TN
Tel: 01923 249711
www.markits.com
Wheels and detailing components

Mike Carrington
Tel: 07801 796864
Email: mikecarrington01@gmail.com
Coach lighting kits

Modelmaster
31 Crown Street, Ayr KA8 8AG
Tel: 01292 289770
www.modelmasterdecals.com
Extensive range of waterslide transfers, including
lining, mostly in 4mm scale

Model Yard
16 Helmsley Road, Leeds, West Yorkshire
LS16 5JA
Tel: 0113 294 8808
www.modelyard.co.uk
7mm scale interior lights and tail lamps

Palatine Models
www.palatinemodels.co.uk
LMS coach underframe kits and other
components for 4mm scale

Parliamentary Trains
13 Wordsworth Road, Rugby,
Warwickshire CV22 6HY
Tel: 07771 508085
www.parlytrains.co.uk
'O' gauge kits, specializing in nineteenth-century
subjects

PH Designs
www.phd-design-etchings.co.uk
Detailing components, kits and BK Systems
couplings

Phoenix Precision Paints
Orwell Court, Wickford,
Essex SS11 8YJ
Tel: 01268 730549
www.phoenix-paints.co.uk
Enamel paints, primers, varnishes, thinners,
masking fluid and painting accessories. Also
distributors of No Nonsense Kits

Precision Labels
Tel: 07800 744170
www.precisionlabels.com
Transfers, coach destination boards and
details, bespoke transfers, 3D printing and
design service

Railtec Models
www.railtec-models.com
Off-the-shelf and bespoke transfers

Scale Model Shop
Tel: 01422 405040
www.scalemodelshop.co.uk
Modelling tools, paints, weathering products,
wood-grain decals

Shapeways
www.shapeways.com
3D printing marketplace, where lots of railway
subjects can be found

Shawplan/Extreme Etchings
2 Upper Dunstead Road,
Langley Mill,
Nottingham NG16 4GR
Tel: 01773 718648
www.shawplan.com
Detailing components, laser-cut glazing

Slater's Plastikard
Old Road, Darley Dale, Matlock,
Derbyshire DE4 2ER
Tel: 01629 732235
www.slatersplastikard.com
Wheels, plastic kits, plastic card and section

Southern Pride Models
9 Manor Avenue South, Kidderminster,
Worcestershire DY11 6DE
www.southernpridemodels.co.uk
Carriage kits and detail parts

Train-Tech
DCP Microdevelopments Ltd,
Bryon Court, Bow Street,
Great Ellingham,
Norfolk NR17 1JB
Tel: 01953 457800
www.train-tech.com
Coach lighting and sound-effect units

Worsley Works
www.worsleyworks.co.uk
Coach kits, conversions, detailing parts and
bespoke etchings in virtually any scale

York Modelmaking
Unit 13,
The Bull Commercial Centre,
Stockton-on-the-Forest,
York YO32 9LE
Tel: 01904 400358
www.yorkmodelmaking.co.uk
Laser-cut plastic, wood and card coach kits and
components. Bespoke laser-cutting service in any
scale

USEFUL WEBSITES

**George Dent Model Maker: A Model
Maker's Diary**
http://georgedentmodelmaker.blogspot.com

Manchester Model Railway Society
www.mmrs.co.uk

Model Rail Magazine
www.model-rail.co.uk

National Model Railway Association
www.nmra.org

National Railway Museum
www.nrm.org.uk

SCALE SOCIETIES

2mm Scale Association
www.2mm.org.uk

3mm Society
www.3mmsociety.org.uk

Broad Gauge Society
www.broadgauge.org.uk

Double O Gauge Society
www.doubleogauge.com

EM Gauge Society
www.emgs.org

Gauge O Guild
www.gaugeOguild.com

MOROP (for NEM standards)
www.morop.org

N Gauge Society
www.ngaugesociety.com

NMRA
www.nmra.org

OO9 Society
www.OO9society.com

Scalefour (P4)
www.scalefour.org

Scale Seven Group
www.scaleseven.org.uk

PROTOTYPE SOCIETIES

Diesel & Electric Modellers United
www.demu.org.uk

Historical Model Railway Society
www.hmrs.org.uk

Great Western Study Group
www.gwsg.org.uk

LMS Society
www.lmssociety.org.uk

LNER Society
www.lner.info

Midland Railway Society
www.midlandrailwaysociety.org.uk

Railway Correspondence & Travel Society
www.rcts.org.uk

Southern Railways Group
www.srg.org.uk

INDEX

3D printing   9, 89–93

adhesives   20–22, 30–31, 37–38, 44, 61, 73, 78, 82, 134–135
aerosol paints   30, 188
airbrushing   182–188

back-to-back gauge   40–41
baggage   240, 242
bearings   62, 64–65, 155–156
bogies   41, 64–66, 75, 78, 93, 117, 154–159, 173–175
buffers   45–46

clear coats   33, 201–203, 215–216, 219, 240
compensation   158–161
couplings   104–112

DCC   8, 242
decals   32–34, 201–205, 213–215, 240
destination boards   232–237

filler   22–23, 43, 47, 63, 73, 77, 91, 97
football specials   238

gangways   111–114
glazing   9, 35–39, 53
graffiti   238–240

handrails   42–44

interiors   27–31, 53, 69–70, 164

laser-cutting   82–87
lighting   113–117, 242–245
lining   210–215

masking   198–201, 222–223
metal, properties of   118–123
    working with   121–161, 170–176
metallic paints   215–216

National Railway Museum   13,

paint   190–192
    application   29–30, 36, 193–197
    stripping   179–181
passengers   29–31
plastics, properties of   58–59
    working with   59–73, 164–170
primer   76–77, 153, 188–189

re-numbering   32–33
resin   74–82, 94, 100
roofs   45–46, 56–57, 67–69, 88, 149–154, 173, 175

scratch building   51–53, 162–177
soldering   17–18, 127–134, 140–142
    tail lamps   242–245

T-cut   32, 218, 220–221, 241
tools   15–19

underframes   10, 14, 53–56, 63–64, 75, 136–144, 170–172

weathering   217–231
weight   70–72
wheels   39–41, 62, 93, 117
window labels   237–238
    bars   241–242
wood effect finish   206–209

RELATED TITLES FROM CROWOOD

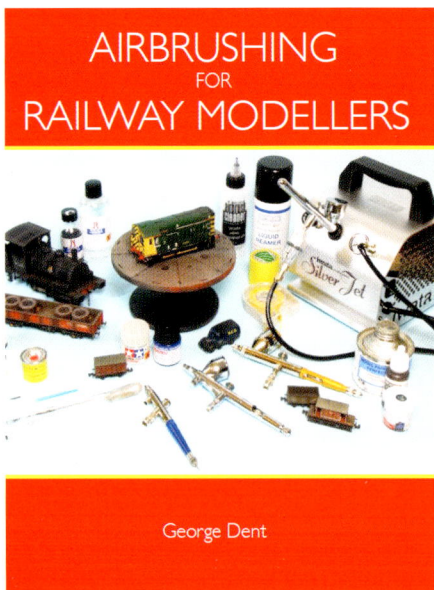

Airbrushing for Railway Modellers
GEORGE DENT
ISBN 978 1 84797 265 1
224pp, 500 illustrations

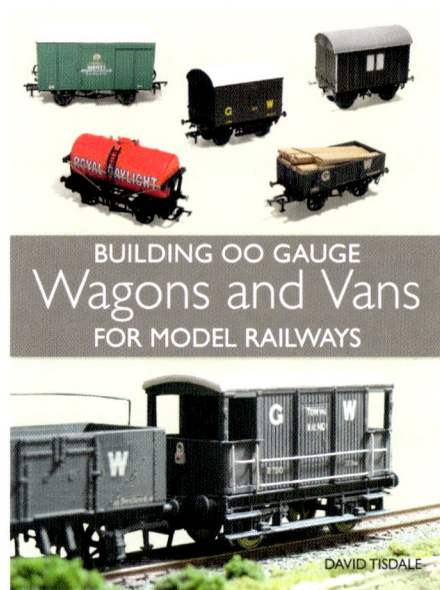

Building OO Gauge Wagons and Vans
DAVID TISDALE
ISBN 978 1 84797 983 4
192pp, 290 illustrations

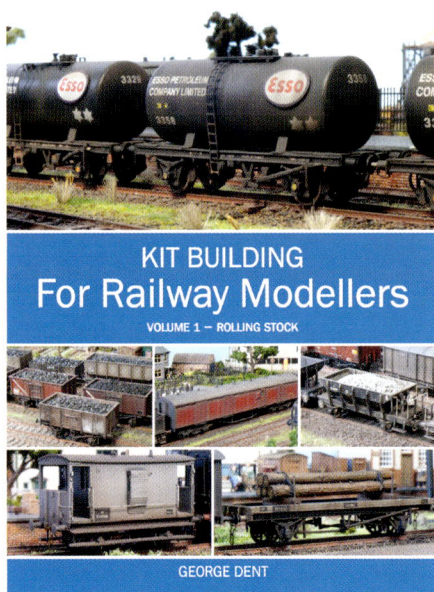

Kit Building for Railway Modellers Vol 1
GEORGE DENT
ISBN 978 1 84797 484 6
224pp, 590 illustrations

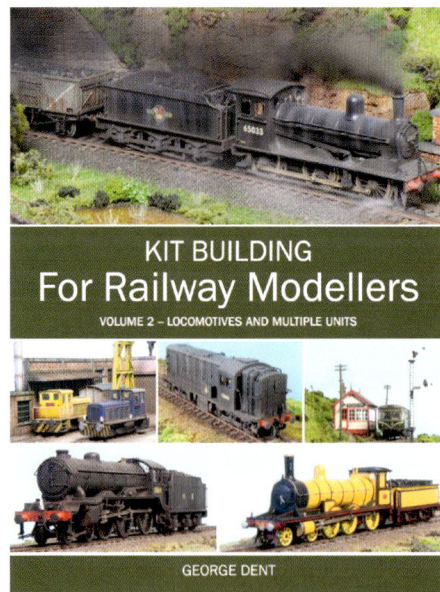

Kit Building for Railway Modellers Vol 2
GEORGE DENT
ISBN 978 1 84797 551 5
224pp, 540 illustrations

RELATED TITLES FROM CROWOOD

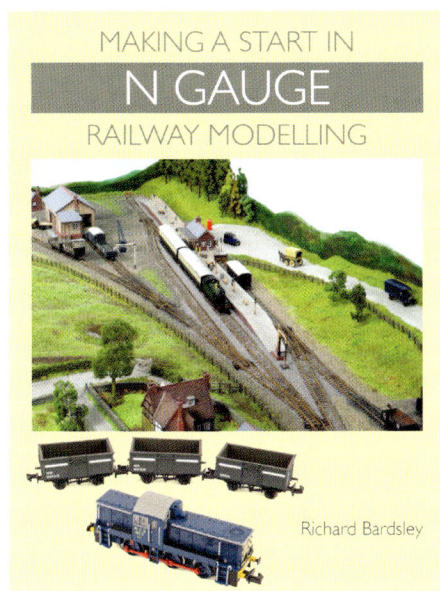

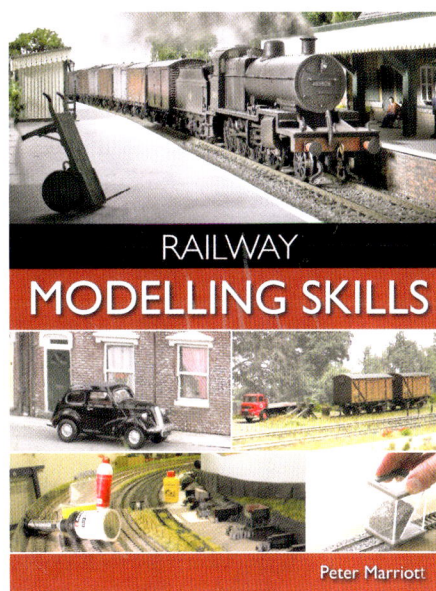

In case of difficulty ordering, please contact the Sales Office:

The Crowood Press

Ramsbury

Wiltshire

SN8 2HR

UK

Tel: 44 (0) 1672 520320

enquiries@crowood.com

www.crowood.com